NO PLACE LIKE MURDER 2

Praise for *No Place Like Murder 2*

"Put away the rose-colored glasses. History isn't always pretty. There is a dark side to Indiana's past that needs to be pulled from the shadows. This gripping true crime collection illuminates some of the most fascinating and chilling cases in Hoosier Heartland history."

CHRIS KENNEDY NIXON, author of *Murder & Mayhem in Early Jay County*

"Thornton brings to life long-forgotten true crimes that will keep the reader riveted and horrified at the brutality one human can have for another."

DIANA CATT, author of *Death Map*, a Lila Kincaid Investigation

"Janis Thornton recounts twenty Indiana murders involving women and children that made headlines in their day but were lost to history until now. True crime aficionados will find her fascinating second volume of *No Place Like Murder* hard to put down."

GARY SOSNIECKI, author of *The Potato Masher Murder: Death at the Hands of a Jealous Husband*

Also by Janis Thornton

No Place Like Murder

Too Good a Girl: Remembering Olene Emberton
and the Mystery of Her Death

The 1965 Palm Sunday Tornadoes in Indiana

Images of America: Tipton County, Indiana

Images of America: Frankfort, Indiana

Images of America: Elwood, Indiana

Dust Bunnies and Dead Bodies

Dead Air and Double Dare

Love, Lies and Azure Eyes

JANIS THORNTON

NO PLACE LIKE MURDER 2

VINTAGE TRUE CRIME IN THE HOOSIER HEARTLAND

Foreword by Stephen Terrell

This book is a publication of

LIFE SENTENCES PUBLISHING, LLC
www.lifesentencespublishing.com

Copyright 2024 by Janis Thornton
All rights reserved

No part of this book may be reproduced or utilized in any form or by any means, electronic or mechanical, including photocopying and recording, or by any information storage and retrieval system, without permission in writing from the publisher.

Manufactured in the United States of America

ISBN: 978-1-7327630-5-0 (paperback)

This book is dedicated to the hard-working newspaper reporters, who wrote the first drafts of the historic murders that appear on the following pages. Their enduring words provide an eye-opening, often shocking glimpse into the past and remind us that human life is as fragile today as it was decades ago, when their stories were rolling off the presses.

CONTENTS

	Foreword by Stephen Terrell	iii
	Acknowledgements	vii
	Introduction	ix

PART I: Victims / Women

1	Dorothy Poore: The Girl in the Dresser Drawer	3
2	The Case of the 'Flaming Youth' Murder	21
3	The Bloomfield Slasher	33
4	Murder at the Lafayette Street Rooming House	43
5	Bushwhacked on Bittersweet Road	51
6	A Bullet for Tacie Mang	59
7	The Deadly Affair of Nora Kifer	67
8	The Mysterious Murder of Madam X	81

PART II: VICTIMS / KIDS

9	LITTLE GIRL GONE	93
10	THE PRIVATE HELL OF HARRIET DINKINS	111
11	PANDEMONIUM AT WILLAM REED ELEMENTARY SCHOOL	121

PART III: KILLERS / KIDS

12	WHEN MURDER IS CHILD'S PLAY	135
13	THE MOTHER GOOSE MURDER TRIAL	143
14	THE SAGA OF SORORICIDE CHARLES MESSEL	157
15	REMEMBERING NELLIE MAYNARD, THE GIRL ON FIRE; AND ROSIE PERKINS, THE GIRL WHO STRUCK THE MATCH	167

PART IV: KILLERS / WOMEN

16	ROCK-A-BYE-BYE, BABY: THE UNSPEAKABLE CRIME OF NORA MOSHER	175
17	THE PROSECUTION OF ALICE LAWSON: 'THE HUMAN ICICLE'	185
18	THE GLASGO FIASCO	195
19	THE CONTEMPTIBLE CRIMES OF CLARA CARL: INDIANA'S FEMALE BLUEBEARD	205
20	CORNBREAD TO DEATHBED: THE DELICIOUS REVENGE OF NELLIE COLLINS	217
	BIBLIOGRAPHY	225
	AUTHOR	236

FOREWORD

There is something about true crime that grabs our attention and won't let go. Our television is populated with NBC's *Dateline*, ABC's *20/20*, and countless other cable and streaming knock offs, telling dramatic stories about tragic events. We all hark to the siren song of a police car, fire truck, or ambulance that makes us stop what we are doing and look. There is a primal attraction. It's why bestseller lists are populated with true crime stories.

There's an old newspaper adage: "If it bleeds, it leads." I found that true when working on my family genealogy in my ample spare time during the first months of the pandemic. Searching for information on a great-uncle I knew nothing about, I was suddenly staring at a headline about the "notorious John Terrell," who ambushed his estranged son-in-law in 1903 in such a spectacular fashion that it ended up making headlines in more than six hundred newspapers across the nation, including the front page of the *New York Times*. The story fired my interest in historical true crime, resulting in my book, *The Madness of John Terrell: Revenge and Insanity on Trial in the Heartland*. But thanks to Janis Thornton, I already had an interest in historical true crime.

A former newspaper reporter, Janis is a master of the true crime genre. Her book, *Too Good a Girl*, about the unsolved murder of her high school classmate, brought a sharp reporter's eye to decades-old evidence. She also brought a sympathetic touch to telling the story of the victim, her family, and friends. The same is true with the first volume of *No Place Like Murder*, which, like this volume, is filled with historic true crime.

Janis writes with an eye for the human side of tragic, often horrible events.

This was never more evident than in her book, *The 1965 Palm Sunday Tornadoes in Indiana*. She recounted the most destructive and deadly day in Indiana history, told through the eyes of more than one hundred survivors.

Janis provides far more than just facts and figures or the titillating shock of outrageous crimes. She never loses sight of the real people involved in these stories—victims, witnesses, police, coroners, and yes, perpetrators, some who are violent thugs, but others who are sympathetic people trapped in unfortunate circumstances.

For example, in 1954, small-town girl Dorothy Poore left home for the big city to find a job. Instead, she was horrifically murdered, her nearly nude body found days later stuffed in a hotel dresser drawer.

In "The Bloomfield Slasher," the doctor of a pregnant, eighteen-year-old wife, became enamored with her and convinced her to leave her husband. When the young woman had a change of heart and reconciled with her husband, the spurned doctor attacked her with surgeon-like precision as she walked down a Bloomfield street.

Tragic school shootings too often lead the news, but they are not new. "Pandemonium at William Reed Elementary" tells of the shocking, 1960 shotgun murders of two Hartford City teachers by, perhaps, the least likely person as their classrooms of stunned fifth-graders watched.

"Bushwhacked on Bittersweet Road" tells of three teenagers, cruising along a country road outside Mishawaka in 1937, when they came upon a car that appeared to have broken down. Concerned, the teens stopped to help but were met with a hail of gunfire from an unknown assailant, killing sixteen-year-old Melba Moore.

"The Mother Goose Murder Trial" recounts the story of an eleven-year-old Starke County boy, Cecil Burkett, who, in 1921, became the youngest child in the nation to face the possibility of the electric chair.

"The Saga of Sororicide Charles Messel" recounts the 1911 tragedy of eleven-year-old Fern Messel, whose father was arrested for "ruining" her. The next day, her seventeen-year-old brother, Charles, shot and killed her after he overheard her say he "was as guilty as Pa." The resolution was as unexpected as the crime.

"Rock-a-Bye-Bye, Baby: The Unspeakable Crime of Nora Mosher" tells of a woman, who in 1907, bashed in the head of her newborn baby. Both she and her father, the suspected father of the baby, were charged with the murder—but only one was convicted.

"The Prosecution of Alice Lawson: The Human Icicle" and "Cornbread to Deathbed: The Delicious Revenge of Nellie Collins" tell of abused women in early 1900s Indiana who found no other way out of their intolerable circumstances than to rid themselves of their tormentors, no matter the cost.

"The Contemptible Crimes of Clara Carl: Indiana's Bluebeard" could have been part of *The Poisoner's Handbook*. Clara poisoned two husbands, and a father-in-law to boot, all within just over a year and got away with it—almost, that is. The men were long cold in the grave, when authorities received an anonymous letter telling them to dig up the bodies and look for arsenic.

There are many more of these historical true crime stories—twenty in total. Think about these stories set in a time when the population was much smaller and society simpler, more law-abiding, more religious, more neighborly. At least that is the perception. How many times have you heard someone, after hearing about a particularly heinous crime, remark, "Why can't people be like they used to be?"

After reading this book, you may conclude that we are, in fact, like people used to be.

So, settle into your favorite easy chair with your favorite comforting drink at hand and enjoy this wonderful book.

Stephen M. Terrell

Stephen M. Terrell is a retired lawyer with a passion for writing. His latest book is a historical true crime saga, The Madness of John Terrell: Revenge and Insanity on Trial in the Heartland. *(Kent State University Press, 2024). Visit him online at www.terrellwrites.com.*

ACKNOWLEDGEMENTS

Despite what you may hear, no book writes itself. This is particularly true of historic nonfiction books that take a deep dive into the past to explore shocking and heartbreaking incidents that were long-forgotten, regardless of how hard they rattled their corner of the world when they occurred.

Such is the case for *No Place Like Murder 2*, which revisits twenty historic Indiana murders, most of them occurring more than one hundred years ago. This, like all nonfiction books, has required incalculable hours of research and hard work, but there is another indispensable aspect of book writing that isn't always obvious. And that is the help, information, inspiration, and encouragement provided by many generous, highly knowledgeable people.

No Place Like Murder 2, like its predecessor, *No Place Like Murder*, has been a long time coming, and I'm enormously grateful to the many special people who helped me get it into your hands. They each have my deepest, heartfelt appreciation, and they include:

> FELLOW AUTHORS—Stephen M. Terrell for writing a most-thoughtful foreword; Diana Catt, Donna Cronk, Michael Dabney, Russ Eberhart (a.k.a. Ross Carley), Chris Kennedy Nixon, Nicole Kobrowski, Keith Roysdon, and Gary Sosniecki for their kind blurbs; Tim Byers, Bob Beilouny, Bruce Cochran, Tom Kohlmeier, Victor MacDonald, Sandy Miller, and Carol Paddock, fellow members of my writers group, for their thoughtful feedback and unwavering support
>
> PROFESSIONAL SERVICE PROVIDERS—Michael Vetman of the Indiana

State Archives for providing the prison records and mugshots of many of the characters in this book; Patrick Pearsey, Indianapolis Police Department archivist, for offering me the use of several photos from the Dorothy Poore case file; the Indiana State Library staff for their beyond-the-call assistance; and copyeditor/proofreader Carol Paddock for her vast editorial abilities and keen eye

HISTORIANS—Sinuard Castelo, director of the Blackford County Historical Society; and Janet Moore of the Madison County Historical Society

CONTRIBUTORS—Shirley Harter Dollar and Nancy Tatman Lenfestey, former students of the William Reed Elementary School, for sharing their recollection of the incident there on February 2, 1960; and John Shaw for the tip about the 1883 murder of Madison County native Susannah Bronnenberg Nelson

AND JUST BECAUSE—Nancy Coy, Mary Frances Fernung, Marcy Fry, Matt Geas, Dixie Ihnat, Ruth Illges, Chip Mann, and William E. Tidler II

Thank you, all! You're the best.

INTRODUCTION
Historic True Crime Never Grows Old

Modern-day stories of true crime abound. It seems that the moment a sensational, horrific murder hits the mainstream news, an enterprising writer starts cranking out a book. And to their good fortune, an ever-expanding market of eager readers is waiting to lap it up.

Our media—print, broadcast, and social—pounce on a grisly crime the moment it occurs, home in on every gruesome detail, elevate it to top-story status, and then, often within hours, move on to the next ratings grab, leaving it behind like yesterday's news.

I enjoy exploring cases that were left behind. It is a wise choice for a true crime writer driven by an almost inexorable enthusiasm for solving puzzles, especially old ones that involve figuring out not only who dunnit, but why. That preference also aligns with my fascination for history and has led me to produce another collection of historic Indiana true crime stories.

While I find nearly all sensational historic true crimes riveting, the ones I seek out, research, and write about are those that have long faded into obscurity. As I cobble together the elements of each story, I most enjoy sifting through the source material for clues to the emotions and motivations that drove the people who committed the crimes. Styles, tastes, habits, landscapes, technology, and societal norms change over time, but the human condition remains steadfast. Therefore, perhaps the only substantial difference between people of 2024 and those of 1924 is the speed at which their lives move.

After the release of *No Place Like Murder* in 2020, I continued to dig for compelling stories to tell. This time I found myself drawn to crimes revolving around women and children, who sadly are frequent victims of violent crime. However, what I found most unsettling was the discovery that oftentimes they themselves are the killers. The product of my research is this book of twenty gripping stories of murder that occurred in a variety of Indiana communities—close-knit rural towns, as well as bustling cities—between 1883 and 1960. Some of the incidents are brutal and premeditated; others are the unintended result of the perpetrator's momentary loss of control. All focus on a woman or child. Sometimes both.

Readers who are drawn to true crime revel in the front-row vantage point it provides, allowing them to experience an array of dangerous situations with morbid outcomes. It also introduces them to numerous characters, ranging from despicable monsters to endearing innocents.

My first collection of historic Indiana crime stories provides a look into the minds of murderers and the motives behind their heinous acts. Assailants hail from all walks of life and pluck their cue to kill from a wide swath of flimsy excuses. Generally, people who take a life are not genetically predisposed to violent behavior, although the jury is still out on the percentage who are. Most often, the cold-blooded killer's motive is prompted by power, greed, retribution, jealousy, anger, or a circumstance that has upturned their chosen place in the universe.

My second collection expands on all of that and confirms there are no absolutes in murder. According to the FBI's most recent data on violent crime, the vast majority of perpetrators are men between the ages of twenty and fifty-nine, albeit gender and age occupy both ends of the spectrum.

For example, this book covers several cases featuring children, including: ten-year-old Alice Cothrell, who vanished from her neighborhood in Allen County and five days later was found drowned in the cistern belonging to her contentious neighbor; eleven-year-old Cecil Burkett of the tiny town of Ora in Starke County who was tried for the shotgun slaying of his seven-year-old neighbor, Benny Slavin; nine-year-old Robert Silvers of Portland who stabbed and killed his nine-year-old playmate, Bernie Teeters, after a quarrel over a baseball mitt; and Alexandria's eight-year-old Nellie Maynard, who died of acute burns caused by fourteen-year-old Rosie Perkins, who set Nellie's dress on fire.

The book also dissects the roles of women in several more sensational Hoosier homicides. Those stories introduce readers to the likes of Greenfield's Clara Carl, who newspapers deemed Indiana's female Bluebeard; Rose

Glasgo, whose alligator tears held sway with the jury that acquitted her in the shooting death of her estranged husband in the city of Brazil; Harriet Dinkins, who caused the gas inhalation deaths of her three young children, thus nullifying her claim as Muncie's Mother of the Year; as well as many more innocent victims, such as Evansville's Mary Elizabeth Robb, Clinton's Dorothy Poore, Lizzie Skinner of Bloomfield, Alice May Girton of Randolph County, and Hartford City school teachers Harriet Robson and Minnie McFerron, all of whom violently lost their lives for no good reason at the hands of men they thought they knew.

Like my first book of historic true crimes, researching the various crimes led me to better understand the people touched by the malevolent deeds that forever changed their lives. Crafting the stories for modern-day readers gave me insight into the victims' and perpetrators' lives, their attitudes, and their outlooks for happiness and heartache. Consequently, I came to realize that crimes of passion and greed are not a modern invention, and people who inhabited Indiana decades before us are not so very different from Hoosiers of today.

Historic true crime never grows old, as long as readers follow their curiosity to unexpected places, where a strategically placed bullet can rip apart far more than its intended target's fate. I hope you find the stories in the book as fascinating and unforgettable as I have. But as you read, I suggest you keep a light burning. And your door bolted.

Happy reading.

Janis Thornton

PART I
VICTIMS: WOMEN

1
DOROTHY POORE:
THE GIRL IN THE DRESSER DRAWER

Dateline: Marion County, 1954

The year was 1954. America was booming, and opportunities abounded. Indianapolis was the perfect place for an ambitious, eighteen-year-old Hoosier woman to test her mettle and start her life.

Dorothy Poore graduated that spring from Clinton High School, and she was dying to escape her tiny, Vermillion County town. The afternoon of Wednesday, July 14, she hugged her mother, Hazel, goodbye and boarded the Circle City-bound bus, promising to return Saturday. After arriving in Indianapolis, Dorothy hoofed the two-and-a-half blocks from the terminal at Market and Illinois Streets to the Lorraine Hotel at 12 South Capitol and registered for a room. The three-night stay would set her back $6, but she hoped to land one of the state's well-paying typist jobs after she took the civil service exam on Thursday.

Saturday evening, Hazel waited at the Clinton bus station, anxious to greet her daughter and hear about her trip. But when the bus pulled in and the passengers disembarked, Dorothy wasn't among them. Hazel couldn't imagine what had happened.

The Girl in the Dresser Drawer
The headline splashed across Monday's *Indianapolis Star* shouted the news that no mother should ever have to bear: "GIRL'S BODY FOUND IN HOTEL."

The story reported that three members of the housekeeping staff of the Claypool Hotel, located downtown Indianapolis on the corner of Washington and Illinois Streets, had discovered Dorothy's "nearly nude, badly decomposed body" Sunday morning in Room 665, where it had been jammed into a dresser drawer. Police couldn't make sense of it.

Dorothy's family and friends couldn't either. They assured investigators that Dorothy had always been a quiet, reserved girl. So, had she been lured to the hotel room by a "sex fiend" as the *Indianapolis Star* suggested? Had she gone willingly? Was she there for a job interview? No one knew.

Marion County Coroner Dr. Roy B. Storms estimated that the young woman had died late Thursday, July 15, or early Friday, July 16, but he could not yet determine the cause of death. The autopsy by Dr. David Rosenbaum was inconclusive. Perhaps she had died of strangulation, he said, but he wasn't sure. She might have been suffocated by a pillow. Swelling and decomposition of Dorothy's body, caused by the scorching July heat, made certainty impossible.

Rosenbaum removed her vital organs and sent them to Indiana University Medical Center for toxicology tests.

A Fine Girl with a Bright Future
Dorothy Lillian Poore was born August 21, 1935, in Chicago. An only child, she lived most of her life in Clinton, Indiana, with her mother, Hazel Poore, and her grandmother, Lilly Dancy. Dorothy's friends remembered her as a beautiful, well-liked girl. Quiet and known for her serious, no-nonsense personality, Dorothy had focused her academic studies on business courses and excelled at typing and shorthand. She figured such skills would open doors to a business career and had set her sights on Indianapolis. She was certain the capital city would offer far more exciting and lucrative opportunities than any available in her hometown.

Dorothy's final journey to Indianapolis was her third in her pursuit of a job. She had made her first trip on Thursday, July 1, and stayed three days—two at the Lorraine Hotel and one at the home of a family friend. When Dorothy returned to Clinton the following Monday, she told her closest confidant, her grandmother, about two strange men who had harassed her the moment she stepped off the bus in Indianapolis—one, who took her suitcase from her; and the other, claiming to be a terminal detective, who gave it back to her. Dorothy said the men had upset her so much that she had been unable to sleep that first night.

Dorothy Poore was a happy, eighteen-year-old Clinton (Indiana) High School senior with everything to live for, when she posed for her graduation photo above. Dorothy's friends described her as "neat" and "meticulous," which is apparent in the photo of her snapped on a sunny day shortly before she left Clinton and headed off for a new life in Indianapolis in July of 1954. *Photos courtesy the Indianapolis Police Department Archives.*

Even so, Dorothy traveled back to Indianapolis on Tuesday, July 6. That time, Dorothy's mother accompanied her, rented her a room at the Adams Hotel in the two hundred block of North New Jersey Street, and returned to Clinton, leaving Dorothy to take her civil service test on Thursday, July 8. However, Hazel called Dorothy Wednesday night and begged her to come home, claiming she couldn't bear to lose her daughter. Unable to withstand her mother's pleas, Dorothy obediently skipped the test and caught the next bus home. Still, she was growing ever more restless. She had dreams to pursue.

Within a few days, Dorothy had worn down her mother's objection and earned her blessing. The following Wednesday, July 14, Dorothy stepped aboard an Indianapolis-bound bus for the last time.

Five days later, Hazel and Lilly traveled to Indianapolis to meet with the coroner. Dorothy was buried in Clinton on Wednesday, July 21. According to that day's edition of the *Daily Clintonian*, two Indianapolis police detectives and a Claypool Hotel bellhop were among the funeral attendees. They hoped to spot their missing "dresser drawer slayer" suspect, but they didn't.

The Claypool Hotel, where Dorothy Poore's body was found on July 18, 1954, was located at the corner of Illinois and Washington Streets in downtown Indianapolis, Indiana. *Photo courtesy the Indianapolis Police Department Archives.*

Desperate for a Woman

As the vigorous investigation continued, several witnesses told police about crossing paths with the guest occupying the Claypool's Room 665 on Thursday and Friday, July 15 and 16. Hotel records showed that the room had been registered to a man named Jack O'Shea of New York City, who had left behind plenty of excellent fingerprints. Although the prints didn't match any in the FBI files at that time, the prints would confirm O'Shea's presence in the room once he was arrested.

Hotel staff described O'Shea as about thirty years old, short with a medium build, and fair-complected with blond hair. A mail clerk at the hotel described him as "something like the sweet Van Johnson type," referring to the popular Hollywood leading man.

Bellman Bruno Widmann escorted the suspect to his sixth-floor room at around 4:20 p.m., Thursday. Widmann, a chiropractic student with a knack for drawing, sketched a likeness of the guest for the police. They, in turn, distributed the drawing to newspapers and law enforcement departments throughout the state in hopes someone would recognize him.

Widmann told the *Indianapolis Star* that "the man seemed frantic for a woman" and had insisted, "If you can get me a girl, I'll go as high as $50."

Victor Lively's hotel guest registration card shows he had registered under the pseudonym "Jack O'Shea," a resident of New York City, when he checked into the Claypool Hotel's Room 665 on July 15, 1954. *Photo courtesy the Indianapolis Police Department Archives.*

According to Widmann, the man seemed to have plenty of money, evidenced by O'Shea's thirty-five-cent tip, but Widmann declined the suspect's request, advising him that the hotel was respectable, and getting him a woman could not be done.

A cab driver told police about transporting a young man, fitting the suspect's description, from the bus station to the Claypool. According to the driver, as soon as the passenger climbed into the cab, he asked the driver to get him a woman. "I don't do things like that," the driver explained. "I have a wife and a couple kids." But as the cab approached the hotel, the passenger tried again. "He told me that he was willing to pay $150 a week for a woman to stay with him," the driver said.

Before the man exited the cab and entered the hotel, he asked the driver to wait. When he came out a few minutes later, he told the driver to send a woman to Room 665. "He paid me $1.50 on the $1.05 meter charge," the driver said, "and I drove away. I thought the guy was a little batty."

The Sweetest Thing

The suspect passed himself off as owner of the O'Shea Employment System, one of the city's busiest employment agencies, which led police to believe Dorothy had made an appointment to speak with him about a job.

The Claypool's manager told police that a young woman wearing a checkered-print dress had approached the desk at three o'clock Thursday afternoon and asked if Jack O'Shea had registered. He had not. But the *Star* reported that one of the hotel's elevator operators claimed to have taken O'Shea from the sixth floor to the lobby at around 5:00 p.m. The same operator, according to the *Star*, took a woman closely resembling Dorothy from the lobby to the sixth floor at 6:30 p.m. but couldn't recall bringing her back down. Other hotel employees did say, however, that they had seen Dorothy leave the hotel shortly past 6:30.

According to another elevator operator, O'Shea returned to the Claypool around midnight with an unidentified, blue jeans-clad young woman. Although the hotel employee could not identify O'Shea's friend as Dorothy Poore, police didn't rule out the possibility.

"They were playing around on the elevator," the operator said, "and he said, 'This is my sweetheart. Isn't she the sweetest thing you have ever seen?' "

Police found no one able to verify whether the young woman with O'Shea was Dorothy, nor could anyone say what time, or if, Dorothy returned to the Lorraine Hotel Thursday night.

The coroner decided Dorothy had died sometime between 1:00 and 3:00 p.m. Friday, which was the approximate time O'Shea called the hotel's housekeeping service and asked that his room be cleaned. Two hotel maids responded. One told police that O'Shea spoke to her quite pleasantly, but the other said he seemed "wild-eyed" when he asked her to remove a spot of blood from his bedsheet, which he blamed on a nosebleed.

After that, he went downstairs to the hotel's barbershop. The barber said O'Shea appeared distraught as he walked into the shop at about three o'clock. He wore a light sports jacket and asked if he could get a shave without taking off the jacket, explaining that his shirt was dirty. While the jacket didn't present a problem, the barber told the *Star* that he thought it curious. Police speculated that O'Shea may have been trying to hide a telltale sign, such as scratches on his arms or traces of his victim's blood on his shirt.

That was the last any of the Claypool Hotel staff saw of the man calling himself Jack O'Shea, even though hotel records showed he had paid for his room for an additional day, extending his checkout time to 4:00 p.m. Saturday.

Not a Pretty Sight

Hotel maids Ella Mae Bobby and Julia Bell entered Room 665 at around 10:00 a.m. Sunday and were immediately repelled by an offensive odor. As they searched the room for the source of the stench, Bell found it when she neared the dresser.

She slid out the top and middle drawers. Both were empty. She attempted to open the bottom drawer, but it was stuck. Although she pulled with all her strength, it wouldn't budge. She summoned houseman William Kimbrough for assistance, but he couldn't extract the bottom drawer either. So he removed the middle drawer, giving him a straight-line view of the bottom drawer's contents.

For a fleeting moment, the shock paralyzed him. He couldn't believe his eyes.

Stuffed into the drawer—measuring forty-eight inches long by twenty-four inches wide by ten inches deep—was the five-foot six-inch, 106-pound body of a young woman. Wearing only her panties, bra, and slip, she had been laid on her back with her legs folded underneath her. Her left arm was draped across her chest, and her head was jammed over her right shoulder into the container's back corner. She was badly bloated, and lividity had darkened the exposed skin from her chest up. She was not a pretty sight.

Shaken, Kimbrough notified W. Bryan Karr, the hotel manager. He, in turn, called the police.

The hotel had been in the process of installing an air conditioning system, but it had not yet reached the sixth floor. Thus, the torrid July heat had accelerated the body's decomposition. The putrid odor wafting from Room 665 necessitated the evacuation of the entire sixth floor and prompted the firemen who removed Dorothy's remains to wear gas masks.

Police immediately set to work searching the room for clues. They found a pair of jeans, a blouse, a plastic belt, and a pair of sandals stashed in the room's utility closet. Under the radiator, they found a purse containing an application for a Social Security card, a pack of gum, an address book, and a nickel. Based on the application form and the high school class ring on the dead woman's finger, police identified the victim and phoned her family.

Dorothy's mother and grandmother, Hazel and Lilly, were devastated. They had expected Dorothy to return home Saturday night. "I waited until midnight last night for her," Lilly explained. "I thought that she just had been delayed and would call today. God, who could have done anything like that?"

The coroner was never able to determine the cause of death, but he ruled out blows, bullets, and knife wounds. He also ascertained that Dorothy had not been raped. He suspected strangulation or suffocation, but the condition of the body prevented him from making a more accurate assessment.

Neither Dorothy's family nor her acquaintances understood why she was in a strange man's hotel room. That was not like her, they said. Hazel told the *Indianapolis Star* that Dorothy was "a wonderful, very fine girl" who would never "go to a room with a man on her own freewill."

Apprehended in the Show-Me State

Police weren't surprised when the Manhattan address O'Shea used at the Claypool Hotel failed to pan out, but three fast-breaking developments reported Thursday, July 22, provided detectives their best hope of locating their man.

A Claypool Hotel maid found Dorothy Poore's dead body stuffed into the lower drawer of this dresser in Room 665 at the Claypool Hotel. *Photo courtesy the Indianapolis Police Department Archives.*

First, police found a witness that had seen a man fitting the suspect's description walking to the Terminal Bus Station at Market and Illinois Streets at noon Saturday. Second, an employee of a northeast Indianapolis laundry identified the suspect as a woman-crazy, former co-worker named Victor Hale Lively, who spoke with a Texas drawl. And third, by comparing the signatures on the registration cards at both the Kirkwood and Claypool Hotels, police ascertained that their suspect had stayed at the Kirkwood as Lively, until Thursday afternoon, when he checked in at the Claypool as O'Shea.

Buses departing the terminal around the time Lively was spotted were destined for Fort Wayne, Muncie, and Terre Haute. Police asked authorities in those areas to be on the lookout for their suspect. Now that police had their man's real name, an accurate description, and the direction he was headed, the manhunt evolved quickly.

Police were confident that Lively's apprehension would be only a matter of time, and they had been right. Lively was picked up the next day, Friday, July 23, by deputies Robert Wilkerson and Carroll Rowland of the sheriff's department of St. Louis County, Missouri. One of them spotted Lively shortly before noon stepping out of a clump of bushes on U.S. Highway 66, twenty-five miles west of St. Louis. Wearing a yellow sport shirt and light blue trousers, Lively had been hitchhiking his way to Texas to see his mother. He might have avoided capture had he not stopped to relieve his bladder.

Lively had no identification on him. When the deputies asked his name, he promptly told them. Under one arm, he carried a small package wrapped in newspaper. The deputies told him to unwrap it. Tearing away the paper to reveal a .32 caliber Mauser automatic pistol, Lively nervously explained that he needed the gun "because there are so many bad men on the highways." Things might happen to a lone guy walking along the road if he didn't have a weapon to take care of himself, he pleaded.

Lively needn't have bothered with the vulnerability act. The deputies knew who he was. Moments before noticing him along the road, they had seen a story in one of the area papers about the Indianapolis murder and the hunt for the suspect. They cuffed Lively in the backseat of their patrol car and drove him to the sheriff's office in nearby Clayton, the St. Louis County seat. There, they turned him over to a pair of formidable interrogators, Captain Harry Newbold and Deputy Sheriff Hugh Bresnahan. Within two hours, Lively admitted to killing Dorothy Poore. Once Indianapolis Police Detective Sergeants Randolph Schubert and Harold Goodman arrived, he filled in details.

Lively claimed he had picked up Dorothy and her friend, whom he knew only as Ruth, at a hamburger stand the evening of Thursday, July 15, and the two women had willingly accompanied him to his room at the Claypool. The three had indulged in gin and tonics for at least two hours before Ruth announced she wanted to go. However, according to Lively, Dorothy wanted to stay. And that, he said, led to a spat and prompted Ruth to tear out of the room, leaving Dorothy behind.

Lively claimed Dorothy was happy to be alone with him. In fact, she stripped down to her slip, bra, and panties to make herself comfortable. She even promised to follow him wherever he went. "She didn't have anywhere else to go," he said. All was fine for the next hour or so, Lively said, until she turned on him, rejecting the gin and insisting he buy her some whiskey. He flat out refused, he said. He didn't want to spend more money.

He claimed Dorothy grew furious and resorted to vile language. But when she started swinging her fists at him, he had no choice but to wrap his arm around her throat to subdue her. After two or three minutes in his embrace, she collapsed onto the bed, he said.

According to Lively's confession, he spent the rest of the night sitting in his room, while he finished off his bottle of gin and pondered his options. Early Friday morning, he folded Dorothy's lifeless body into the bottom drawer of the dresser, deposited her jeans, blouse, and sandals in a ventilator, and left the hotel to grab a bite to eat and clear his head.

She Was Asking for It
Although Lively was unable to formulate a story that exonerated himself as Dorothy Poore's killer, he cavalierly painted a tale designed to pin at least part of the blame on his victim. She was drunk, he asserted, and she was selfish. Worst of all, evidenced by the scant clothing she was found wearing, she was loose.

Schubert and Goodman weren't buying it. Two days before, they had traveled to Clinton for Dorothy's funeral and talked with one of her friends, William Marts, whom she had occasionally dated. According to the July 21, 1954, *Indianapolis Star*, Marts had told the detectives, "She wouldn't even go with me in my car until I had known her for quite a while." Marts was certain Dorothy would not have gone to the man's room, unless she had a very good reason, such as a job interview. Because the alleged killer had passed himself off as the owner of the O'Shea Employment System, Marts and the detectives believed Dorothy had naively visited "O'Shea's" hotel room in an effort to obtain a job, according to the *Star*, and not for a love tryst.

Lively's reputation was not nearly as sterling as his victim's. He had grown up in Beaumont, Texas, the adopted son of Jack and Sadie Lively. He left home in 1951, five months before his father died, and returned only three times. He was on his way back, when he was picked up in Missouri. He hadn't known that his mother had died on April 1. Lively had been in minor trouble in Beaumont, according to Beaumont Police Captain J. D. Wingate. The officer said Lively had been running employment opportunity ads in the local paper in a scheme to lure young women to his hotel room. Once they were there, he persuaded them to strip down to their undies and parade around the room. Although someone finally reported him, he was never arrested.

Revises Confession
Lively signed a waiver of extradition on Saturday morning, July 24, in Clayton, Missouri. Shortly after, his hands were secured to a belt to prevent him from striking at Schubert and Goodman, and they headed east for Indianapolis.

Murder suspect Victor Lively *(second from right)* is accompanied by Indianapolis Police Captain Robert Reilly *(center)* and Detective Harold Goodman *(right)*, when they arrived in Indianapolis on July 24, 1954, after Lively fled to St. Louis following Dorothy Poore's murder eight days before. *Photo courtesy Indianapolis Police Department Archives.*

The detectives reported that during the four-hour car trip, Lively expressed a growing dread of the electric chair, repeatedly groaning, "I know they'll burn me."

After reaching the Indianapolis police headquarters, Lively was interrogated by five investigators. Within thirty minutes, he changed the story he told the Missouri officers and admitted he had choked Dorothy for resisting his repeated assaults of rape. As the *Indianapolis Star* noted, Lively's revised statement restored his victim's exemplary reputation as a "respectable" young woman, who was in Indianapolis to find a good job.

Further amending his confession, he added that he lied about Dorothy insisting on whiskey. "I lied about an argument arising over the drinking," he reportedly told police. "She didn't have anything to drink at all."

He also added that neither Dorothy nor her friend, Ruth, acted like a prostitute, and neither woman had made an advance on him. In fact, he said, once Ruth left, he put the moves on Dorothy, and she successfully resisted.

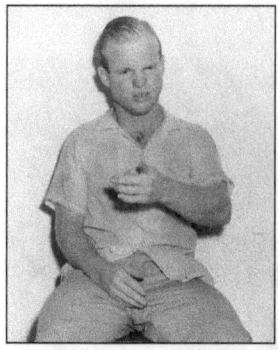

Victor Lively—suspected of killing eighteen-year-old Dorothy Poore at the Claypool Pool and stuffing her body in a dresser drawer—is shown here during his first interrogation by Indianapolis police detectives on July 24, 1954. *Photos courtesy Indianapolis Police Department Archives.*

But her continued resistance frustrated him, taxed his manly pride, pushed his determination, and lit the flame to his indignation.

It was during his third futile sexual attack that he snapped. When Dorothy began to scream, he said, he wrapped his hands around her neck and choked her. He told the police that with her still-warm, lifeless body stretched out on the bed, he settled into a nearby chair until dawn, drinking gin, and contemplating how he could best save his own neck. By morning's first light, he had figured out a plan. He put Dorothy in the dresser drawer and left the building.

When one of the officers asked Lively why he killed Dorothy, he replied weakly, "I don't know."

The grand jury indicted Lively on Thursday, August 12 on the charge of first-degree murder by strangulation or suffocation with premeditated malice by means unknown. Fulfilling the promise made to Lively two weeks before, Marion County Prosecutor Frank H. Fairchild vowed to demand the death penalty. After two state-appointed attorneys quit the case, Lively managed to scrape together $500 to hire defense attorney Ferdinand Samper.

Lively's new lawyer—a forty-year-old, life-long Indianapolis resident in his fourth year of legal practice—promised to make the prosecutor's job a nightmare. He would subpoena "everybody" connected with the case, he said, including the St. Louis County deputy sheriffs who arrested his client along Route 66. A week later, on August 19, after implementing a variety of stall tactics and bogus claims about Lively's rights, Samper's hot-tempered client appeared before Judge Saul I. Rabb in criminal court, division 2. Despite previously signing a confession to the murder, Lively entered a plea of "not guilty," claiming his confession was coerced.

Samper stonewalled the procedure for two months. His stall tactics included calling for a new judge, dismissing habeas corpus proceedings, and throwing out the confession. The trial was finally scheduled to begin October 11, but on September 29, Marion County Prosecutor Fairchild was admitted to Robert W. Long Hospital for high blood pressure and died a few days later. The deputy prosecutor took over and postponed the trial until Monday, November 15, despite Samper's irate objections. Samper's plate was overflowing, however. A third indictment, charging Lively with murder during attempted rape, was entered on October 13; and the search for the elusive Ruth, was still underway.

Order in the Court
The trial finally started on the assigned day in Judge Rabb's dingy, Marion County criminal courtroom in the courthouse basement. The room had space to seat only sixty spectators, but more than two hundred jammed the outer hallway, hoping to get in. Day one was spent selecting the twelve members of the jury from a pool of fifty candidates. While questioning them, Lively's attorney revealed that he intended to seek a lesser charge of manslaughter for his client, a penalty that carried a sentence of a mere two to twenty-one years.

During that first day of his trial, Lively sat quietly at the defense table, chomping on gum and picking wax from his left ear, while his attorney laid out his strategy—that his client had been in a drunken stupor the night of Dorothy's death and remembered nothing; thus, he had to be innocent. In questioning the first several prospective jurors, all of them male, Samper asked if they would "hold it against a man who took an unmarried girl to a hotel room."

Judge Rabb deemed that line of questioning a cunning way to imply that such a girl was promiscuous and, therefore, asking for trouble. He put a stop to the question, warning Samper that trying to plant doubt about the victim's moral character was out of order. "The girl is not on trial," the judge said.

Thinking he could bend the male jurors' perspective to his favor, Samper had hoped for an all-male jury panel. However, to his great dismay, when all twelve jurors were seated five days later, one of them was female.

The first day of testimony followed on Monday, November 22. John Daily and James Rocap, Jr., for the prosecution, called eleven witnesses—hotel employees, taxi drivers, police, the coroner, and medical personnel among them—and methodically started building the state's case.

First called was hotel maid Julia Bell, who testified about finding Dorothy Poore's body. Bell described how she "broke away and ran" when her co-worker, houseman William Kimbrough, pulled out the middle dresser drawer and exposed Dorothy's swollen, decomposing remains in the drawer below. Next, the coroner told the court why he had returned a verdict of death by strangulation, and the toxicologist testified that there was no evidence of poison or drugs in the girl's vital organs. Indianapolis Police Sergeant John Sullivan followed, recounting how he'd found Dorothy's clothing hidden in an air duct in the hotel room and revealing publicly, for the first time, that a pamphlet and pornographic pictures had been found there too. Sullivan also described a nasty bruise on Dorothy's neck that had already bred flesh-eating worms.

Two days later, on Wednesday, November 24, the defense entered a motion, asking the court to release Lively on the grounds that the arrest was illegal because his client had been coerced into signing a confession he "supposedly" made in Clayton, Missouri. Lively took the stand and swore that Captain Harry Newbold of the sheriff's office had threatened physical harm if he refused. "I was scared," Lively said. "I was afraid of getting whipped." Newbold strongly denied making any such remark, noting that Lively was in public view the entire time he was in the St. Louis County jail.

Lively took the witness stand again on Friday, November 26. That time he claimed he had signed the confession to avoid the electric chair. He explained that when he was eight, he had seen a man burn to death on high-voltage power lines in his neighborhood. It had been horrible to watch, he said, and terrified him that he might die the same way in the electric chair. "They couldn't touch the man's body for three hours without the flesh coming away from the bones," Lively blubbered.

With that, Chief Deputy Prosecutor Daily snarled, "You know the flesh fell off Dorothy Poore's bones, don't you?" At that, Samper shouted an objection. The judge sustained it.

The Story of Ruth
Indianapolis Police Detective Sergeant Harold Goodman gave testimony on November 26 about Lively's third confession that he made to Goodman and his partner, Detective Sergeant Randolph Schubert, on July 24 in the car as they drove Lively back to Indiana from Missouri.

According to the November 27 *Indianapolis Star*, Goodman testified that as he, Schubert, and Lively were en route to Indianapolis, Lively sat in the backseat happily chewing on a wad of his favorite tobacco as he told stories about how he'd met and murdered Dorothy Poore.

Among the stories, Goodman said, was Lively's account of meeting a woman named Ruth the evening of Friday, July 16, and that when he had asked her to get him a woman, she agreed to do it. Sometime later, as Lively claimed, Ruth and a shy, eighteen-year-old girl named Dorothy came to his hotel room. After he and Ruth shared a few gin and tonics, Dorothy agreed to go out with him for something to eat. Ruth stayed behind and, according to Lively's story, when they returned to the room, she was gone.

Goodman said Lively told him that he "made a pass at Dorothy," but she "brushed him off." Lively said he then became physical with Dorothy, struggling with her to remove her clothing, and then trying to have "sexual relations with her," but it was impossible.

"She was screaming like she was trying to hit high C," said Goodman, quoting Lively. He continued reciting Lively's words: "Someone turned the light on in the hallway, and I tried to shut her up. I put my arms around her throat. When I realized what I was doing, I let go of her, but she was gurgling and sucking air. Blood was coming out of her mouth." Afterward, according to Lively's story as told by Goodman, Lively sat in the room drinking gin. When the sun came up, he crammed Dorothy's body into the dresser drawer and tied her legs together with her blouse.

Goodman said he asked Lively if he had sex with Dorothy after she was dead, and Lively reportedly said, "I couldn't do a thing like that. I just couldn't."

Looney Lively Testimony
The Tuesday, November 30 *Indianapolis News* reported that Lively had taken the stand that day and delivered a slightly different rendition of the story Goodman had given Friday. In his revised version, Lively told the court that he and Dorothy had been gleefully making love until "all of a sudden, she let out a scream like a high C." While it was the same note Goodman disclosed

on Friday, in Lively's story on Tuesday, the scream caused him to "black out." Furthermore, when he came to several hours later, Dorothy was dead and he was clueless.

Lively told the court that Dorothy had "seemed shy and almost blushing" when she went up to the room with him around midnight. But after a while, she got to "playing around" and became more than a willing partner, even taking the initiative of stripping down to her underwear. According to Lively, after she helped him remove his shirt, she had said, "You look like a man. … How much of a man are you?" When he woke up and found her dead, he had tried to revive her with wet towels. Realizing he couldn't, he thought of reporting the situation to the police, but because he had been drinking, the idea scared him.

As the *News* reported, Lively continued his bizarre story, explaining, "I just sat there trying to figure out what had happened. I started getting really scared. This didn't make sense to me."

Samper next asked his client if he was finally telling the truth. Lively replied, "Yes, sir, I am. All those other stories, I just made up."

When Lively's attorney asked if he placed Dorothy's body in the dresser, Lively said he must have, "Because I was the only one in the room."

Samper then called Grace Lawson, who, according to Lively, was the mysterious "Ruth," who had accompanied Dorothy to his hotel room. Lively previously described "Ruth" as a "big-busted" woman, so in an apparent attempt to corroborate her identity, Samper asked Lawson to remove her coat. She did, prompting chuckles from the spectators, and Samper promptly dismissed her.

After a ten-minute recess, Chief Deputy Prosecutor John Daily shredded Lively's preposterous testimony about his gin-induced blackout with a razor-sharp cross-examination. When Lively repeated that he didn't remember strangling Dorothy, Daily surprised the courtroom with a photo enlarged to forty-eight by thirty-six-inches showing her badly decomposed body in the dresser drawer. Turning to Lively, Daily snapped, "Maybe this will refresh your memory." Lively sank back in his seat, his revulsion exposed, and sheepishly said, "It doesn't look like Dot."

The Thirteenth Day
The defense rested late that Tuesday. The state's rebuttal ended shortly before noon the next day, Wednesday, December 1. Closing arguments followed, each side limited to two hours. Daily implored the jury to send Lively to the

chair "for the foul and premeditated" murder, suggesting that Lively had engaged in sex with his victim after he had strangled her. Samper argued that because Lively had been in a gin stupor at the time Dorothy was strangled, the charge should be reduced to manslaughter. After receiving the instructions from Judge Rabb, the jurors retired to the jury room at 4:30 p.m. and began deliberating. It was the trial's thirteenth day.

The jury reached its unanimous decision at 1:35 a.m. Thursday. The jury foreman said none of the jurors questioned Lively's guilt. The matter up for debate was the punishment. Three of the members held out for death. On the fifth ballot, the jury reached unanimous agreement—nine hours and five minutes after departing the courtroom.

The bailiff notified the Marion County jail, where Lively was being held, that the verdict had been reached. When Lively was awakened, he was visibly shaking. He asked for a hamburger to calm his nerves. The *Indianapolis Star* reported that as Lively was led into the courtroom, he commented to the bailiff, "I feel like a bride at a shower."

Trembling, Lively fixed his gaze on the floor as he stood before Judge Rabb awaiting his fate. Lively nearly collapsed when the judge read the jury's verdict: guilty of first-degree murder. The judge immediately sentenced Lively to life in prison. Awash with relief, Lively fell onto his attorney's shoulder and sobbed amid a barrage of flash bulbs popping all around him. Samper said to him, "I saved your life," to which Lively could only wheeze, "Yeah." He was quickly handcuffed and led from the courtroom. It was 2:00 a.m.

Reporters immediately gathered around the attorneys and shouted questions: "Are you satisfied with the verdict?" … "Will you appeal?" … "What about the sentence?"

Squeezing through the crowd, Samper was heard saying, "He isn't going to die. That's all I can say now."

Regarding the verdict, Daily offered, "It's fine. I knew we had a good jury."

On Friday, as dawn was breaking, Victor Lively, accompanied by two Marion County deputies, left Indianapolis bound for the Indiana State Prison in Michigan City. Stepping into the vehicle, in answer to an *Indianapolis News* reporter's question regarding his future plans, Lively said, "I'm going to study real hard and get myself a degree."

It wasn't likely. According to Lively's aunt in Nederland, Texas, once her nephew reached the ninth grade, he "flatly refused" to attend school, and he quit, never again cracking open a textbook.

Epilogue

Judge Rabb denied Lively's request for a new trial, leaving the Indiana Supreme Court his only option, assuming the high court would accept the case. However, while a favorable decision by the high court may have been Lively's last chance to get his life sentence overturned, a new trial did not come without the risk of another jury sending him to the electric chair.

Lively did seek a new trial but not until the spring of 1977, when he filed a petition asking to be declared a pauper. Had his petition been granted, he could have asked the public defender to review his case and possibly get him his long-awaited, new trial. Ironically, later that same year, Ferdinand Samper died, taking with him the invaluable knowledge and experience gained in trying Lively's case.

Eventually, Lively won his freedom. It came in the form of a parole on July 25, 1980—almost twenty-six years to the day that he strangled the life out of Dorothy Poore. Lively met his own death after suffering a heart attack just six months later. He was fifty-two, which had given him thirty-four more years than Dorothy had.

Many decades have passed since the starry-eyed, young woman from Clinton stepped off the bus in the Capital City, eager to start her life. Dorothy Poore had prepared well for the career she dreamed of and should have enjoyed the future that was hers. The odds of her stepping off that bus into the waiting hands of death were infinitesimally small, and yet she did. The irony couldn't be more blatant and tragic. ❖

2

THE CASE OF THE 'FLAMING YOUTH' MURDER

Dateline: Vanderburgh County, 1933

The trial opened January 3, 1934. Eight days later, Cyril Staab sat stiffly behind the defense table in Judge Union Youngblood's Vanderburgh County courtroom gnashing his teeth and rubbing his moist palms together. He was intent on projecting a facade of cool composure, despite the tension surging through his veins. Within minutes, he would learn the jury's decision: guilty or not guilty. Did he or did he not shoot and kill twenty-year-old Mary Elizabeth Robb during the wee hours of October 15, 1933, following a drunken "flaming-youth" party at a seedy Evansville roadhouse? The girl's shocking, untimely death had been the talk of Evansville for nearly three months; and the trial had kept the city spinning for a solid week, proving the old adage that one man's entertainment is another man's nightmare.

Seated to Cyril's left was his attorney, Orville Reeves. To Cyril's right was his father, George Staab, and his audibly sobbing grandmother, Carrie Schwering. The trial had been a test of stamina for each of them.

The overflowing courtroom was abuzz with chatter, until the door suddenly swung open and twelve men paraded in and took their seats in the jury box. Foreman Eugene Eisterhold passed a folded slip of paper to Bailiff James Stockwell, who, in turn, handed it to Deputy Clerk Ed Sauer. The spectators held their breath, and stillness enveloped the room.

The clerk unfolded the paper, and Cyril's heart rate spiked. He thought back to Deputy Prosecutor James Meyer's ridiculous opening argument, labeling Cyril as "not just a killer" but rather "a super killer," painting him as "heartless, callous, and vicious, with a soul filled with malice."

Cyril was incensed. How could anyone believe that the popular, mild-mannered, twenty-two-year-old son of an Evansville police officer, a graduate of Lockyear Business College, and a promising, hard-working bookkeeper with no prior criminal record was a super killer? He rolled that distinction around in his head, and his thoughts flashed back to that Saturday night last October. It was supposed to have been an enjoyable night on the town with friends—dancing, imbibing some cheap booze, and making a little whoopee. Where had it all gone wrong?

A Date with Death
On the crisp afternoon of Saturday, October 14, 1933, Cyril took a break from his duties at the collections office, where he worked for Edward Gumble, Sr., and phoned Mary Elizabeth Robb. The two had met that spring at the Lockyear Business College and dated occasionally. After three rings, Mary Elizabeth answered with a tentative, "Hello," and Cyril wasted no time getting to the point.

"Hi ya', Mary," he blurted out. "How 'bout I pick you up around nine o'clock tonight, and we'll go out to Smitty's and have some fun?"

After an uncomfortably long pause, Mary Elizabeth told him, "Oh, gosh, Cyril, I don't know. I'm not sure that's such a good idea."

Her reservations were well-founded. She didn't know Cyril well, certainly not well enough for a late-night date at a roadhouse dance club. Who knew what might happen? What if he drank too much? What if he tried to get fresh with her? With these concerns swirling through her head, Mary Elizabeth wasn't comfortable committing, and that's what she told him.

Cyril was peeved, but he didn't give up. He explained that his friends, Edward Gumbel, Jr., twenty-three, and his fiancée, Beulah Bender, eighteen, would be joining them. Learning she would have a female ally, Mary Elizabeth relented and accepted Cyril's invitation, even though nothing in her proper, small-town Indiana upbringing could have prepared her.

The Robb family—Roy and Polly and their daughters, Norma and Mary Elizabeth—was known well throughout the Robb Township community of Stewartsville, located twenty miles northeast of Evansville in Posey County. Mary Elizabeth had been a brilliant student, who excelled in dramatics and

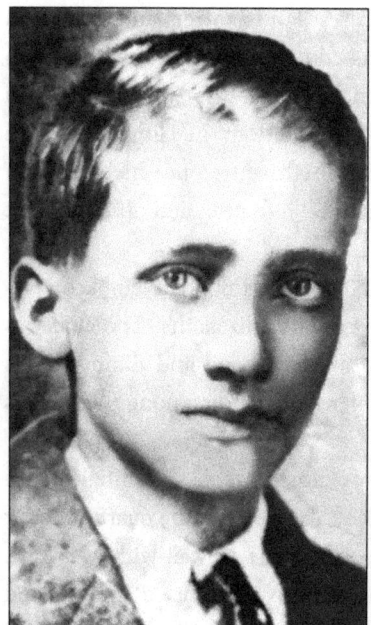 

Cyril Staab *(left)*, a twenty-two-year-old, Evansville, Indiana, bookkeeper, was convicted for the shooting death of twenty-year-old Mary Elizabeth Robb *(right)* of Stewartsville in 1933. The two had met the previous year, while attending the Evansville-based Lockyear Business College.

was a prominent member of the Stewartsville High School Drama Club. Had her family's worldview been broader, she might have traveled to Chicago, or perhaps even New York, to pursue a career on the stage. Instead, after graduating high school in 1930, she moved to Evansville and attended business school. However, after completing her courses, she settled for a position as a domestic.

Roadhouse Rendezvous
Edward and Beulah picked up Cyril that evening at his office and proceeded to the Staab residence on West Indiana Street. The couple waited in Edward's roadster while Cyril entered the house and talked with his dad. The father-son relationship had taken a bumpy turn of late, and when Cyril returned to the auto a few minutes later, he grumbled that his father, an Evansville motorcycle patrolman, had suffered a bike accident a few hours before and was in a lot of discomfort, not to mention a bad mood.

"I wish something would happen to him so he would kick off," Cyril complained, "then I could get his insurance money."

The three next made a stop on Northwest Fourth Street and purchased two pints of liquor. According to Beulah's courtroom testimony, they then made their way to Mary Elizabeth's residence on Delaware Street. After Cyril brought her out to the car and made the introductions, he climbed into the seat next to Beulah and helped Mary Elizabeth settle onto his lap. With everyone crammed into the car, Edward shifted into gear, and off they went. Destination: Smitty's.

Located at the busy intersection of Lincoln and South Weinbach Avenues, Smitty's was a three-mile drive from Mary Elizabeth's. The club was open nightly until 1:30 a.m. and offered a dance band and dining for its twenty-five-cent admission. It was a popular destination among Evansville's younger, fun-seeking clientele.

Once the four arrived at the club, they claimed a table and mingled with others—talking, laughing, and dancing. They also downed the quart of liquor they picked up earlier. Unfortunately, alcohol didn't sit well with everyone. Around midnight, Edward became nauseous, so he excused himself and strolled outside for fresh air.

"The rest of us were still in the club at one-thirty, when it closed and the orchestra began putting their instruments away," Beulah later explained, neglecting to note that they were all tipsy. "That's when we went out to the car and found Eddie."

He was feeling better but not well enough to drive. He and Cyril had a brief exchange with Beulah and named her the designated driver. Everyone piled into the roadster, with Mary Elizabeth again sitting on Cyril's lap, and they were off for their next adventure.

Around two o'clock, the foursome arrived at the Brown Derby Restaurant and Cottages at U.S. Route 41 near the Evansville-Henderson Bridge. The attendant, twenty-one-year-old William Burnett, greeted them. Edward asked for a room, and William stepped onto the car's running board, directing Beulah to the back row of cabins. He stopped her at Cabin 12 and proceeded inside to turn on the heat. Beulah and Edward stayed in the car, but Cyril and Mary Elizabeth climbed out and disappeared into the shadows.

Beulah told police that as she waited, she heard a sound "like a cap pistol." Her head spun in the direction of the noise, and in the penumbra of the roadster's headlights, she saw Mary Elizabeth lying facedown in the cinder driveway and Cyril standing five-to-ten feet away. He looked up at Beulah for a beat before crying out, "My God, she's shot herself with my gun. Scoot over.

I'll get in and we'll act as if we never met the girl."

Until that moment, Beulah and Edward had been unaware Cyril had brought a .25 caliber pistol.

A Mortal Wound

William was still inside the cabin when he heard the gunshot. Looking out the rear door, he saw Cyril pacing toward a crumpled body on the ground. William rushed out and ran to the young woman. He told the police, "With Staab's aid, I turned her over. I saw the hole in her forehead and a criss-cross cut around it. I asked Staab what happened, and he told me the girl had fallen and injured herself."

William said he was certain Mary Elizabeth's injury was a gunshot wound, but he didn't see the gun.

"Staab asked if he could leave her at the cabin," William said, "and I told him, 'No, you have to get her to a hospital.'"

William helped Cyril and Edward pick up the unconscious woman and place her in the roadster's rumble seat. Because of the situation's critical nature, William firmly believed Mary Elizabeth should not be alone in the seat. But when he suggested someone ought to climb into the back and sit with her, Cyril snapped, "Not me!"

When the car drove away with Mary Elizabeth slumped in the rumble seat alone, William assumed it was headed for the hospital.

"I told them to hurry because she was hurt bad," he said.

Beulah drove down U.S. 41 toward the hospital, but when she reached Riverside Drive, Cyril insisted she continue to Waterworks Road, and she did. There, he told her to turn and pull over. According to Beulah, she stopped the car and Cyril climbed out, clenching the gun.

"He wiped it with a handkerchief and thrust it into the dirt," she told the police. "That's to take the fingerprints off," Cyril explained when he returned. "It's a stolen gun," he added offhandedly, "and if it's found, I'd be ruined."

Cyril proposed dumping their mortally wounded companion in a cornfield, Beulah claimed, but she ignored him and resumed driving. When they reached the Welborn-Walker Hospital, Cyril rang the night bell. Three nurses came out and helped carry Mary Elizabeth inside. Cyril stayed at the hospital, while his friends hightailed it to Edward's house to break the news to his dad.

By sunrise Sunday, October 15, Edward Gumbel, Sr., had escorted his son to the police station and informed the two emergency officers on duty what

The popular Brown Derby's restaurant and cottages were located outside of Evansville on U.S. Highway 41 near the Evansville-Henderson Bridge. Mary Elizabeth Robb was shot in the head in the area of the cottages shortly after she, Cyril Staab, Edward Gumble, and Beulah Bender made a stop there at around two o'clock the morning of October 15, 1933. *Photo courtesy of the Willard Public Library Archives.*

had transpired at the Brown Derby tourist campgrounds. The officers immediately went to the hospital and arrested Cyril. Detectives scoured Gumbel's route between the campground and the hospital for the gun, but their efforts were futile.

Mary Elizabeth was pronounced dead at approximately 4:30 p.m., and within hours, two of the hospital's doctors on staff had performed an autopsy at the Klee and Burkhart Funeral Home. In examining the bullet hole in the center of Mary Elizabeth's forehead, they found no powder burns, which suggested the shot had not been self-inflicted. The bullet was lodged deep inside her brain, an inch and a half behind her left ear, despite Cyril's efforts to dig it out with a sharp instrument. The only other mark on Mary Elizabeth's body was swelling and discoloration around her left eye, which the doctors attributed to her fall. Anticipating the unexpressed question on everyone's mind, the doctors confirmed that she had not engaged in sexual relations, nor was she pregnant. And with that, they released her body to the Robbs' home in Stewartsville.

Murder Most Brutal

Police detained Cyril, Edward, and Beulah for questioning early Sunday. By nightfall, they had released Beulah. They held Edward and Cyril overnight, although the prospect of Cyril walking away scot-free wasn't promising. On Monday, William Burnette was taken into custody but was released after making a statement and swearing he had not seen Mary Elizabeth handle Cyril's gun. Cyril, however, reportedly clung to his story that Mary Elizabeth shot herself.

Evansville newspapers reported that, according to Vanderburgh County Prosecutor Winfield Denton, a murder charge would "undoubtedly be filed" as soon as the investigation was complete and a grand jury assembled. In the meantime, Denton and Vanderburgh County Coroner Edward Kraft traveled to Stewartsville to visit the Robb family and take a closer look at the cut around the fatal wound in Mary Elizabeth's forehead.

The October 16 edition of the *Evansville Journal* reported that the cut extended from her hairline to "almost the top of her nose." The story went on to state:

> It is clean, as if it had been cut with a razor, except where the instrument was gouged into the actual wound. According to Kraft, it appears that the knife or other instrument used was first inserted into the bullet hole and forcibly turned, tearing out small fragments of bone from the skull, evidently while the girl was still alive.

Denton told the *Journal* on Monday that the murder of Mary Elizabeth Robb was one of the "most brutal" he had ever come across. On Tuesday, he charged Cyril with premeditated, first-degree murder for which bail would be denied. Edward, who also had been held in jail since Sunday, was set free. Two weeks and two days later, the grand jury indicted Cyril Staab. His request for bail was denied again, and the trial was set for December 18 but later postponed to January 3.

Dirty Lick

Following jury selection, the Staab trial kicked off on the afternoon of Thursday, January 4, 1934, with the attorneys' opening statements. "Staab was five feet away from the girl, and we have evidence to show conclusively that he shot her," prosecuting attorney Denton asserted.

But Ollie Reeves, for the defense, took the opposite view. He insisted the case was based purely on circumstantial evidence and that he had the evidence to show conclusively that the girl had killed herself, either accidentally or intentionally. But when Reeves blatantly declared that Mary Elizabeth willingly went to the Brown Derby campground to spend the night, her father, Roy Robb, jarred the courtroom when he sprang from his seat at the prosecution table, banged the tip of his cane into the hardwood floor, and cried out, "It's a lie! My daughter never would have done that!"

Beulah Bender was the first witness called by the prosecution. She described the "whoopee party's" activities that evening, starting with Cyril's introduction of Mary Elizabeth through the foursome's arrival at the campground and ending with the shooting. She also described the confusion that erupted on the drive to the hospital and the stop Cyril insisted she make along the way.

Bolstering the prosecution's case was Beulah's disclosure of a brief, but stunning, verbal exchange she'd had with Mary Elizabeth at the club.

"I remarked that she had a pretty dress," Beulah testified, "and Mary answered that it was dirty because Cyril had knocked her down and given her a 'dirty lick.'"

Equally helpful to the prosecution was Beulah's declaration that prior to the group's arrival at the Brown Derby campgrounds, "the Robb girl did not know where we were going, as nothing had been said in her presence about going there."

Beulah's statement, in essence, laid the groundwork for the prosecution's final argument, that Cyril had killed Mary Elizabeth because she refused to spend the night with him. And further, Denton maintained, throwing away the gun, as Cyril had done en route to the hospital, was clearly the act of a guilty man. Thus, in his closing argument on Wednesday, January 10, the prosecution asked the jury to convict the "heartless, callous, and vicious" defendant with first- or second-degree murder. "There couldn't be any other verdict," he said. Throughout the prosecution's summary, Mary Elizabeth's mother wept inconsolably, her father sat bent forward with his chin resting on the crook of his cane, and Cyril, seated a few feet away, appeared emotionless and unmoved.

On the other side of the coin, the defense strenuously argued that the case was "wholly circumstantial." Defense attorney Reeves insisted that Mary Elizabeth had shot herself; and yes, his client had disposed of the gun, but he did so out of fear. Furthermore, he said, no one had witnessed the shooting. According to the *Evansville Journal*, during his final argument, Reeves hammered home that point with a fiery appeal to the jury:

> You are asked by the state to infer that the defendant fired the shot with premeditated malice. The girl was out there in front of the car by herself. No one

saw her, and no one knows what happened. You do not have to send a man to the electric chair or the penitentiary on such flimsy, ridiculous evidence as found in this case.

With that, Reeves rested his case and sat down. During the course of the week-long trial, the courtroom had been packed, tears had flowed, emotions had surged, and Cyril had not taken the stand. The case was handed over to the jury at 3:05 p.m. Wednesday. After deliberating less than four hours, the jury returned its verdict.

The Jury Speaks
The courtroom was still jammed with the curious spectators when the foreman handed the decision to the deputy clerk. The court clerk unfolded the paper, and a hush fell over the room. As the decision was read aloud, Cyril clenched his sweaty fists and his impassive expression turned dour.

"We, the jury," the clerk recited, "find the defendant guilty of murder in the second degree."

The January 11 *Evansville Journal* reported that immediately after the verdict was read, Cyril's grandmother "wept violently and tears burst from his shaken father's eyes." Once the meaning of the clerk's words sunk in, Cyril's dark demeanor began to lighten. After a moment, he patted his grandmother and draped an arm around his father's shoulder as he whispered to him with a thin smile. Judge Youngblood dismissed the jurors and instructed the defendant to return the following afternoon for sentencing. Seven deputies and police officers then ushered Cyril back to his jail cell across the street.

Mary Elizabeth's father told the *Journal* reporter that he and his wife were comfortable with the outcome. "Nothing can satisfy us for the loss of Mary Elizabeth," he said, "but we are content with the verdict."

Cyril's father, however, was not. He remained firmly convinced that his son was innocent and vowed to fight for his freedom for as long as it took.

Perhaps no one was more pleased with the trial's outcome than Winfield Denton. In a statement to the *Evansville Journal*, the prosecuting attorney said:

> The defense tells us [Mary Elizabeth] wanted to fire a pistol and shot herself. Do you honestly think she wanted to go out to a camp and shoot a gun for target practice that time of the night, or fire a salute to let everybody know she was there? I'm satisfied Mary Elizabeth was a good girl. I'm satisfied Staab shot her, and she died fighting for her virtue.

Prison-bound

Thin and pallid, Cyril returned to the crowded courtroom on Thursday, January 11 for sentencing. Looking down at the young man seated at the defense table, Judge Youngblood asked, "Do you have any reason your sentence should not be passed?"

Cyril replied, "No, sir."

The judge ordered Cyril to stand. His expression devoid of interest, he rose and faced the judge.

"A jury has found you guilty of murder in the second degree," the judge said. "Therefore, the court now finds that you shall spend the remainder of your natural life in prison."

He then remanded the prisoner to the custody of the sheriff and adjourned the court. Minutes later, on the way back to his cell, Cyril brazenly declared to spectators, "I could have given the judge the Bronx cheer, and he couldn't have given me anything more."

Cyril was removed from his Evansville jail cell at 2:30 a.m. Saturday, January 13, securely shackled and whisked away by Deputy Sheriffs Walter Crowther and Ollie Weaver. The gates to the Indiana State Prison in Michigan City opened for him at 9:15 a.m.

Weaver told the *Evansville Press* that Cyril had vowed to do his stretch "in the easiest way" in hopes of an early parole. "We told him goodbye when we left him with the receiving guard and advised him to be a good boy," Weaver said.

According to the *Press*, as the two deputies left Cyril at the entrance to the inner gate, he shook their hands and told them, "Whenever you're up here, look me up." And with that, he smiled and stepped inside the impenetrable, towering walls that surrounded his new home.

Epilogue

Within days of Cyril's imprisonment, his attorney filed a motion for a new trial, but ultimately, it was denied. His father died on April 10 that year, following an appendectomy; and Cyril, accompanied by a prison guard, was allowed a brief trip home to attend the funeral. The following August, Cyril's elusive .25 caliber pistol finally turned up in Evansville's Bee Slough, a natural waterway that drained a large portion of the city's southside. Mary Elizabeth's father died of a heart attack on April 10, 1936—exactly two years following the death of Cyril's father.

Three-and-a-half years later, the *Evansville Press* carried a page eight story headlined, "Evansville Man Active in Publication of Magazine at Michigan City Prison." According to a letter to the paper from Cyril, the publication, *Bourne*, had been established as an experiment in "promoting a better understanding between those inside and those outside." Cyril served as editor.

He continued his editorial pursuit until he was paroled by Indiana Governor Henry Schricker in January 1945. He had served eleven years of his life sentence—a sliver compared to the years remaining for the life he stole. Upon release, Cyril immediately relocated to Gary, where he found work in a steel mill and met his future wife, Rose Drake. The couple married the following September. For the rest of his life, Cyril maintained his innocence in the death of Mary Elizabeth Robb, insisting she had shot herself.

Cyril Staab, the once notorious flaming youth, died quietly in 1974. He was sixty-two. ❖

3

THE BLOOMFIELD SLASHER

DATELINE: GREENE COUNTY, 1898

The raw, winter breeze stung twenty-three-year-old Malissa "Lizzie" Skinner's cheeks and whipped up the hem of her ankle-length coat. Pacing southbound along Bloomfield's bustling Franklin Street shortly before noon on Thursday, December 29, 1898, she paid no mind to the horse-drawn wagons clattering by. Nor did she acknowledge the Bloomfield citizenry strolling about. Her attention was fixed on the decision she made the evening before.

She unfolded Dug's note as she approached the Monon depot and gave it another read. "Wonder what now. You better go home and go at once. I am not in a very bright humor today." Lizzie was disgusted. Giving that man five years of her life was a humiliating mistake. Now, an opportunity for redemption dangled before her, and she was determined to snatch it.

A Case of Mistaken Fidelity
Lizzie had met Dr. Ephraim Ellsworth "Dug" Gray in early 1894, when she was eighteen years old, five months married, and six months pregnant. Nevertheless, the long-married, thirty-five-year-old doctor was smitten. It had been no accident when he bumped into her husband, Richard Spears, at the Bloomfield fairgrounds racetrack and cornered him with a proposition. Gray introduced himself and explained that he had noticed Lizzie's "delicate condition" and would gladly take her on as a patient. "I'll give her excellent service," he promised, "and don't worry about paying. I'll give you more than enough

time to settle up."

Richard and Lizzie talked it over and agreed to accept the kind doctor's offer.

As promised, Gray dutifully tended to the needs of his beautiful, young, pregnant patient. The day Lizzie went into labor, the good doctor was there to skillfully guide her baby boy down its birth canal and into the world. Post pregnancy, Lizzie was slow to regain her health, thus requiring frequent visits with the doctor—sometimes at his office, sometimes at his home.

The doctor-patient arrangement continued even after the obvious return of Lizzie's strength and good health. As Richard's suspicions grew, he quizzed his wife incessantly about the doctor-patient relationship. The Spearses eventually opted to separate, and they divorced in 1897. Lizzie took back her maiden name, and Richard relocated to Paris, Tennessee. Gray, likewise, left his wife, Louise, and their ten-year-old daughter, Nellie.

Despite Gray's frequent episodes of moodiness and cruelty, the adulterous relationship flourished. However, a few months after her divorce, Lizzie confided to close friends that she had grown fearful of Gray. She also lamented that she was sick of her wayward life and regretted having ruined her reputation. Longing for her past role as a wife and mother, she reached out to her former husband and begged for forgiveness. The couple reconciled on Christmas Day 1898, and Lizzie and their son, Floyd, were to join Richard in Tennessee shortly after the start of the new year.

A Surgeon's Precision

Gray hustled to Bloomfield's southside via Seminary Street, two blocks west of Franklin. He felt certain Lizzie was on her way to the Monon depot to catch the midday train to Bedford to meet a new lover, and he'd be damned if he allowed that to happen. She was his property, and he was going to remind her of that fact.

At the culvert near Jones Mill, Gray cut through the log yard and proceeded straight to the depot to await her arrival. When he saw her step onto the southeast corner of the mill some fifty feet away, he moved into the sunlight and called out, "Lizzie, go home. Go home, and I'll forgive you."

Lizzie hesitated as she considered Gray's absurd order. A second passed, and she resumed walking in his direction. "Get out of my way," she said somberly. "You have no business telling me what to do."

Each step reduced the distance between them, and when she was within

Artist sketches depict Dr. Ephraim Ellsworth "Dug" Gray, who attacked and brutally killed his lover, Malissa "Lizzie" Skinner, as she approached the train depot in Bloomfield on a cold, late-December day in 1898.

arm's length, Gray raised his left palm in front of her face to stop her from passing.

"Oh, no, you don't," he hissed as he slid his right hand into his coat pocket and withdrew a surgeon's knife, its blade almost eight inches long. Flicking it at her, he shouted, "You're not leaving me again!"

Lizzie's eyes widened. She turned to run, but her attempt proved futile as Gray plunged the knife's blade deep into her back, causing her to fall face-down. Gray lurched forward. Straddling her prostrate body, he thrust his blade into the flesh between her left shoulder and her neck, slicing the jugular. He immediately rammed the toe of his boot under Lizzie's midsection and rolled her over.

Her eyes glazed with terror. She struggled to speak, but as the blood rose in her throat and gushed past her lips, her words became mere gurgles. Gray's fury was insatiable. He jammed his knife into Lizzie again, sinking it into her right breast, near her shoulder. A subtle shudder rippled through her body, her eyes rolled upward, and Lizzie Skinner ceased to be.

The hint of a satisfied smile tugged at Gray's mouth, but he wasn't finished. He raised his hand for one final assault and drove the blade deep into her left breast, severing the aortic valve with a surgeon's precision.

He huffed a pent-up breath, and looked around. He spotted a dozen or more bystanders rushing his way, and they didn't appear friendly. With no time to spare, he yanked the knife from Lizzie's chest, swiped its bloody blade across her coat, and shoved it back into his pocket.

Shifty Shades of Gray
The January 6, 1899, edition of the *Bloomfield News* described Gray as a "reputable physician" but "more or less dissolute." Physically, according to the *News*, he was slightly built, not tall, and intelligent looking with a thin mustache and light-colored hair swept across his forehead.

The son of a long-time, highly respected Bloomfield physician, Gray was born in 1861 in Hobbieville, Indiana, twelve miles southeast of Bloomfield. He, his sister, and two brothers had grown up in Springville. He married Louise Newsome in 1882. The marriage produced five children, but only his daughter, Nellie, survived. In 1892, Gray attended the St. Louis, Missouri-based Marion Sims Medical College, whose namesake was regarded as the "Father of Gynecology."

Following graduation, Gray returned to Bloomfield, where many considered him one of the city's up-and-coming doctors. In time, however, the Grays' family history of insanity tugged at the young doctor's resolve. He began to experience bouts of depression for which he habitually sought relief through liquor and opiates. His relationship with Lizzie Skinner suffered because of his self-destructive behavior, which routinely manifested in harsh emotional, verbal, and physical abuse.

Lynching Bee
Determined to outrun the approaching mob, Gray leaped over the expanding pool of blood surrounding Lizzie's lifeless form and hastened uptown to turn himself in. As he sprinted up Franklin Street, Oliver Ferguson's horse-drawn wagon passed him, and Gray hitched a ride. When it reached the courthouse, he jumped off and dashed inside to the sheriff's office, but the clerk informed him that he would find Sheriff John McLaughlin at the jail.

Undeterred, Gray headed for the jail, but as he crossed the courthouse lawn, Lizzie's father, Tom Skinner, stopped him. The news of the savage murder was spreading like an inferno through town. The stunned and grieving father stepped up to his daughter's killer and snarled, "I hope you're ready to die."

A sneer spread across Gray's face, and he assured the old man, "I'm as ready as I'll ever be."

Gray's cavalier response tested Skinner's restraint. "If I had a gun," Skinner said brusquely, "damn you, I'd kill you on the spot."

Skinner glared at Gray, and his eyes blazed with contempt. Several seconds of prickly silence passed between them before Skinner brushed past Gray and hurried to the depot.

If Gray was unnerved by Skinner's threat, he kept it to himself. What he feared most was a "lynching bee." Without further obstruction, he resumed his trek to the jail, where he found the sheriff and sputtered, "I've killed the woman." The puzzled sheriff asked "*Which* woman?" and Gray shouted, "*The* woman. There is but one."

An angry crowd gathered outside the jail demanding the sheriff hand over Lizzie's killer. McLaughlin called in his legal advisors for a hurried consultation about the situation, and they advised him to get his prisoner out of town quickly. By 2:40 p.m., he and a deputy had slipped Gray out a side door, loaded him onto a wagon, and started the arduous, twenty-eight mile journey to Bloomington.

Noose News

Scores of people hovered over Lizzie's body for hours, while it laid on the muddy ground waiting for Coroner William Axe to return from his outing to the Greene County countryside. Upon his arrival, Axe had the body moved to a local mortuary, where he conducted his post-mortem examination. When he finished, the undertaker prepared Lizzie for burial.

While the funeral was underway the next afternoon, Axe opened the courtroom to witnesses' testimonies about Gray's lethal attack on the helpless woman. The testimonies, coupled with the examination of the body, resulted in the coroner's verdict of murder in the first degree.

As Lizzie was lowered into the ground at Grandview Cemetery, Gray and McLaughlin were on a train en route to the Jeffersonville Reformatory, a hundred miles southeast of Bloomfield. The sheriff's quick action in secretly whisking his prisoner out of town had foiled the lynch mob's plan and saved Gray's neck. Gray would not return to Bloomfield until his trial.

In an attempt to influence the public's opinion of Lizzie, an article in the January 20, 1899, edition of the *Bloomfield News* advocated for her redemption. "In justice to the dead woman," the page one article stated, "it is right for the people over the state to know that she was not a 'common prostitute,' but that Gray was undoubtedly her only companion in adultery for some time after her separation from her husband."

Gray was indicted on Thursday, February 16, and the trial was set to begin nearly three months later.

Trial Gets Underway

The trial opened Monday morning, May 8, before a courtroom bursting with Bloomfield residents eager to witness Gray's comeuppance. Back in town after a four-months-long confinement at Jeffersonville, Gray dragged his feet and staggered as the sheriff led him to the defense table, where he slid into the seat beside his attorneys. Once the arraignment was underway, Gray sat quietly with his head bowed and eyes downcast. Absent was his cocky air of self-importance. When the judge asked for his plea, Gray surprised no one.

He pleaded insanity.

The following day, with the jury in place, prosecuting attorney Webster V. Moffett delivered the opening statement for the state, while Gray slumped in a rocking chair and paid no attention. The first witness called was Lizzie's father. Tom Skinner testified that months before Lizzie's murder, she had grown so fearful of the young doctor that she moved into her brother's home, south of the town square.

Moffett handed Skinner a bundle of letters Gray had written to Lizzie and asked him to read excerpts to the court. Several passages expounded on Gray's infatuation with Lizzie, as well as his hatred for Richard Spears. Others boasted of brutal, but cowardly threats.

Richard Spears took the stand next and spoke of his relationship with his ex-wife, their marriage, their breakup, and their reconciliation. He confirmed that they planned to remarry as soon as Lizzie joined him in Tennessee.

Among other key witnesses for the state was Bloomfield saloonkeeper Louis Kidd, who stated that a week before the murder, Gray was in the bar showing off a large knife.

"Dr. Gray said he was going to use it to do one of the damnedest deeds," Kidd told the court.

Moffett smiled and reached inside his coat, withdrawing the knife Gray had used to kill Lizzie. He raised it over his head, making it visible to everyone in the courtroom. Then, turning back to Kidd, Moffett asked, "Is this the knife?"

"Yes," Kidd replied, "that's the one Dug showed me."

Defense of the Indefensible

Cyrus E. Davis, for the defense, made his opening statement on day six of the trial, Monday, May 15. He assigned the blame to Lizzie Skinner, herself, for his client's fatal infatuation with her, and excused her murder because of Gray's mental instability. Davis laid out his case, emphasizing that Gray's ancestors had been prone to insanity and melancholy. Thus, Davis insisted, even though his client knew well the difference between right and wrong, he lacked the resolve to do the right thing.

To prove his case, Davis called his witnesses. One of his strongest was Gray's father, Dr. John W. Gray, who was asked to recount a verbal exchange with his son at the Jeffersonville Reformatory. The elder Gray had asked his son if he had ever been abused, harmed, or mistreated by Lizzie Skinner, and he replied, "No, indeed. She was a perfect woman. I thought more of her than I do of my own soul."

Reacting to his son's statement, the father gasped, "Then why, in the name of God, did you kill her?"

The defense counselor was attempting to prove insanity, and the younger Gray's answer did not disappoint.

"I don't know," was his response.

Other defense testimony was equally damning as witness after witness spoke of seeing Gray drunk, depressed, angry, or threatening suicide.

The next day, the defense called Dr. W.B. Fletcher to the stand. Fletcher, a specialist on nervous diseases and insanity, had previously been the superintendent of Central State Hospital in Indianapolis. Davis asked Fletcher how he would diagnose the defendant's mental acuity, considering the influence of hereditary insanity that ran through Gray's family, the illnesses he suffered as a child, his conduct and habits, the state of his melancholy, and the crime he had allegedly committed.

Without hesitation, Fletcher answered, "Dug Gray is of unsound mind."

Conversely, over the next two days, the state called a stream of witnesses, who thought otherwise. All were well-acquainted with the defendant, and each confirmed that in the days preceding Lizzie's murder, Gray had appeared "of sound mind."

On the evening of the trial's ninth day, attorneys representing both sides of the case were ready for final arguments; and the following day, Friday, May 19, was dominated by blusterous oratories.

The day's showstopper, as reported by the *Indianapolis Journal*, was delivered by Ephraim Inman, an attorney for the prosecution retained by Richard Spears. Inman was a Greene County native and future legendary legal

Dr. Ephraim Ellsworth "Dug" Gray posed for his prison mugshot upon his arrival at the Indiana State Prison in Michigan City in May of 1899. Although Gray was sentenced to serve a life term, in July 1913, Indiana Governor Samuel Ralston honored Gray's request for a pardon. *Photo courtesy the Indiana State Archives.*

counselor, who, in 1925 would gain recognition for his defense of Ku Klux Klan leader D.C. Stephenson in the murder of Madge Oberholtzer.

"Such a speech never fell from the lips of man before in this county," the *Journal* wrote of Inman's closing argument. "It was intensely dramatic, and he had part of the jury in tears." Inman ended his speech with an admirable, theatrical flourish—hurling Lizzie's blood-soaked garments at Gray and proclaiming, "Thou shalt not kill!"

The case went to the twelve jurors at 2:00 p.m. Saturday, May 20. They reached their verdict within twenty-four hours.

Verdict Spawns Threats

Sheriff McLaughlin ushered the defendant into the courtroom at 2:40 p.m. Sunday. The jury took their seats, and the foreman handed the sealed verdict to the clerk.

The clerk unfolded the paper and read the verdict aloud: "We, the jury, find the defendant, Ephraim E. Gray, guilty of murder in the first degree and fix his punishment at imprisonment in the state's prison for life."

Most Bloomfield citizens expected Gray to pay for his crime with his life, and their dissatisfaction with the prison sentence quickly erupted into threats of mob violence.

In an effort to protect Gray, the sheriff dressed him in women's clothes and escorted him to a carriage waiting to drive them to a coal mine east of town, where they spent the night. Monday morning, calmer heads prevailed and the anger abated when McLaughlin returned Gray to the courtroom for sentencing. Defense made a motion for a new trial, but it was overruled.

Shortly past noon, on Monday, May 22, 1899, the sheriff and Gray boarded a train on the first leg of their long journey north to the state penitentiary in Michigan City. According to the *Indianapolis News*, the men reached their destination around midnight, and as they parted ways, Gray promised to be a good prisoner.

Epilogue
Ephraim Ellsworth Gray settled into his new life as an inmate at the Michigan City prison and conducted himself amicably. He even practiced medicine at the facility's hospital. Fourteen years later, the July 19, 1913, edition of the *Indianapolis Star* reported that Indiana Governor Samuel Ralston had granted the diabolical doctor a parole. Ralston justified his decision by citing Gray's purported recovery from his addiction to booze and drugs.

According to the *Star*, Ralston blamed Gray's excessive use of intoxicants for altering his judgment and causing him to commit the brutal murder. However, ten of the twelve jurors who prosecuted Gray, as well as his prestigious father, had pushed for the parole and likely influenced Ralston's decision.

Gray was fifty-two years old when he regained his freedom. Following his release, he settled down and resumed his medical practice in the Knox County city of Bicknell, where his daughter, Nellie, made her home. Gray's wife, whom he had abandoned before killing Lizzie Skinner, died in 1906.

Gray died February 19, 1929, of liver cancer. Today, the doctor occupies a modest spot in Bloomfield's Grandview Cemetery. His tiny tombstone bears only his name. ❖

4

MURDER AT THE LAFAYETTE STREET BOARDING HOUSE

Dateline: Allen County, 1938

Alice May, the oldest of Gail and Maude Ann Girton's three daughters, grew up in rural Randolph County, Indiana, near the county seat of Winchester. After a childhood accident impaired the motion of her right arm, she was no longer able to raise it over her head. Because the disability made her eligible for vocational preparation assistance from the Indiana State Rehabilitation Department, in September of 1938, just four months after graduating from McKinley High School, the attractive, petite, eighteen-year-old Alice May Girton packed up and moved sixty-five miles north to Fort Wayne and began her studies in secretarial science at the esteemed International Business College.

She first moved into a ladies-only boarding house, operated by the Woman's Christian Temperance Union. Six weeks later, however, she relocated to a co-ed rooming house on Lafayette Street. Initially, according to her classmates at the college, she was bashful and introverted. But as her confidence blossomed, her popularity and her circle of friends grew, including interested young men.

The night of Wednesday, October 12, Alice May went to a movie with furnace repairman Howard Zimmerman, also eighteen. The next morning, Alice May's landlady, Lillian Kelly, knocked on her tenant's door. After numerous raps evoked no response, Kelly entered the room and shrieked. Alice May's nude body was sprawled on the floor, her bra was twisted tightly around her neck, and her silk bloomers were crammed down her throat.

As a student at the International Business College in Fort Wayne, eighteen-year-old Alice May Girton was happily preparing for her future. Unfortunately, her life was ruthlessly cut short in the early morning hours of October 13, 1938, when the man who lived across the hall forced his way into her room at the Lafayette Street boarding house and murdered her.

Kelly raced to the phone and called the police.

Neighbor Quick to Confess

Fort Wayne Police Detective Captain John Taylor responded to Kelly's call and took Zimmerman into custody for questioning. According to the detective, the repairman said he had been with Alice May from 8:20 p.m. Wednesday until about 3:15 a.m. Thursday, and during that time, she was unharmed, fully clothed, and very much alive.

Zimmerman was exonerated within twenty-four hours after Adrian H. Miller—a thirty-one-year-old engineering student, who lived in the room directly across the hall from Alice May—confessed to the murder.

Taylor claimed he had trapped Miller into the confession thanks to the latest crime detection techniques he had recently learned at the Washington, D.C.-based FBI National Academy. The police talked with Miller Thursday evening and, letting him believe Zimmerman was their prime suspect, they sent him home.

"We waited until he was asleep," Taylor said of Miller, "and we broke into his room and got him up for questioning. We hurried him to the station and had his admission in ten minutes."

Shady Background
Adrian Miller was born in Lackawanna, New York, in 1907. He claimed that he left home in 1928 and headed to Mobile, Alabama, where he landed a job on a cargo ship and traveled the world. Through the years, he experienced numerous run-ins with the law—vagrancy, opium usage, bar fights, pimping, threatening a man's life, etc. He relocated to South America in 1933 to work as a construction foreman and allegedly married the niece of Oscar Benavides, then-president of Peru. Miller said he returned to the States in 1937 and landed a job on a Pennsylvania river boat. One night, he surprised a burglar in the captain's office and got into a tussle. Miller ended up killing the man and throwing him overboard. "The authorities held me for a day," Miller said, "but after the body couldn't be found, they gave me a pat on the back and let me go."

Miller moved to the Fort Wayne boarding house in mid-1938, while attending classes at Indiana Technical College, where he was employed as a janitor.

Arrested and Charged
Fort Wayne police arrested Miller on Friday, October 14, and held him without bond for the Allen County Grand Jury on a charge of first-degree murder. The penalty for first-degree murder in Indiana was death or life imprisonment. However, after Allen County Coroner Walter Kruse found that Alice May had been raped, Prosecutor C. Byron Hayes vowed to change the charge to "murder in commission of an assault," making the death penalty mandatory.

The next day, Miller's attorney announced that if his client was indicted for murder, he would plead insanity. Miller's mother had been a patient at a Racine, Wisconsin-based psychiatric hospital for more than twenty years, and one of his brothers also was a psychiatric patient. Thus, the family history provided a valid basis for the insanity plea.

The grand jury indicted Miller on November 10 on two counts of first-degree murder. The indictment charged that Miller forced "an article of women's underwear, commonly known as 'step-ins,' into his victim's mouth, thereby preventing the access of air into her lungs and causing her death." He also was charged with murder in the commission of rape.

Indeed, as promised, Miller pleaded insanity.

The Trial

Following two postponements, Allen Circuit Court Judge Harry Hilgemann gaveled Adrian Miller's murder trial into session on Monday, May 1, 1939.

Jury selection was the first order of business. Accordingly, the attorneys began the arduous task of questioning nearly one hundred prospective jurors. Because so many of them admitted to having already formed opinions regarding Miller's guilt, final selection wasn't completed until Wednesday. Throughout the process, Miller spent his time studying the bas-relief sculptures decorating the courtroom walls and nodding off.

Once all twelve jurors were picked and sworn in on Wednesday, May 3, Prosecutor Hayes made his opening statement to the jury asking for the death penalty. As Hayes described Alice May's murder, her father, Gail Girton, buried his head in his hands and wept. At the end of the day, Girton said he hoped Miller would be found guilty and sentenced to death. "Nothing less," the grieving father said. "Society owes that to itself." None of Miller's relatives was present in the courtroom.

The state introduced numerous exhibits, including Alice May's pink under slip that had been found mixed up with the bedsheets, as well as a green skirt and pink sweater that had been neatly folded and placed at the foot of the bed. The state claimed the items showed that Alice May had been preparing to retire when Miller forced his way into her room. The prosecution also introduced the handkerchief that Miller had intended to stuff into her mouth before he lost it in the dark, as well as Miller's orchid-colored pajamas, the top half of which had been ripped during the struggle.

When Hayes completed his opening argument, he called the state's first witnesses—Lillian Kelly and Howard Zimmerman.

Damning Evidence

The highlight of Thursday, May 4, was the testimony of clinical pathologist Dr. Bonnelle W. Rhamy, who had made the post-mortem examination of the body with Coroner Kruse. The *Times-Gazette* of Union City asserted that the state "hoped to weave an intricate web of scientific evidence" that would prove Miller's guilt and guarantee his punishment.

When Rhamy took the stand, the prosecutor asked him about his investigation at the crime scene.

"I found a very much disordered bed and a naked female lying on the floor," Rhamy explained. "The female appeared to be about seventeen years old. She was lying prone with arms akimbo, her body was stiff, and her fingers were tightly clenched. I observed heavy friction abrasions at the crest of the hip bones and four finger scratches on her throat. Rigor mortis had set in, so I judged that the girl had been dead seven to eight hours."

Rhamy next described the gruesome reflex by Alice May's body when he extracted her underpants from her throat.

"There was an immediate heavy rush of air into her lungs," the doctor said, "which was plainly audible. The step-ins were so tightly jammed into her throat that they had jammed the tongue back, completely shutting off the air from air passages. Her tongue was crumpled up and out of shape from the pressure."

Rhamy disclosed more damning evidence against Miller when he told the court about the bloodstains found in Miller's room. The blood tested as the somewhat rare Type 3, he said, which, more significantly, also was Alice May's blood type.

When the prosecution submitted the doctor's slides of the blood specimens as evidence, the defense attorney objected fiercely. Judge Hilgemann overruled the objections and admitted the slides into evidence.

A Father's Love

Gail Girton, among the final witnesses for the prosecution, also took the stand Thursday. His wife, Maude, and daughters, Dorothy, twelve, and Wanda, ten, listened from their front-row seats.

As Girton began his testimony, the details of his oldest daughter's death became too graphic for her young sisters to bear. After the girls were removed from the courtroom, the grief-stricken father clasped his shaking hands and fought back tears as he spoke of Alice May and how happy she had been as she adjusted to her school life away from home. He said he had last seen Alice May alive on October 8, the Saturday before her death. The defense did not cross-examine him.

Following Girton, Deputy Prosecutor Otto Koenig reminded the court that shortly past midnight on October 14, police escorted Miller to the jail for a grilling by Fort Wayne police officers Taylor, Smith, and Kammeyer about the murder. Miller caved within thirty minutes and confessed.

Koening introduced Miller's signed confession into evidence and read it to the jury, despite the defense attorney's vehement protest. The prosecution rested.

The Jekyll-and-Hyde Defense

Late that afternoon, defense attorneys Miller and Rothberg launched their case. The Union City *Times-Gazette* reported that the defense planned to present Miller as an emotional "Dr. Jekyll and Mr. Hyde," meaning he was "a bright student with unusual control over his mental processes by day and an irresponsible sexual sadist with no control by night."

Dr. Kermit Perrin, director of the Fort Wayne Health Clinic, testified that he had treated Miller for syphilis, which was known to cause psychiatric disorders. But when the defense asked to enter as evidence a letter from a doctor for the San Diego, California, Police Department claiming that Miller harbored homicidal tendencies, the judge refused. Instead, Miller's attorney called Dr. Norman Sweet, a psychoanalyst from the Chicago Seminary of Science, who had examined Miller at the Allen County jail two days before. Sweet declared that, in his opinion, Miller was a "sexual sadist."

During his testimony, Sweet said, "I found from questioning [Miller] that he has been a very lonely man since he was six years old, and that among the evidence of his sadistic tendency is an incident where he once saturated a cat with kerosine and burned it alive."

The state strenuously objected, explaining that the defense was trying to introduce evidence which the court had already ruled inadmissible. Despite the objection, Sweet was able to speak of incidents contained in the letter from the San Diego doctor questioning Miller's sanity.

On Friday, May 5, in an effort to draw further evidence of Miller's impaired mental state, the defense called Edward Mildebrandt, a faculty member of the Indiana Technical College. Mildebrandt told the court that Miller was "a good student" who often arrived at "illogical conclusions" and held "illusions of a glorious past." Mildebrandt said Miller calmly passed a difficult chemistry test the afternoon following Alice May's murder as if nothing unusual had happened. Mildebrant considered such behavior "abnormal."

Judge Hilgemann had appointed psychiatrist Dr. Lewis P. Harshman to examine the defendant and report to the court after both the state and defense rested their cases. Harshman had determined Miller was sane. Additionally, Harshman confirmed that Miller's blood tests showed no signs of syphilis.

And the Verdict Is …

The case went to the jury the afternoon of Saturday, May 6. After deliberating less than two hours, the jurors reached an agreement on the third ballot.

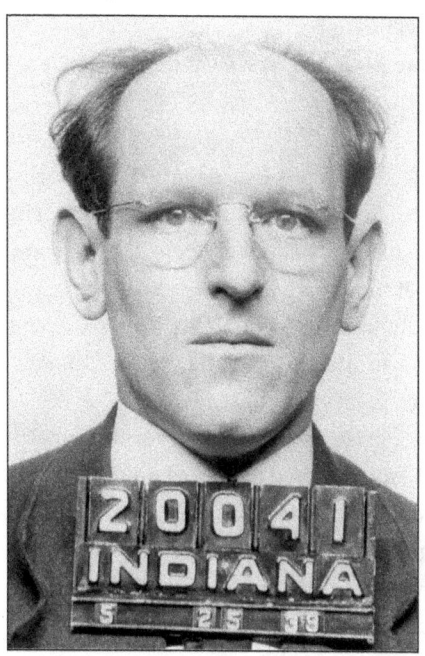

Thirty-one-year-old engineering student Adrian Miller, who confessed to murdering Alice May Girton, paid for his crime on August 16, 1939, when he was electrocuted in the Indiana State Prison's electric chair. *Photo courtesy the Indiana State Archives.*

At 6:00 p.m., they filed back into the courtroom, and the foreman handed the typewritten verdict to Judge Hilgemann. Miller's face tightened, and he chomped his gum as the judge read the verdict aloud. "We, the jury, find the defendant guilty of murder in the first degree as charged in the indictment."

Hilgemann asked Miller if he wished to have the sentencing deferred to a later date. Miller shook his head vigorously.

The judge continued, "Under the law, I am required to ask if you have anything to say before sentence is passed. Have you anything to say?"

Miller grunted, "No."

Hilgemann proceeded to sentence Miller to the mandatory penalty—death in the electric chair—on August 16. As Miller took it all in, his breathing grew heavy, his eyes turned glassy, his complexion paled, and he fainted. Deputies roused him with a dash of cold water to his face and escorted the dazed convicted killer back to his cell.

Waiting for Hilgemann to issue the death warrant, Miller remained jailed in Fort Wayne another sixteen days. During that time, Miller wrote a letter to his victim's father, claiming he had found religion and, therefore, sought forgiveness. Miller's two-hundred-word apology suggested that after he was put to death, he would again see Alice May, so he hoped to tell her that he had been forgiven by her parents—"as God has done."

Whether the Girtons responded to Miller's request was never reported.

Epilogue

On Monday, May 22, Allen County's sheriff and two deputies transported Miller to the Indiana State Prison in Michigan City. Miller appeared cheerful as he left the jail in Fort Wayne, thanking its staff for their kindness and urging the newspaper reporters to visit him.

"I am ready to die," he reportedly told the Union City *Times-Gazette*, emphasizing "there is still some good in me." To that, he added, "In some slight measure, this might atone for my great sin against society."

Shortly after his arrival at the state prison, Miller was processed, photographed, assigned his number, 20041, and escorted to his cell on death row.

When his date with death arrived, he accepted it calmly. No one visited him during the final few preceding hours, other than a priest with whom he prayed. At dinner time, Miller ordered a tasty meal of filet mignon, fried potatoes, corn, peas, and butterscotch pie a la mode. He finished with a cigar and a pack of smokes.

Prison officials said he had spent his time on death row in a more agreeable frame of mind than previous residents, reading books on chemistry, engineering, and philosophy. Perhaps it was an effort to expand his understanding of his impending death.

Finally, the clock struck midnight on Wednesday, August 16, 1939, and Miller calmly and without assistance was escorted from his cell to the execution chamber. Seconds after he declined to make a last statement, the executioner threw the switch, sending two thousand volts of electricity through Miller's wasted body. He was pronounced dead at 12:11 a.m.

Because no one claimed his fried remains, Miller was buried in the prison cemetery. ❖

5

BUSHWHACKED ON BITTERSWEET ROAD

Dateline: St. Joseph County, 1937

Under the starlit October sky, the Chevy sedan tore through the quiet, Granger, Indiana, residential neighborhood. Sidewalks were empty and, except for a smattering of muted porch lights, the street was dark, which wasn't surprising. It was nearly ten o'clock.

The auto slowed as it reached the Moore home, where it abruptly whipped into the driveway and jolted to a halt. The driver's door flew open, and out jumped twenty-year-old Adolph Stopper. Vaulting over the car's front end to the passenger-side, he flung open the door, and seventeen-year-old Charles Walton scrambled out. The two young men worked in tandem, carefully lifting out the limp body of Stopper's fiancée, Melba Moore. The sixteen-year-old girl was tiny, barely weighing a hundred pounds. Stopper had no trouble scooping her up in his arms.

"I've got her," he said to Walton. "You go on up to the house and tell her folks what happened."

As Stopper made his way across the lawn to the front door, he felt Melba's warm blood soaking through his shirt sleeve. Tears filled his eyes, but his resolve to stay calm for her only grew stronger. "You'll be okay, sweetheart," he said softly to her and stepped up his pace.

This shouldn't have happened, he thought. He still couldn't believe some crazy fool had shot at them. How was he going to explain this to Melba's family?

What would he tell Melba when she came to? And what if she didn't?

Any Given Tuesday—At First

Tuesday evening, October 12, 1937, started out as rather ordinary. Stopper, who lived in Mishawaka, had driven the twenty miles northeast to Melba's home, arriving around seven o'clock. Her neighbor, Walton, was already there. For the next two hours, the three young friends engaged in animated chatter and unceasing laughter as melodious tunes wafted from the family's Philco radio.

Nothing memorable happened until about nine o'clock, when they climbed into Stopper's car and headed for the Mishawaka Rubber & Woolen Manufacturing plant to pick up his dad, Leo, and drive him home. During the trip to Mishawaka, the trio eagerly watched the road for unwitting rabbits to chase, an activity that they, like many Hoosiers, considered fun sport. As Melba's father, Harold, told the *South Bend Tribune,* "Rabbits abound in the region, and motorists frequently chase them in the glare of the headlights."

According to Stopper, after dropping off his dad, the threesome drove to the nearby Wayside Inn on East Jefferson Boulevard and picked up some barbecue sandwiches.

"We went east on Jefferson, eating the sandwiches," Stopper told the *Tribune,* "and turned north."

Cruising through the remote St. Joseph County countryside, far from the city lights, the trio sat shoulder-to-shoulder in Stopper's front seat. Except for a pair of muted yellow light beams leading them down a lonely stretch of Bittersweet Road, they were shrouded in darkness. At about 9:30 p.m., they passed a driverless sedan idling along the side of the road. Stopper wondered if someone might be in trouble, so he braked to a stop, shifted to reverse, and started backing up.

Illuminated by the Chevy's backup lights, a large man cursing loudly in broken English stepped from the shadows, raised a revolver, and started shooting at Stopper's car. Reflexively, Stopper threw the gear stick into first and stomped the gas pedal. As Stopper sped away, the shooter riddled the car with bullets, the last one drilling through the back window and into the base of Melba's skull. Neither young man was struck, although Walton's left shoulder had been grazed by a fragment of lead.

Stopper soared the remaining mile and a half to Melba's home. When he arrived, she was unconscious and losing a considerable amount of blood.

Melba Moore was only sixteen years old that chilly October night of 1937, when she lost her life to an unknown stranger's bullet as she and two friends, Adolph Stopper and Charles Walton, drove through the St. Joseph County countryside.

Placing Melba on the Moores' couch, Stopper began blurting out what had happened. But before he could finish, he fainted and fell to the floor.

The Moores rushed their daughter to the hospital, rather than wait for the ambulance. Mr. Moore drove, while Stopper held Melba in his arms. She died en route.

Investigation Begins
The family immediately notified the police. Both Stopper and Walton spent the night at the St. Joseph County sheriff's office answering a barrage of ques-

Melba Moore's fiancé, Adolph Stopper *(left)* and their friend Charles Walton were questioned at the St. Joseph County Sheriff's Department about the mysterious gunman on Bittersweet Road. Neither of them was considered a suspect in Melba's shooting death. *Photo courtesy* The South Bend Tribune.

tions. Sheriff William J. "Big Bill" Hosinski was satisfied that the young men were telling the truth and released them the next morning.

The coroner performed an autopsy, extracting a .38 caliber slug from Melba's brain. The sheriff and his deputies drove out to the scene of the crime and recovered six spent bullet casings. They photographed the shooter's skid marks, showing he had turned the car around at a high speed and proceeded west toward Mishawaka. However, they found nothing pointing to the mysterious gunman's identity or why he had fired at Stopper's car. Hosinski was reportedly inclined to believe a criminal or fugitive from justice was responsible for the unprovoked attack. He pursued his investigation accordingly.

Nobody Didn't Like Melba

Melba's family and close friends were nearly paralyzed with grief. Front doors throughout the Moores' neighborhood were shut and the air was silent. "Melba was a sweet child," one neighbor said. "We haven't an idea in the world why anyone would want to shoot Melba. She had no enemies, only friends.

She worked hard. She never did anything wrong."

Harold and Ruth Moore and their five children—Mildred, eighteen; Melba, sixteen; Harold Jr., twelve; Josephine, ten; and Eugene, six—had moved to Granger from Mishawaka the previous May. Even in that short time, the family developed many friendships. When Melba was killed, the community turned out to support the Moore family, and hundreds attended Melba's funeral on Friday at the First Baptist Church in Mishawaka and her burial in the Mishawaka City Cemetery.

Among the mourners at the funeral were the sheriff and several of his deputies, who were on the lookout for new clues. Although the investigators were still batting zero, Hoskinski told the *Tribune*, "We are following every trail, checking every story, and sifting everything that looks like a clue. We are leaving nothing undone, but up to this point, we are without a single clue."

Absent much-needed leads, the sheriff yielded to his mounting frustration and insisted that Stopper and Walton submit to lie detector tests. Consequently, on Sunday, October 17, the two voluntarily journeyed to the Indiana State Police headquarters in Indianapolis, where they were hooked up to a polygraph and questioned for nearly seven hours. The exercise was futile, producing no new information.

Hosinski also sent the six spent shells recovered at the scene, as well as the bullet removed from Melba's head, to the FBI in Washington, D.C., on the chance their analysis would lead to clues to the shooter's identity. Nothing came of it.

Suspects Emerge
Hosinski's optimism rose on Tuesday, October 19, when Dewey Garland of Grace, Kentucky, was arrested in Danville, Illinois, and implicated in Melba's murder. Garland confessed to murdering his wife and wounding his daughter twelve days before. In a letter to Hosinski, Garland's sister-in-law placed Garland's getaway in the vicinity of Granger on the night of October 12. Furthermore, he had fled Kentucky armed with a .38 special revolver. When he was arrested, the revolver was missing. However, within a few hours of the arrest, the Illinois State Police eliminated Garland as a suspect in the Melba Moore case after they ascertained that shortly before Moore's killing, Garland was visiting his brother in Slidell, Illinois, sixteen miles southwest of Danville and more than 150 miles southwest of the scene of the crime.

Thrust back to square one, Hosinski was growing desperate as pressure

No one worked harder to find Melba Moore's killer than St. Joseph County Sheriff William J. "Big Bill" Hosinski. Much to his regret, after spending months pursuing seemingly viable suspects, motives, and theories to no avail, he eventually had no choice but to set the case aside and move on. He never forgot it, however.

mounted to solve the Moore case. The description of the shooter had been widely publicized—a big man donning an overcoat and a hat. And the car had been described as dark-colored. Conveniently, Dr. Douglas Owen, owner of the St. Joseph Valley Sanitarium north of South Bend, who had interviewed Stopper and Walton, matched the assailant's physical description. He also drove a dark-colored Pontiac sedan. In addition to those damning similarities, Owen's car was equipped with a short-wave radio and was loaded with firearms. And worse, Owen's hobby was crafting gun barrels in his basement.

Hosinski became aware of Owen early Monday morning, October 18, after the constable of the town of Roseland found him sleeping in his car near the sanitarium. Learning that no one had seen the doctor since the day of the shooting, Hosinski asked Owen to come to the jail for questioning.

During the doctor's voluntary, two-day stay in the sheriff's quarters, he was interrogated extensively, federal agents searched his home and office for evidence that would link him to the murder, and Stopper and Walton were called there to identify him. None of the sheriff's endeavors was fruitful, and Thursday afternoon, Owen was released. The doctor's release returned the crime to its previous status as "one of the most baffling in the county's history."

The press made little of Owen's sudden sale of his sanitarium in mid-November. The *Tribune* allocated just four paragraphs to the sale on page one of its November 17, 1937, edition. According to the story, Owens and his estranged wife, Marjorie, transferred the property back to the couple from whom they purchased it the previous year. The selling price was a veritable steal—$1.00. Owen's name next appeared in the South Bend paper on December 30, 1937. The page seven story reported that Marjorie Owen had divorced her husband on the grounds of cruelty. She testified that he continuously berated her in the presence of sanitarium employees, insisting she was crazy and belonged in a straight jacket.

Perhaps it was the doctor who was off balance, but if the sheriff regretted letting him go, that too was never reported. Owen departed South Bend before the divorce was final and never returned.

By the last day of December 1937, the Moore murder case was relegated to the sheriff's dead file, while the *Tribune* writers rated it their number one story of the year.

"Today the tire tracks on lonely Bittersweet Road are long since obliterated," the paper stated, "the cartridge chambers are but insignificant relics of the case, and nowhere, except in the murderer's heart, is known the secret of who killed Melba Moore and why."

A New Suspect Emerges
But seven days into the new year, Sheriff Hosinski received a tip that the Indiana State Police was seeking ex-convict and alcohol runner Lawrence McCarty in St. Joseph County, where he would be visiting places he was known to frequent. Hosinski, with his deputy and a state police officer, headed for the six hundred block of East Mishawaka Avenue to hunker down and watch. A few hours later, McCarty drove up, parked directly in front of the officers' car, and climbed out. He didn't have a chance.

McCarty had taken over a South Bend barn, in which he stripped parts from stolen cars. When the barn's owner, Carmelita Hawkins, discovered the criminal activity, McCarty had threatened her. On the night Melba was killed, Hawkins was driving home from a trip to Michigan. McCarty had previously pressed Hawkins for details of her intended route home, which would have placed her in the vicinity of Bittersweet Road. However, at the last minute, fearing McCarty would be waiting for her, Hawkins had taken a different route. When she learned that a young woman had been killed that night on Bittersweet Road, she went to the authorities.

Following McCarty's arrest, Hosinski launched a vigorous, days-long investigation that concluded with a lie detector test conducted by the state police. While McCarty was no Boy Scout, the evidence wasn't there to connect him to Melba's murder. But there was an abundance of evidence linking him to auto theft, and on February 23, 1938, he was sentenced to ten years in the Indiana State Prison.

With Hosinski out of motives, theories, and ideas, he had no choice but to set aside the Melba Moore murder case and allow it to quietly die. It would haunt him for the rest of his life.

Epilogue
Hosinski died January 27, 1963, when he suffered a heart attack while driving to church and crashed into a parked car. Melba's father, Harold, passed away in 1953, and her mother, Ruth, in 2002. Melba's fiancé, Adolph Stopper, died in 1994. He was seventy-six.

All had lived out their lives in the South Bend area without ever learning who fired the bullet that had stolen their beloved Melba from them. ❖

6

A BULLET FOR TACIE MANG

Dateline: Grant County, 1897

Tacie Mang was a natural beauty with full, rosy cheeks framed by voluminous, bouncing blonde curls. Her graceful demeanor, lilting laugh, and pleasing personality set her apart as Upland, Indiana's darling. But it was Noah Johnson, a rough, twenty-three-year-old Upland farmer, who won her heart; and when Tacie fell in love, she fell hard. However, after playing Johnson's handmaid for eighteen months, she finally grasped that a seventeen-year-old woman was ill-prepared to think about marriage, especially to an emotionally immature man six years her senior. Consequently, in late August of 1897, following weeks of quarrels, Tacie broke off the engagement. Rejection did not sit well with Johnson, and his ego began to brew a deep, untapped anger directed at Tacie.

Sweethearts No More
Johnson decided early in his relationship with Tacie that he had found his bride. Although he loved her with all his heart, the shame of losing her overshadowed his capacity for humility and self-reflection, and his dark side began to take control.

With hopeful expectations, he visited Tacie on Saturday, September 18 and took her for a buggy ride. Before long, however, they were arguing. The following Thursday evening, September 23, Johnson gave it another try by attending services at Tacie's church. Afterward, he and Tacie, her best friend, Artie Zula Pierce, and a young boy named Curtis climbed into Johnson's buggy and headed for Tacie's house. At first, the foursome's laughter filled the buggy, but predictably, Johnson and Tacie's lightheartedness quickly devolved into another angry spat. At that point, caving to his petulance, Johnson stopped the buggy and ordered everyone, including Tacie, to climb out. Johnson proceeded directly home, but sleep wouldn't come. Still angry when he rose the next morning, Friday, September 24, he sneaked his father's .38 caliber pistol out of the bureau drawer and stashed it in his pants pocket.

An hour later, pacing south along the road between Van Buren and Upland, Johnson came face-to-face with Tacie, Artie, and their fourteen-year-old chum, Marshal Pence, strolling north on their way to the Monroe Center schoolhouse. No one stopped, but Johnson and Tacie exchanged awkward greetings as they passed. Johnson had continued walking south for a tenth of a mile, when he abruptly stopped, reversed course, and bolted to catch up with Tacie. Once he was within a few feet of her, he drew the revolver from his pocket and fired at the back of her head. The bullet knocked her forward, and she landed facedown on the dirt road.

Johnson froze as he absorbed what he had done. Then suddenly, in a disgraceful display of cowardice, he vaulted over the fence and dashed away toward Gas City.

Cruel and Cool
Johnson meekly entered the Gas City police station and turned himself in to Chief Isaac M. Hoagwood. The *Fairmount Weekly News* reported that as the slightly built, blue-eyed, fair-haired Johnson explained what had happened, he maintained an air of cool detachment. He lost control only briefly when the sheriff confirmed that the bullet he fired into Tacie's head had been fatal.

Hoagwood escorted Johnson from Gas City to the Grant County jail in Marion. Within hours, Sheriff A.C. Alexander received word that more than a hundred angry Upland-area residents had formed a lynch mob, and with the help of their bloodhounds, they were hot on Johnson's trail. They wouldn't be satisfied until Johnson was dangling from a rope. Anticipating the looming danger, Alexander transported his prisoner twenty-nine miles to Kokomo, where Johnson was locked up in the Howard County jail.

According to the *Indianapolis Journal*, Howard County Sheriff W.H. Sumption placed extra guards on duty in readiness for the mob. He also obtained a dozen extra rifles with sixty rounds from the local armory and gave orders to arm the prisoners in the event of an attack.

"If the mob forming in the Upland neighborhood comes here to lynch Noah Johnson," Sumption said to reporters, "they will meet with a warm reception."

The precautions worked. The lynch mob never showed up.

A Lynchee in Waiting
While Johnson awaited his lynching, or arraignment, whichever came first, he agreed to be interviewed by a reporter for the *Marion Leader*. "I realize the seriousness of the crime I have committed," Johnson asserted. "It is impossible for me to say what prompted me to commit the deed. It was a feeling from within that I haven't words to describe. Did I love Miss Mang? Well, I should say I did."

Tacie's funeral was held Sunday, September 26 at the Methodist Protestant Church, within walking distance of the murder site. It drew an estimated 3,000 mourners—the largest in the town's recent memory. She was buried nearby at Atkinson Cemetery.

The Grant County Grand Jury indicted Johnson on Tuesday, September 28 for first-degree murder. According to the *Indianapolis Journal*, Johnson cried "almost constantly," at last realizing the enormity of his crime and the consequences awaiting him.

Johnson was transferred back to the Grant County jail prior to his arraignment on Monday, October 4 before Circuit Court Judge Joseph L. Custer. He pleaded not guilty. No date was set for his trial.

Johnson Goes to Court
The trial commenced the morning of January 3, 1898, the first Monday of the new year. Once Judge L.L. Kirkpatrick gaveled the court to order, the first item of business was Johnson's plea. To no one's surprise, Johnson claimed his mind had been "unsound" when he murdered Tacie Mang. Therefore, he pleaded "not guilty by reason of insanity."

The next item was jury selection, typically a fairly straightforward process. However, according to the *Indianapolis Journal*, because of the county's large Quaker population, finding twelve men in favor of the death penalty became a challenge for the prosecution. After eliminating all but eleven members of three jury panels, the attorneys could not agree on their twelfth juror until Friday, January 7, delaying the start of the trial by a week.

The trial finally began on Tuesday, January 11, with some eight hundred

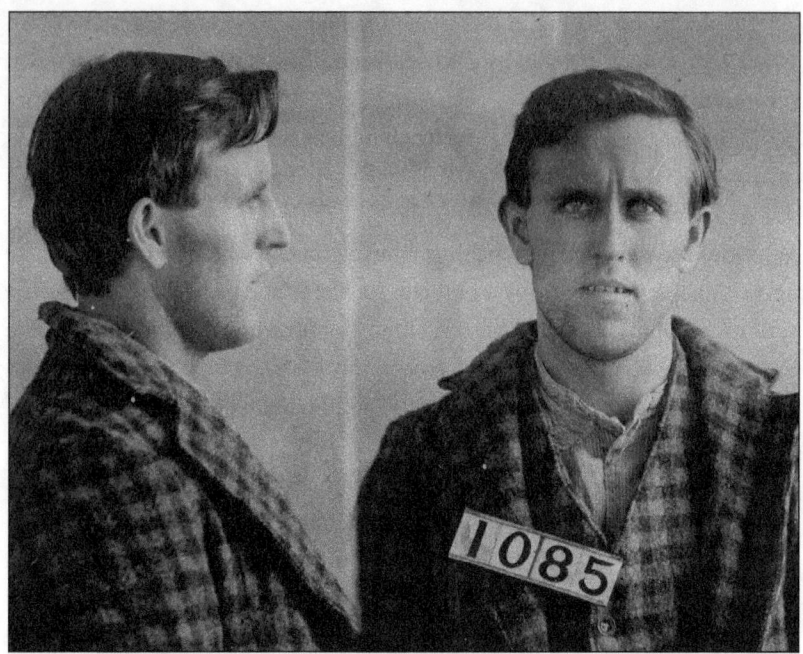

Noah Johnson shot and killed his seventeen-year-old girlfriend, Tacie Mang, on September 24, 1897, in rural Upland, while she walked to school. Johnson immediately turned himself in, and on January 20, 1898, he was sentenced to life at the Indiana State Prison, where died of tuberculosis five years later. *Photo courtesy the Indiana State Archives.*

spectators crammed into the courtroom. Over the next three days, witnesses for the prosecution generally painted Johnson as a troubled young man with an explosive temper, although, according to the *Indianapolis News*, throughout the trial, he "preserved an expression of dullness and apathy."

Tacie's Mom Takes the Stand
The prosecution's strategy peaked just before noon on Thursday, January 13, when attorney John Strange called Tacie's mother, Etna Mang, to the stand. Amid tears and a quaking voice, Mrs. Mang testified to having last seen her daughter alive the morning of September 23 as Tacie was leaving for school. That evening, Tacie sent word that she was spending the night with a girlfriend. Mrs. Mang also discussed her daughter's relationship with Johnson and admitted that her concern was not about Johnson. Rather, she felt Tacie was too young for courtship and marriage.

Before Mrs. Mang was dismissed from the witness stand, Strange held up a small, brown-paper package and slowly unwrapped it, revealing a simple, blue gingham sunbonnet. The bonnet bore large stains of Tacie's dried blood. Shock rippled through the courtroom. Although the attorneys for the defense tried to downplay the bonnet's significance and move on, Strange would have none of it. While tears rolled down Mrs. Mang's cheeks, Strange asked her to point to the bullet hole. He then handed the bonnet to the jury, who passed it from man to man.

The *Kokomo Daily Tribune* reported Johnson's reaction to seeing the bloodstained bonnet.

> When the bonnet had nearly gone the rounds, [Johnson] raised his eyes and stared as though he had seen a specter. There was a rush of blood to his face. As the sunbonnet was handed back to the prosecutor, the elbows of Johnson went down on his knees, and his face was buried in his hands. ... His body shook, and he was convulsed with great sobs. He moaned and cried, but no articulate word was uttered. Johnson's grief was infectious. ... Tears were in the eyes of many spectators as Johnson was removed from the courtroom, sobbing like a brokenhearted child.

After that somber display, the state rested. Providence could not have planned a stronger conclusion.

Insanity Anyone?
The defense opened the next morning—Friday, January 14. Insanity was the Johnson team's only card. To prove their case, they called witnesses who claimed first-hand knowledge of the Johnson family's mental and emotional acuity.

Johnson's half-brother, Monroe, testified that Noah had acted "peculiarly" during the three days preceding the murder. Monroe said his brother had slept in the barn the night before shooting Tacie, and early that morning, when he came into the house, "he seemed very sad and downhearted."

According to the *Upland Monitor*, Perline Moore, Johnson's elderly aunt by marriage, testified that several members of her deceased husband's family had been insane. Among them was Johnson's maternal grandfather, whom she referred to as a "raving maniac" that died of "nervous prostration." She also spoke of Johnson's uncle, a preacher, who had ripped the Book of St. John from his bible and "ate it up," as well as her "weak-minded" first husband, whom she claimed thought he was president of the United States.

The prosecution felt incredibly optimistic, while the defense team surely knew their witnesses' testimony had fallen short of its purpose, when the court turned the case over to the jury at 5:00 p.m. on Thursday, January 20. Thus, it was no surprise when eight hours and five minutes later, the jury returned its verdict: guilty of murder in the first degree.

Life Conquers Death

According to the *Indianapolis Journal*, eleven jurors likely would have called for the death penalty if not for juror Reuben Jones, who originally voted "not guilty by reason of insanity." However, on the fifth and final ballot, Jones acquiesced to a life sentence, and that was the penalty the jury settled on.

Johnson was among the twenty people present in the courtroom when the verdict was announced. A weak sigh of relief passed Johnson's lips upon hearing his fate: he would not hang. A few hours later, he appeared before Judge Kirkpatrick for the final time. The judge denied the defense's request for a new trial and handed down Johnson's sentence.

The *Fairmount News* reported that after Kirkpatrick asked Johnson if there was any reason the court should not pronounce the sentence, Johnson only shook his head. With that, the judge stated:

> It is never a pleasant duty to sentence a man to prison, even for a short time, and it is more unpleasant to sentence a man to prison for life, and especially a young man like you. …
>
> Your punishment is severe, but not as severe as it might have been. The jury that tried you has been more lenient with you than you were with your victim. They have spared your life but have provided that it must be spent restrained of your liberty, and behind prison walls. …
>
> I hope you will accept the conditions that are the result of your rashness and folly, and that you will try to lead an upright life. The judgment of the court is that you be confined in the Northern Prison during the remainder of your natural life.

On Saturday, January 22, 1898, Grant County Sheriff Alexander, with Johnson in tow, boarded the afternoon train in Marion headed for its final destination in Michigan City. The *Fairmount Weekly News* described Johnson's demeanor as "stolid to the last" while "bidding his brothers and weeping sisters goodbye without apparent feeling." The Fairmount paper also noted that Johnson's attorneys predicted that within a year, their client would be "a hopeless lunatic."

While the attorneys' prophecy was sobering, Johnson's ultimate fate was worse.

Epilogue

In April 1902, Johnson was diagnosed with tuberculosis and transferred to the prison hospital. The Johnson family asked Indiana Governor Winfield T. Durbin to allow Noah be brought home for treatment, but their request was denied. The following January, Andrew Johnson, made a trip to Michigan City to visit his brother for the last time.

The February 5, 1903, *Upland Monitor* reported that Johnson's father and brother, Jesse, had traveled to Michigan City and brought his body back to Upland, where the local funeral director had prepared it for burial. A funeral was held at Center Church, and according to the *Monitor*, "an immense throng of people surged about the church and many could not gain admission." Johnson was buried in nearby Atkinson Cemetery, where Tacie Mang also was interred, and where his father would be laid to rest two years later.

In death, Johnson at last received the respect he had longed for. ❖

7

THE DEADLY AFFAIR
OF NORA KIFER

Dateline: Vanderburgh, Warrick, and Gibson Counties, 1900

On the bright, sunny morning of Wednesday, May 23, 1900, a Warrick County farmer driving his rig across Stephens Bridge, north of Oak Hill Cemetery Road in Vanderburgh County, noticed a strange object floating in the creek below. Assuming it was a dummy placed there by a jokester, the farmer pointed it out to two men approaching on foot and continued on his way. The men, like the farmer, were amused but wondered why so many flies were swarming around an inanimate object. When they descended the creek bank for a closer look, what they found sickened them.

They hightailed it to the nearest farmhouse and sent for the Vanderburgh County authorities. Among the responders was the coroner, who confirmed that the item in the creek was a decomposed body, its head and torso weighted below the water by a thirteen-pound stone tied around the victim's neck, which in turn caused its legs to rise above the water and catch in a fallen tree. The remains likely would have been swept away and never discovered if not for those constraints.

Based on the shreds of clothing clinging to the corpse, the coroner determined the deceased was a woman. But two overriding questions prevailed: who was she, and how did she wind up in the muddy waters of Pigeon Creek flowing alongside Evansville's northeastern boundary?

Recognizing the Remains

The remains were transported to the morgue in Evansville, where they were immediately autopsied. The doctors found the skull splintered into pieces by some sort of heavy instrument, the nose broken, both cheekbones crushed, and the brow ridge smashed in. All the hair had slipped from the head, and decomposition of the face was well underway. Identification would be dubious, although two distinguishing marks remained: a portion of one front tooth blackened by decay, and the back of the neck adorned by a birthmark.

The autopsy revealed little else, but rumors of the unidentified, markedly deteriorated body spread quickly. An Elberfeld resident visiting Evansville that day heard the rumor and told an *Evansville Courier* reporter that one of his neighbors, a young woman named Nora Kifer, had not been heard from for weeks.

The *Courier's* reporter sent word to the girl's father, Zachariah Kifer. The next morning, Kifer made the trip to Evansville to view the remains. He had prayed they wouldn't be his daughter's. However, as the *Courier's* May 24 edition reported, "a grizzled, sun-browned, toil-bowed Zachariah Kifer bent over the cheap coffin containing the body of the young woman found in Pigeon Creek and pronounced, 'Yes, that's Nora.'"

Who was Nora Kifer?

Eighteen-year-old Nora, the second oldest of Zachariah and Elizabeth Kifer's four children, was described by the May 25 *Evansville Courier* as "not a beautiful girl." Nonetheless, the *Courier* claimed she had held "a marvelous power over men," perhaps because of the "baby innocence" reflected in her large blue eyes.

"Her hair of dark brown crowned a face of wondrous sweetness," the *Courier* wrote. "Her complexion was clear, save for a few freckles across her nose, and her lips were full and rather sensual." But, it countered, "Her flat nose was her weak point and marred what otherwise would have been a beautiful face."

The *Courier* shamelessly cited a rumor that characterized Nora as a "wild girl," who had cavorted with scalliwags since she was sixteen. Worse, Princeton, Indiana, journalist Stanley Garrison suggested she was a prostitute.

Without a Trace

Nora had last been seen alive near her Elberfeld home the evening of April 3, standing on the Stephens Bridge. Her father told police that Jesse Keith,

Eighteen-year-old Nora Kifer had been missing from her Warrick County home for seven weeks when, on May 23, 1900, a farmer found her decomposing body trapped in the muddy waters of Pigeon Creek, under the Stephens Bridge, north of Oak Hill Cemetery Road in Vanderburgh County.

the sixteen-year-old son of the Kifers' well-to-do neighbor, Joseph Keith, had visited Nora earlier that day, and the two had walked out to the orchard to talk. Afterward, according to Zachariah, Nora had "dressed up in her best clothes" and left the house. She told her father she was going to a "spelling match" in town.

Along the way, she called on the Figleys, who lived about a half-mile from the Kifers. After visiting for an hour, she announced, "I have to go as it is getting late." Nora then proceeded for another mile, where she took a turn to the south, according to neighbors who noticed her on the road.

The April 3 sighting at Stephens Bridge was the last Zachariah knew of Nora's whereabouts until April 9, when the family received a suspicious letter dated "April 9, Elberfeld," and postmarked "April 8, Evansville." The message was written in red ink and would become a key piece of evidence, spitefully referred to as "the scarlet letter." It read:

> Dear Mother,
>
> I start this evening for Chicago on a trip. I may be gone three months and might be six, with a friend. I expect to have a fine trip. Do not be uneasy about me.
>
> From your loving daughter,
> Lora

This 1900 view of Stephen's Bridge looks east over Pigeon Creek in Vanderburgh County. Nora Kifer's body was discovered in the water directly below the three women standing on the bridge.

The Kifers were most definitely uneasy. Nora had not been spotted in Elberfeld since April 3, the handwriting was large and bold—nothing like Nora's dainty script—and it was signed "Lora." Nora's parents were baffled.

A Speedy Arrest
Elberfeld residents were heartbroken by Nora's death and wanted answers as much as the Kifer family did. Whispers naming thirty-nine-year-old Joseph Keith as the girl's likely murderer quickly wafted through the village and drew the attention of law enforcement.

Early Friday, May 25, Warrick County Sheriff Cherry, accompanied by Evansville Police Department Sergeant William Heuke and Detective William Wilson, surprised the Keiths at their rural Elberfeld home and arrested Joseph and his son, Jesse.

The caravan of officers and prisoners arrived at the Evansville city jail at approximately one o'clock that afternoon. The evidence against Joseph Keith was mounting.

Investigators had compared his handwriting to that of the April 9 letter allegedly penned by Nora. The police decided the handwriting was indisputably Keith's. Additionally, "Lora," as the note was signed, was a nickname for Nora that only Keith used.

The above drawings depict Nora's father, Zachariah Kifer *(left)*, and her lover, Joseph Keith *(right)*, the prime suspect in Nora's murder.

Keith's situation worsened when a set of brass knuckles was found in his coat pocket. According to the Saturday, May 26 *Evansville Courier*, police speculated Keith had used the weapon to strike Nora, knocking her senseless, and then completed the job with a stone or heavy hammer. The discovery prompted police to sharpen their focus on Keith's whereabouts prior to Nora's disappearance.

Dozens of witnesses were interviewed, but it was Keith's son who provided the most compelling lead. Jesse told police that on April 3, he delivered a note from his father to Nora, asking her to meet him that night at the bridge.

When police interrogated Joseph Keith, they asked about the note, but he coolly shrugged it off as a lie. He did, however, admit to having been intimate with the young woman, but only once, in December 1899, when they traveled together to Evansville. Keith claimed he had not seen Nora since and had nothing further to offer.

Police confined Keith to a solitary cell, where he could stew in his own guilt without distraction. Saturday morning, however, the interrogation resumed, and Keith took a new tack by implicating a peddler named Michael Cassidy. According to Keith, he had paid Cassidy $50 to whisk Nora out of the area and keep her quiet about the affair. Keith swore he had not wanted her harmed.

New Song for Eventide

Before sunset, Keith was singing a different tune. Police had located and arrested Cassidy, who strenuously refuted Keith's claims. Cassidy swore he had never even heard of Nora Kifer, let alone agreed to make her disappear. The police shrewdly brought him and Keith together and continued the interrogation.

At first, the men held fast to their stories, but on Sunday, May 27, Keith's resolve abandoned him, and he broke down, shouting, "I lied! I lied! I never gave this man money to get Nora out of the way." Keith confessed that he had observed Cassidy the previous week in Elberfeld and figured that, within a few days, he would be miles away. "My idea was to lay the crime on some man that was out of range of the officials," he insisted. "I would not make an innocent man suffer, even if I were sent to the gallows."

Keith likely hadn't realized that he had foreshadowed his own fate. Cassidy was promptly released from custody.

That same day, the police visited Keith's home, where they confiscated his bloodstained buggy carpet and a bloody wrench. As a result, he admitted to writing the note that lured Nora to the bridge and, as police suspected, he was indeed the writer of the so-called "scarlet" letter. Consequently, law enforcement officials were almost certain Keith had committed the murder without assistance from anyone. All they needed to seal their certainty was a full confession. And that, Keith promised, would come Monday morning.

Maintains Innocence

Despite Keith's vow to come clean on Monday, he didn't. As the *Indianapolis News* reported, "With a careworn look upon his face and trembling like a man being led to his execution," Keith was escorted to his preliminary hearing in Judge Jordan G. Winfrey's city courtroom, where he was arraigned and bound over to the circuit court without bond. When asked if he was innocent or guilty, in a voice barely audible, he muttered, "I am not guilty."

Keith was quietly transferred Saturday, June 2, from the Evansville city jail to the county jail, where he would await the next step of his legal nightmare, a decision by the grand jury. The Vanderburgh County Grand Jury convened on June 4, but its progress was bogged down by the many witnesses to be questioned, and even more so by the continuing discovery of incriminating evidence.

A new search was made of the grounds surrounding Keith's property in late June targeting a wooded area, situated along a direct line between Keith's house and the Stephens Bridge. The search yielded a piece of sisal rope that exactly matched the rope tied around the stone and Nora's neck.

Within days, another search party stumbled upon a forgotten, dilapidated well located on farmland adjacent to the Keiths' property, about a quarter mile from the bridge. A member of the party peered into the deep well and spotted a lock of light brown hair clinging to the rough interior wall. The searchers dragged the bottom of the well and retrieved another sizable wad of hair, matching that found near the top. They also retrieved a hammer and a pair of crudely made grab hooks. A few yards away, a team stumbled upon a pair of slippers matching those Nora had worn the night she disappeared. Zacharia Kifer identified the hair and shoes as his daughter's, and two neighboring farmers recognized the grab hooks and hammer as Keith's. In addition, detectives returned to the well and found drops of blood on the wooden rails that surrounded it.

The grand jury released its report the afternoon of Friday, July 6. It was no surprise that the collection of physical evidence was more than sufficient to indict Keith. However, locations where the evidentiary items had been found clearly indicated that the murder had not occurred in Vanderburgh County. Rather, the evidence left no doubt that Nora Kifer had been murdered in her home county.

Therefore, Keith was hurriedly transferred to the Warrick County jail in Boonville, where the legal process would restart at square one.

Keith on the Move
The week following his transfer to Boonville, Keith appeared before Justice of the Peace Thomas Youngblood for his preliminary hearing. With head bowed, a trembling Keith perched beside his attorneys, Frank B. Posey and Dewitt Q. Chappell, as witness after witness eviscerated any doubt to his guilt. At the hearing's conclusion, Youngblood bound Keith over to the Warrick Circuit Court without bail to await action by the grand jury, which would not meet again until September.

The two-and-a-half-month wait for Keith's indictment by the Warrick County Grand Jury riled up a great many Elberfeld-area citizens, and their impatience soon mutated to rumblings of a lynch mob. On Saturday, August 18, the threat fully materialized when a hundred masked men—armed with guns, knives, clubs, and even a telephone pole to serve as a battering ram to break into the jail—gathered in a grove a mile outside of Boonville. Fortunately for Keith, Warrick County Sheriff Ben Hudson got wind of the plan in time to discreetly move his prisoner back to Evansville. In the days following, Elberfeld folks scoffed at the scuttlebutt about a mob, and Keith told the *Princeton Daily Clarion* that he thought it was funny.

Keith made himself at home at the Evansville jail, but not for long. On September 8, the Warrick County Grand Jury indicted Keith for murder in the first degree, and in less than a month, at the request of Keith's attorneys, the case was venued to Gibson County. Keith was moved to the Gibson County jail in Princeton on October 3. His trial was set for December 17 but subsequently was rescheduled for Monday, December 31.

Trial Gets Underway

Blustery winds propelled shards of frigid rain through Princeton those first days of Keith's trial, but the disagreeable weather couldn't discourage hundreds of curious spectators, including news reporters representing five states, from jamming Judge Oscar M. Welborn's courtroom. The jury selection was completed by 10:30 a.m. Wednesday, January 2, 1901, and within minutes, Thomas Lindsey for the prosecution launched into his opening statement.

Addressing the judge and jury, Lindsey proclaimed that the murder of Nora Kifer was carried out with premeditation and malice; thus, Joseph Keith must pay the death penalty. "Because no human saw the striking of the blow which killed Nora Kifer," Lindsey stated, "the facts of the case are largely circumstantial. However, there is a chain of evidence so strong that no jury can pass it by."

Lindsey gestured toward a table designated for the state. Several items related to the Kifer murder were piled on it: the stone that had kept Nora's body submerged in Pigeon Creek, the rope still tied to it; a hammer, grab hooks, a swatch of matted human hair, a corset, all retrieved from the well; the pair of lady's shoes found in the woods, the iron knuckles pulled from Keith's pocket, and the bloodstained carpet that had lined the floor of his buggy.

Lindsey continued his opening statement, alleging that Keith's infatuation with Nora Kifer had not only cost him a great deal of money, it had prompted threats from his wife to leave the marriage. Thus, driven to desperation, Keith committed the crime, believing it would be the easiest way to save both his bank account and his home. Lindsey laid out other aspects of

Gruesome relics of Nora Kifer's murder are pictured. They include her silk skirt, corset, and shoes. Also shown are the brass knuckles pulled from Joseph Keith's pocket, the hammer and grappling hooks retrieved from the well, Keith's bloodstained buggy carpet, and the thirteen-pound rock that had been tied around Nora's neck to keep her submerged.

the case—the timing, the physical evidence, the personalities involved, Keith's alleged confessions, and his attempts to establish an alibi that would throw the blame onto others—and concluded with a vow: "The state will prove conclusively that the defendant, Joseph Keith, is guilty beyond a reasonable doubt."

With that, the prosecution's case was underway. According to the *Evansville Courier*, over the next four days, the state called seventy-nine witnesses. They included law enforcement officials, physicians, Keith's fellow inmates at the Evansville jail, members of the Keith and Kifer families, and numerous Elberfeld-area residents. The testimony helped establish Keith's guilt and make clear that he and Nora had been an item and made little effort to keep it private.

Damning testimony was offered Thursday, January 3 by Joe Duffy, a rural Elberfeld resident, well-acquainted with the Kifers and the Keiths. Duffy said he had last spoken with Keith on May 20 as they passed each other on the road near the canal bridge, south of Elberfeld.

"During our conversation," Duffy told the court, "Mr. Keith asked if I had heard talk about him and Nora Kifer."

"And had you?" said prosecuting attorney Lindsey.

"Yes," Duffy replied, "and I told him so."

"What did Mr. Keith say to that?" Lindsey inquired.

"Joe said it was a lie, and he would see that someone paid for it."

"Pay for it?" prompted Lindsey. "How?"

Nodding, Duffy answered, "He said she was probably in a sporting house in Evansville, and if she has lied about people at Evansville as she has done around Elberfeld, she's liable to be killed and thrown in the river with a big rock around her neck."

The defense cross-examined Duffy but produced nothing to neutralize his damaging testimony.

Testimony even more damaging was given Friday morning by Keith's son, Jesse. The prosecution called him to the stand to explain the note he delivered to Nora on April 3 on behalf of his father. Jesse reluctantly testified:

> It was in the afternoon. The school teacher came to me and said I was wanted outside. My papa was there, and he took a piece of paper and wrote on it with a lead pencil. Papa said to take the note to Nora Kifer at her home. He said to give it to no one but Nora. ... I asked him what he wanted with her, and he said she had been telling lies on him, and he wanted to talk to her about it. ... In the note were these words: 'Lora, meet me at the [bridge] about dark.'
>
> After Nora read the note, she ripped it into pieces and said, 'Tell your papa all right.' ... When I told father that Nora said it was all right, he said nothing. ... The day my father was arrested and taken to Evansville, I was with him. He said to me, 'If they ask you if you took the note to Lora, tell them no.'

The State Rests

The state rested its case on Saturday, January 5, and on Monday morning, attorney F.B. Posey delivered the opening statement for the defense. Posey passionately declared that his client had not murdered Nora Kifer, claiming Joseph Keith was home the night of April 3, and he certainly had not written the so-called "scarlet letter." Moreover, Posey insisted, Keith had no motive, adding, "The only blot on the defendant's character was a brief intimacy with the girl that had been dropped long before she disappeared." Posey concluded his opening argument after a mere thirty minutes. According to the *Princeton Daily Clarion*, "The statement was made hurriedly and disconnectedly and was not the oratorical effort many expected."

Witness testimony followed and droned on until late afternoon, painting Keith as a good guy. The *Daily Clarion* reported that "a dozen or more witnesses testified to Keith's good reputation, while the reporters yawned and spectators pretended to be interested, simply staying in the hope that something more sensational would turn up."

When the trial resumed Tuesday morning, January 8, Posey's first witness was Keith's wife, Jennie. After accounting for her husband's activities on the day of April 3, 1900—the last day Nora Kifer was seen alive—Jennie said, "[Joseph] and I were in the sitting room until bedtime. We retired about eight o'clock and got up about six the next morning."

"Did your husband leave the house at any point before sunrise?" asked Posey.

"No," Jennie adamantly replied. "My husband was not away at any time that night."

In his cross-examination, prosecuting attorney Lindsey reminded her that she had sworn to the Warrick County Grand Jury, "I don't know where my husband was on the night of April 3, unless he was at home." Jennie admitted having made the statement but dismissed it due to the stress she had suffered at that time.

Excitement rippled through the crowded courtroom at 2:55 p.m. Tuesday, when the defense called Keith and he stepped to the witness stand. Not even the defense attorneys had been certain Keith would testify in his own behalf. Unfortunately, Posey's constant coughing and the wails of a fussy baby dominated the room for the balance of the day, hindering the courtroom's comprehension of Keith's testimony.

Keith returned to the stand at nine o'clock Wednesday morning, January 9, for a rigid cross-examination by the state. The press described him as a calm, composed "good witness." The *Evansville Journal* stated that not once did Keith answer a question with a "yes" or "no." Instead, it reported, "Keith's answer invariably was, 'I don't remember.'" According to the *Cincinnati Post*, Keith's testimony was a general denial of every circumstance adduced against him.

And Last of All, a Murderer

The trial opened Thursday with closing arguments by Keith's defense team. Spectators' expectations ran high and, according to the *Evansville Journal*, defense attorney Posey did not disappoint. He assured the jury that Nora Kifer's character as a "wayward girl" was a matter of evidence, and he was duty bound to speak of it. Conversely, Posey stated, Joseph Keith lived with the respect of his neighbors and had strayed from the righteous path only one time, when he met Nora in Evansville. "Keith committed one error at the hotel," Posey insisted. "But so did others. Does not the same circumstance point to all these men? Why should Keith be singled out?" Posey continued until almost 5:00 p.m.

Although the jury was weary and hungry, Judge Welborn permitted Lindsey to get the state's closing argument underway. Within the hour, however, he shut it down for the night. When Lindsey resumed his spellbinding oratory Friday morning, January 11, he lambasted the defense.

"Since my friend, Mr. Posey, tried to convince you that Keith is a martyr," started Lindsey, "I will tell you what Keith really is. He is a liar, he is a perjurer, he is a thief, he is a seducer, an adulterer, and last of all, a murderer. ... In denying everything, he tried to make out that over seventy-five of our witnesses were perjurers." To that, Lindsey added with sarcasm, "It's as if we are to believe he is the only saint in the 'whole shooting match.'"

After a brief recess following Lindsey's summary, Judge Welborn gave the jurymen their instructions and sent them to the jury room. It was 12:14 p.m.

Three Hours and Thirty-Six Minutes

Word reached the judge at 3:50 p.m. that the jury had reached its verdict. Thus, one of the most celebrated cases in the history of Gibson County had been decided in a mere three hours and thirty-six minutes.

Deputy Sheriff Will Walters escorted Keith back to the courtroom, where he sat stiffly, drummed his fingers, and scanned the jurors' faces for clues to their decision. Keith's attorneys likely felt anxious, aware that short deliberations typically resulted unfavorably for the accused.

"Gentlemen of the jury," said the judge, "have you reached a verdict?"

Foreman Martin Meyers replied, "We have, your honor."

Silence engulfed the courtroom as a sealed envelope was passed to the court's deputy clerk, Rollin Maxam. At the judge's request, Maxam ripped open the envelope, withdrew a paper, and recited the handwritten verdict: "We, the jury, find the defendant, Joseph Keith, guilty of murder in the first degree and fix his punishment at death."

Keith did not even flinch.

Later, once the excitement had subsided, a reporter with the *Evansville Courier* approached Keith and asked, "What do you think of the verdict?"

Keith grinned sardonically and without hesitation said:

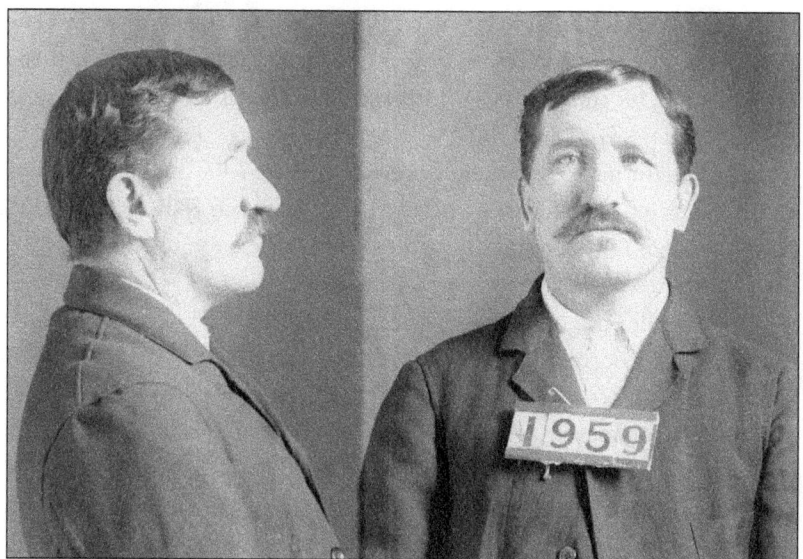

On Friday, January 11, 1901, Joseph Keith was found guilty of the murder of Nora Kifer and sentenced to death by hanging. After his appeal for a new trial was denied, his execution was set for May 24, and he was transported to the Indiana State Prison in Michigan City. Another appeal, this one to the Indiana Supreme Court, resulted in another postponement of the execution. Ultimately, however, the justices agreed with the lower court's decision, and Keith was hanged on November 15, 1901. *Photo courtesy the Indiana State Archives.*

I am surprised. I had not expected anything less than an acquittal. How the jury could find me guilty on *this* evidence is more than I can understand. You may think it strange that I am holding up under this strain, but it is because I am an innocent man. God knows I am not guilty of this awful crime, and I will someday prove my innocence.

The defense team appeared before Judge Welborn the morning of Friday, February 8 to argue for a new trial. The judge overruled the motion, and at 4:20 p.m. that day, a stone-faced, defeated Keith returned to the courtroom for sentencing.

"It is the judgment of the court," Welborn began, "that defendant Joseph D. Keith convicted of the murder of Nora Kifer, shall suffer death, and I fix Friday, May 24, 1901, as the day for his execution at the Indiana State Prison at Michigan City."

Epilogue

Accompanied by the Gibson County sheriff and his deputy, Keith boarded a train bound for Michigan City in the predawn hours of Saturday, February 23.

Once Keith entered the Indiana State Prison, he traded his stylish traveling attire for prison garb and was escorted to the cell in which he would spend his remaining life in solitary confinement. The cell was a mere twenty steps from the gallows.

Keith's attorneys pledged to appeal the case to the Indiana Supreme Court, renewing hope for their condemned client. Their commitment manifested on May 14, when the court stayed the execution until November 15, 1901, and agreed to hear the appeal on October 2.

Alas, in the end, the Keith v. State appeal fell through. Although Posey and Chappell performed admirably when they argued Keith's case in Indiana's highest court, it was all for naught. Unconvinced of Keith's innocence, the supremes unanimously decided that his death sentence must stand. Keith was crushed.

His only remaining hope for escaping the gallows was the commutation from Indiana Governor James Mount that never came. Regardless, Keith staunchly denied his guilt up to the final few minutes before his execution.

Seconds past midnight on Friday, November 15, the prison warden, James Reid, came to Keith's cell to escort him to the gallows. Keith greeted him with a two-page, typewritten confession.

At last, Keith admitted that he alone had killed Nora Kifer. And yet, he relinquished responsibility by pinning the blame on *her*.

"Nora was the cause of her death her ownself," he wrote. "She might have known that a man would protect his wife and family."

Keith went to his death cheerfully crooning the hymn, "I'm Going Home to Die No More." When the gallows' trap door was released at 12:12 a.m., he dangled at the end of his rope until the prison doctors pronounced him dead seven minutes later.

None of Keith's family was present, so the kindhearted warden took it upon himself to have the body shipped back to Elberfeld. After Keith's funeral at his home, he was buried in the nearby Barnett Chapel Cemetery. His son, Jesse, joined him there eight years later.

The execution of Joseph Keith brought the end to what many had called "the most atrocious murder committed in Warrick County." Perhaps the *Evansville Journal* expressed it best: "Keith's name will go down in tradition and story as the boss prevaricator, the most detestable hypocrite and moral leper that this part of the country has known." ❖

8

THE MYSTERIOUS MURDER OF MADAM X

DATELINE: VIGO COUNTY, 1883

The autumn sun was sinking into Indiana's western horizon that chilly Saturday evening, casting elongated shadows of James W. Porter, his son, Joseph, and neighbor, Henry Ishmel, across the lonely Vigo County countryside as they traipsed along Clinton Road, four miles west of Terre Haute. Porter's mongrel dog accompanied them, running ahead, pausing frequently to sniff the air, and darting off in pursuit of small game.

As the threesome neared Mary's Road, the canine spotted a rabbit and chased it into the ravine. Moments later, clenching an odd-shaped object in its mouth, the dog scampered back to his master and dropped a newfound treasure at his feet. Porter took one look and shuddered. On the ground before him lay a human skull. The cranium was severely fractured, and the front, where the face had been, was crushed.

Pieces and Quiet

By the next afternoon, Sunday, October 7, 1883, Vigo County Coroner Andrew Drought, assisted by County Clerk W.H. Duncan, Porter, and some thirty-five curious neighbors, turned up many more bones, broken false teeth, shreds of clothing, and a woman's button-up shoe that still contained the foot. Within twenty-four hours, what was left of a woman's badly decomposed corpse had been uncovered in the ravine amid the shrubbery and leaves. Much of the

Susannah "Susan" Bronnenberg Nelson, of Anderson, whose remains were discovered in rural Vigo County on October 6, 1883, was a member of the revered Madison County-based Bronnenberg family.

body was gone, thanks to ravenous hogs and wild animals. Nonetheless, based on the condition of the skull, Coroner Drought determined the cause of death was murder.

According to the *Terre Haute Weekly Gazette*, "The place where the remains were found, of all other dark and lonely spots in Vigo County, is the most adapted to the commission and concealment of some desperate crime. The hollow is the deepest in the ravine and the furthest spot that could be reached from any of the roads."

Lacking a clue to the victim's identity, as well as a missing person report, county law enforcement officials could not know exactly how long the remains had lain there or to whom they belonged. The discovery was shrouded in mystery.

Three weeks later, however, an area resident poking around the crime scene found a bloodstained fire insurance policy made out to Susannah "Susan" Bronnenberg Nelson of Anderson. A little checking revealed that Mrs. Nelson had been the daughter of the late Frederick and Barbara Bronnenberg, well-known spiritualists and quite wealthy Madison County residents. She had been missing since Thursday, September 6—one month prior to the discovery of her body.

The revelation opened the door to two questions, assuming the body was Mrs. Nelson's: Why had she been in Vigo County? And, who wanted her dead? The mystery deepened.

Madison County Madam

Sixty-nine-year-old Susan Nelson was one of ten Bronnenberg children, five of them brothers whose collective worth was rumored to be roughly a million dollars. Prior to the death of her husband, William Nelson, in 1869, she had been financially well off, too. But after he died, making ends meet was a struggle. Consequently, as the money ran low, she transformed her spacious North Main Street home into a boarding house. Over the years, she rented to many fine people; but after she was murdered, gossip mongers claimed she ran an "assignation house" that let men "decoy innocent girls under her roof and start them on the road to ruin."

The *Daily Wabash Express* noted that Susan Nelson's death was the "all absorbing" topic throughout Anderson. Many people openly called her "Madam."

"Men were discussing it in the hotels, the saloons, the restaurants, and on the street corners," the *Express* wrote. "In all the town, not one person would say a good word about her. Even her own relatives kept their lips closed. No one lamented her death. If she had fallen dead in the street, people would have exclaimed 'glory!'"

Shortly after news of Susan's demise spread statewide, Madison County Sheriff Thomas Moore learned that on September 6, she had withdrawn her entire $750 savings from the Exchange Bank of Anderson, scraped together an additional $300, packed her possessions in a trunk, and boarded a train bound for Indianapolis and on to Nebraska, where her son, Carl, made his home. It had been no secret she had been on the losing side of a number of civil lawsuits, prompting the *Express* to speculate she had left town to protect her financial stability. Unfortunately, traveling with a large sum of money tucked into her bosom may have provided the incentive for her murder.

Familial Suspect

Deeper digging by Thomas Moore and Terre Haute Police Detective C.E. Vandever turned up troubling information about Susan's thirty-seven-year-old son, Jasper, of Cape Girardeau, Missouri. The officers learned she frequently had said she considered Jasper "the joy" of her life, while Jasper considered her his meal ticket. And worse, people familiar with the family told Moore and Vandever that Jasper's disdain for his mother was lethal, often manifesting as physical abuse and verbal threats on her life.

Questioning Jasper became an urgent priority for the investigators, prompting Vandever and Vigo County Sheriff John Cleary to make a trip to Cape Girardeau. The *Muncie Daily News* reported that upon their arrival on Monday, November 12, Vandever and Cleary found what they believed was Susan's trunk in Jasper's possession and arrested the "alleged matricide." The officers then escorted their prisoner and his wife back to Terre Haute.

According to the *Cincinnati Evening Post*, Jasper cried bitterly when he was arrested, and on the journey home, he told Vandever and Cleary that he'd had a premonition that his mother had been murdered at Terre Haute, that her head had been broken with a club, and her body buried in a ravine. During his interview at the Terre Haute jail, Jasper insisted that he and his wife had been in Illinois when his mother was murdered. However, his wife claimed that on the day of the murder, she and Jasper had been in Terre Haute, and he had gone out that night and hadn't returned to their hotel until three o'clock the following morning. In addition, she said, he often pretended to see his mother's spirit and talked to it.

Suspicions intensified after the November 20 *Indianapolis Journal* reported that Madison County Prosecutor William A. Kittinger had obtained a letter from Jasper to his mother, asking her to meet him in Terre Haute on September 6 or 7 so they could attend the local spiritualist organization's seance. The letter was postmarked "Brazil, Indiana," sixteen miles east of Terre Haute, and dated August 23, 1883, two-and-a-half weeks before she left Anderson.

Jasper's prospects weren't looking good, unless he was laying the groundwork for an insanity plea.

Enter Suspect Number Two
The odds of Jasper's insanity plea diminished as speculation about a new suspect grew. Perry Manis, the self-anointed man of God who dubbed himself "Reverend Manis," was a cash-strapped low-life that had resided in the Anderson area for years. According to local scuttlebutt, Manis was a close friend of Susan Nelson's and had served as the pimp for her brothel.

The November 15 *Cincinnati Evening Post* reported that Manis departed Anderson the same day Susan had. Although he had not taken much money

In late November 1883, Perry Manis emerged as a suspect of the Susan Bronnenberg Nelson murder and was charged and arrested. At his trial in January 1884, the prosecution overwhelmingly pointed to Manis's guilt, leading him to confess. As a result, the judge sentenced Manis to spend the rest of his life in the Indiana State Prison South in Jeffersonville. Manis died there in May 1887. *Photo courtesy of the Madison County Public Library in Anderson.*

or a trunk with him, when he returned to Anderson a couple weeks later, he was flush with cash and possessed a trunk that looked suspiciously similar to Susan's. He also was driving a newly acquired horse and buggy. Shortly after, he was arrested for stealing horses and associating with prostitutes. The *Evening Post* stated, "The charge will keep Manis behind bars until it can be ascertained whether he has any guilty knowledge of the murdered Mrs. Nelson."

On Wednesday, November 28, Terre Haute's Detective Vandever boarded a train to Anderson, where he met with the Madison County sheriff. When Vandever returned the next afternoon, Perry Manis was with him. Manis was soon charged with the murder of Susan Nelson and locked up.

The reporter for the *Terre Haute Weekly Gazette* observed that Manis's "general appearance is that of a bad man, and he is much tougher looking than Jasper Nelson. If looks could convict, Manis would be convicted and Jasper would go free."

The sheriff discharged Jasper from custody on the morning of Thursday, December 13, after the Vigo County Grand Jury failed to indict him. The *Gazette* quoted one of the jurors saying, "I am convinced beyond all doubt that Jasper is innocent. There was not a scintilla of evidence against him."

The same could not be said about Manis. The grand jury indicted him that afternoon.

Cock and Bull
Manis's trial was set for January 24, 1884, in the Vigo Circuit Court, but according to the *Terre Haute Weekly Express*, on Friday, January 4, Manis convinced Sheriff Cleary and Detective Vandever to take him to Noblesville, where, he promised, he would produce hidden letters documenting that he and three unnamed cronies had killed Susan for her money. According to the *Express*, Cleary and Vandever fell for Manis's "cock-and-bull story" and escorted him to Noblesville.

"Tuesday afternoon, Manis was secretly taken to the Vandalia train and taken to Noblesville," reported the *Express*. "They arrived about 10 o'clock, and while Vandever went after a sleigh to take them to the spot, Cleary and Manis remained near a lumber yard."

The *Express* story continued:

> When Vandever had been gone a few minutes, Manis broke and ran with the sheriff after him. Cleary fired at Manis just as Manis turned the corner of a lumber pile. Manis then attempted to run across a railroad track but struck his foot against a rail and went sprawling in the snow. Cleary was on him in a second and gave him a hard thump on the head with his revolver.

Manis admitted he had invented the story to facilitate his escape and was taken back to the Terre Haute jail to await his trial. The *Express* reported that evidence of Manis's guilt was so strong, a hanging was almost a certainty.

'Oh, yes!'
On the morning of Thursday, January 24, Judge H.D. Scott called the courtroom to order, and a smiling Bailiff Tolbert proclaimed, "O, yes! O, yes! O, yes! The Vigo Circuit Court is now in session!"

The *Express* described Manis as composed and well-rested, thanks to the "good living afforded the prisoners by the liberal taxpayers of Vigo County." Manis's not-guilty plea set the trial in motion. By two o'clock, the jury had been selected and sworn in, and John W. Shelton—representing the state with Madison County prosecuting attorney William A. Kittinger—delivered the opening statement.

The prosecution came up short on eye witnesses and evidence; however, Shelton leaned heavily on Manis's attempted escape in Noblesville.

The opening statement by defense attorney William Mack lasted all of fifteen minutes, much of which was spent reminding the jurors that someone charged with a crime is innocent until otherwise proven guilty. He pointed out that his client was a stranger to Terre Haute and, therefore, was locked in the grip of a police force eager to close a murder case, a community hungry for a guilty verdict, and a newspaper more interested in spreading sensationalized fake news than in telling the truth.

The prosecution called only two witnesses the first day. Both were from Anderson, and both had been well-acquainted with Susan Nelson. One told of overhearing her and Manis discuss opening a boarding house in Nebraska. The other identified scraps of blue calico fabric found at the crime scene as pieces of the dress Susan had worn the day she boarded the train to Indianapolis.

Strong Case v. No Case
Expectations ran high when court was called to order the next day, and the prosecution didn't disappoint. Shelton first called Jasper Nelson, who identified several articles found in Manis's trunk as belonging to his mother—a tablecloth, a pair of chain bracelets, a silver watch chain, a necklace, a ring, and a clothes brush he had given her with pencil marks around the bottom that he, himself, had made. Other witnesses told of seeing Manis and Susan boarding the same train on September 6, and Frederick Bronnenberg Jr., Susan's brother, testified that Manis had no money when he left Anderson but returned with a wad of bills.

After the noon break, the room was packed almost to suffocation, according to the *Express*. Of the witnesses called, the star was Dr. Thomas Moorhead, who brought Susan's skull, from which a piece of dry skin dangled. Moorhead explained that the day the skull had been found, it was covered with hair and dry skin. The skin over the right temple was loose, and when he scraped it off, he found a fracture that began above the right temple, extended across the right eye socket, down to the upper jaw bone, and continued almost to the base of the skull.

"Was the blow that caused this fracture severe enough to cause death?"

the prosecutor asked.

"In my opinion, yes, it was," Moorhead said, placing the skull on the table at which the prosecuting attorneys and an *Express* reporter were seated. According to the reporter, a worm crawled out an ear hole.

For the balance of Friday and all of Monday, the prosecution called a string of witnesses who testified to Manis's detriment. The most damaging was Charles Green, Manis's fellow inmate at the Terre Haute jail, who testified that after Manis returned from his failed escape attempt in Noblesville, he told Green, "I'm in a bad fix."

"He told me all that had happened," Green said. "He asked if it might be best for him to have his attorney see the judge and prosecutor and plead guilty."

"What did you tell him?" asked Shelton.

"I told him he might as well say he killed Mrs. Nelson," Green replied.

"And how did he respond?"

"He said, 'They know I'm the man anyway.'" Green paused and huffed a little laugh. "Then he said if he'd known things would turn out like they did, he might as well have joined Jesse James."

A Verdict Compromise

When court convened Tuesday, January 29, William Mack stated that the defense had no evidence or testimony to offer and was willing to rest its case. The judge adjourned until 2:00 p.m. When court resumed, Mack and Shelton conferred privately in the anteroom and worked out an agreement for the jury's consideration: Manis would plead guilty in exchange for a life sentence.

The jury accepted the defense attorneys' proposal and brought back a guilty verdict that fixed the punishment as life at the Indiana State Prison South in Jeffersonville. After discharging the jurors, Judge Scott told the defendant to stand. Manis rose slowly, grasping the table for support. His eyes were moist; his breathing was shallow.

"Perry Manis, you have been accused of the crime of murder," the judge said. "You have received a fair and impartial trial, and you have heard the verdict of the jury to which you have agreed. Have you anything to say why the sentence should not be passed upon you?"

Manis blurted out, his voice quivering, "I am not guilty. I have been surrounded by adverse circumstances, and it was impossible for me to do better. The whole truth will be known someday, and I hope to see a time when

The Bronnenberg family historical marker is located inside the entrance to Mounds State Park near Anderson. Shown is a photo of Bronnenberg family patriarch Frederick Brandenberg, born in 1775 in Germany. As a youth, he migrated to America and changed his name to Bronnenberg. Frederick and wife, Barbara Easter, settled in Indiana in 1819. According to the marker, the Bronnenbergs recognized the importance of the historic mounds and were instrumental in their preservation. The marker includes a quote by early Madison County historian Samuel Hardin: "To write the pioneer life of Madison County, Indiana, without mentioning the Bronnenbergs would be like visiting Massachusetts without seeing Boston."

I will be a free man again."

Judge Scott then read the sentence and Manis was led from the packed courtroom. Many of the spectators had believed Manis would be acquitted, but the majority thought he would hang.

The *Express* reporter stopped Manis in the courthouse vestibule and briefly spoke with him. Manis told the reporter he was eager to get to prison and intended to be good, to study religion, and work into the graces of the prison officials.

"I believe in a just God," Manis said. "He is just and this imprisonment is only a mysterious way He has to fulfill his works. I will bear the burden and trust in God."

To the contrary, Jasper Nelson was satisfied with the trial's outcome. He left the courthouse smiling with his mother's skull wrapped in a newspaper tucked under his arm.

Epilogue

The Nelson murder case stood out as one of the shrewdest pieces of detective work Indiana had ever seen, so claimed the January 31, 1884, *Terre Haute Weekly Gazette*, particularly because the clues were so frail and flimsy.

"At the time the [woman's] bones were found in a dark, lonely spot across the river," the *Gazette* stated, "how many people thought that in a few short months, a man would receive a life sentence in our county court for being her murderer?"

Even though Manis declined to testify on his own behalf, many speculated he could not have committed the crime alone and eventually would name his accomplices. He never did.

The July 22, 1886, *Terre Haute Express* ran a brief, page one report that Sheriff Cleary had returned the previous day from the state prison at Jeffersonville, where he had found Perry Manis in the last stage of laryngeal consumption and quickly approaching death.

Manis had hoped for a pardon, but in the end, he asked only for permission to die outside the prison walls. That too was denied, and he died there on Saturday, May 14, 1887. Although he still had family and friends back home, six fellow inmates placed his remains in a wooden coffin and buried it in the prison cemetery. ❖

PART II
VICTIMS: KIDS

9
LITTLE GIRL GONE

Dateline: Allen County, 1901

Ten-year-old Alice Cothrell was adored throughout her hometown of Wallen, nestled in the outskirts of northwestern Allen County. Mischievous, precocious, and bright, Alice didn't know a stranger. Yet, on Tuesday, July 2, 1901, she vanished without a trace.

At one-thirty that afternoon, a barefoot Alice, clad in a light-blue sailor suit, told a playmate that she was embarking on a secret, six-mile trek to Fort Wayne to surprise her grandma. When Alice failed to come home for dinner, her parents became concerned. Their worry escalated as the hours passed with no news of her whereabouts. Fierce thunderstorms saturated the town overnight, and by dawn, the Cothrells were nearly crazed. They didn't know whether little Alice was lost, stolen, injured, or worse.

Search and Geezer

The police and an outpouring of friends and neighbors joined the heartsick parents in scouring the county in hopes of finding the little lost girl. The search continued around the clock for four days but reaped no success. The local press followed closely, and on Saturday, July 6, the *Fort Wayne Sentinel* reported, "[Alice] seems to have completely disappeared as though the earth had opened up and swallowed her."

The next morning, Sunday, forty-five members of the Regulators, an association of lay detectives from nearby Huntertown, met with their captain,

George Warcup. He suggested that Alice may have fallen into a well or a cistern. The men laid out a plan, and the search took a new turn. They gathered garden implements, hooks, and ropes and began dragging wells and cisterns throughout the area. At five o'clock that evening, a few dozen neighbors accompanied Regulators James Noonan and J.E. Ballou to the home of the Cothrell's well-to-do neighbor, sawmill owner Charles W. Dunn.

The tall, white-haired, white-bearded, sixty-one-year-old Dunn met the crowd at his front gate. Appearing irritated, he barked, "I suppose you people have come to look for the missing girl, but you will not find that silly little thing anywhere here. She's probably miles away."

Noonan introduced himself and asked if Dunn would object to two or three of his men searching the cistern.

Dunn scowled at the onlookers. Clearly, he wasn't happy. Glaring at Noonan, he said, "Two. Two is enough."

Noonan motioned to Ballou, and Dunn led them inside his house and into the kitchen, where he moved the table aside and pointed at the trap door to the cistern below. Noonan flung the door open and reached in. Sliding aside the lid to the cistern, he looked into the dark water tank.

"Can somebody get me a long stick?" Noonan asked.

Dunn walked away and returned with a stick about seven feet long and a quarter-inch thick. Ballou took it and poked it into the cistern.

"Do you feel anything?" Dunn said.

"No," Ballou answered, "I can't touch bottom."

"Even if you could," Dunn said, "you would find nothing there."

Ballou asked for a longer stick, and Dunn walked away, returning quickly with a rake and a ball of twine. Ballou understood. He cut off an arm's length of the twine and used it to tightly bind the stick and the rake together, extending his reach to nearly ten feet. He plunged the rake back into the cistern. When it reached the bottom, he immediately announced, "I feel something."

"You are liable to," Dunn said with a bitter laugh. "I don't know when that cistern was last cleaned out."

Ignoring Dunn, Ballou looked up at Noonan and said, "I've got something." Ballou gave the rake a hard push and pulled it up. Squinting into the water, he gasped.

Noonan leaned over Ballou's back and peered into the cistern. "It's the girl," he shouted as Alice's lifeless body, still clothed in her blue sailor suit, rose to the surface.

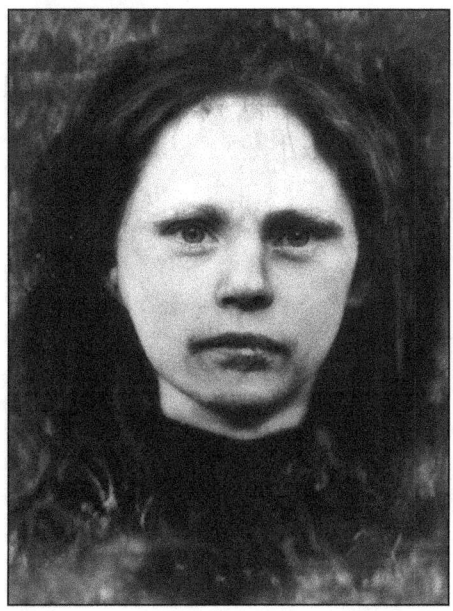

Ten-year-old Alice Cothrell went missing from her home in the tiny Allen County town of Wallen on July 2, 1901. The police and the community pulled together for a vigorous search for the beloved little girl. Five days later, all hope was doused, when police found Alice's body submerged in the cistern of the Cothrells' wealthy neighbor, Charles Dunn.

Dunn blinked at the sight of the dead, waterlogged child and leaped backwards. "My God," he exclaimed. "We have been drinking that water!"

One Mystery Ends, More Begin
Noonan and Ballou carried the girl's body to Dunn's backyard to await the arrival of Allen County Sheriff George W. Stout and the coroner, Dr. Wynn Barnett. Meanwhile, curiosity seekers and members of the press surrounded the house. The *Fort Wayne News* went out on a limb the next day, advising its readers that the tricky accessibility of the Dunns' cistern made it unlikely that Alice's death had been accidental. "The [Dunn] cistern is possibly more difficult to access than any other cistern ever built," the *News* expounded.

The cistern was originally constructed in the back of the house, and the kitchen was later built above it, leaving an eighteen-inch crawl space between the kitchen floor and the cistern's wooden top. A sixteen-inch-wide trap door was added to the wooden ceiling of the cistern and another to the kitchen floor. And when the kitchen's trap door was closed, one of the kitchen table legs stood on it.

Ballou told the *News* that falling into the Dunn's cistern would not be an easy feat, even for a small child. Dropping through both doors to the cistern would require anyone, even a youngster, to pin their arms against their body

An artist's sketch depicts Charles W. Dunn, the wealthy neighbor of the Ed Cothrell family. Dunn was arrested Tuesday, July 9, 1901, by the Allen County sheriff on suspicion of murdering little Alice Cothrell. He was indicted the following day.

and drop down "straight as an arrow."

"And if not," Ballou said, "there would be marks on the body, and Alice's body showed no scrapes or bruises."

Testimony Leads to Arrest

Wasting no time, the next day, Monday, July 8, Barnett and Allen County Prosecutor Emmett V. Emrick convened an inquest. The first witness was Alice's father, Ed Cothrell. Alice often visited the Dunns' seventeen-year-old housekeeper, Marie Sampleson, he said, and often watched Sampleson draw water from the cistern. According to Cothrell, the day Alice went missing, she left home between one and two o'clock and went to the Dunn home. "Several of the neighbors saw her go into the house," Cothrell said, "but no one remembers seeing her come out."

Barnett next called Sampleson. She told him she had been doing the wash the day Alice disappeared. Dunn had drawn the water for her from the cistern before he left for the sawmill, she said, but failed to close the trap doors. Sampleson noticed the trap doors open at about one o'clock, when Alice strolled into the yard. The two exchanged a few pleasantries, and Alice wandered off about fifteen minutes later. Barnett asked Sampleson what time Dunn returned home that day, and she recalled seeing him at around two o'clock, while she was pinning the day's wash on the clothesline to dry.

Dunn's seventeen-year-old hired man, Del Reed, testified next. He had accompanied Dunn and Ed Cothrell to the sawmill to haul logs. Shortly past noon, the three were about three miles outside of Wallen, when Dunn picked up a saw and headed home on foot. Reed and Cothrell continued working until evening.

Reed said he had never observed suspicious activity of any type at the Dunn household. In fact, he said, Alice Cothrell frequently visited the Dunns to sing, while his wife, Elizabeth, accompanied her on the organ. "The little girl was a favorite with Mrs. Dunn," he said. At least twice during the week Alice was missing, he had overheard Mrs. Dunn tell her husband that she feared the little girl had fallen into the cistern. Each time, Dunn assured her that she was mistaken but promised he would rake it, if that would satisfy her. Reed reportedly said Dunn never followed through with his vow. When the prosecutor asked Dunn why he had not checked the cistern as his wife requested, Dunn answered with a shrug, "I didn't think it was possible for someone to get in it, so I figured it wasn't worth the trouble."

A neighboring farmer, Felix Grosjean, testified that when he talked to Dunn about the missing girl, Dunn told him that he had "thoroughly raked the cistern."

Another neighbor, Alex Huguenard, claimed he had seen the girl enter the Dunn home at approximately one o'clock the day she went missing. He testified that for the past week, Dunn had helped himself to four or five pails of water daily from Huguenard's well, most recently Sunday afternoon.

Dunn the Doer of Dastardly Deed
Dr. Frank Greenwell had been called into the case Sunday night to confirm the coroner's findings. Testifying at Monday's inquest, he said, "The girl's body was free of fresh cuts and scrapes, but I did find her thyroid gland swollen." Greenwell explained that the condition of her neck indicated a criminal assault shortly before her death.

Furthermore, he said Alice's lungs were full of air, and he found no water in her throat, trachea, or lung tissue. The doctor asserted that Alice had been choked to death before she was dropped into the water. Greenwell's judgment aligned perfectly with Barnett's.

Finishing off the inquest, Dunn was questioned for more than two hours, far longer than any other witness. He said he had returned home at two o'clock that Tuesday afternoon. Dunn contended he then strolled through his garden to search for the missing girl, even though the Cothrells hadn't inquired about Alice until after seven o'clock that night. He also asserted that, independent of the search parties, he had spent several hours each day that week hunting for the girl.

According to Tuesday's *Fort Wayne Sentinel*, law enforcement officers considered Dunn's testimony detrimental to his innocence, and Barnett and Emrick were convinced of his guilt. At the conclusion of the inquest, they stepped across the hall to the sheriff's office and instructed Stout to take Dunn into custody. The *Sentinel* reported that Dunn was pacing the hallway when the sheriff arrested him and had not expected the murder charge. Initially, he remained cool, but as the sheriff escorted him to the jail and locked him in a cell, Dunn protested incessantly and continually reiterated his innocence.

"I don't see why in hell they've fastened this thing onto me," he exclaimed. "I ain't guilty. I didn't touch the girl."

Tuesday's *Sentinel* also revealed the coroner's previously undisclosed conclusion, that to prevent Alice from screaming, her assailant had strangled her before hiding her body in the cistern. In fact, Alice's death certificate—completed and signed by Barnett on Tuesday, July 9, 1901—declares "choked with a hand" as the "immediate cause of death."

Two Key Witnesses Jailed

Wednesday's papers were abuzz with the Cothrell murder. Charles Dunn had spent his second night in jail, charged with the murder of a little girl, while most recently, his housekeeper, Marie Sampleson, and his handyman, Del Reed, had been taken into custody. They had been arrested as material witnesses, both accused of holding back information, and both held for non-payment of a $2,000 bond.

Oddly, both swore they knew nothing more about Alice's disappearance and death than what they told the coroner during the inquest. But, according to the *Sentinel*, the two had been independently questioned for more than an hour that morning and had remembered "considerably more" than they revealed at the inquest. For example, Marie admitted that Dunn had made "improper advances toward her, but she had struck him over the head with a dipper." Officers were optimistic that the Dunns' hired help knew still more incriminating information and would eventually talk.

Ratcheting up the drama, Alice Cothrell was supposed to be buried that

Wednesday morning, but due to a last-minute request by Dunn's attorney, she wasn't. According to the Fort Wayne papers, the defense interrupted Alice's funeral at the Methodist Church in Wallen and demanded her body be returned to her home for examination by doctors of the defendant's choosing —Maurice Rosenthal and G.L. Greenawalt.

Once their examination was complete, Alice was returned to her coffin and transported to Bethel Cemetery for burial. Afterward, Barnett told the *Sentinel*, "The doctors for the defense discovered absolutely nothing to impair the contention of the state that the girl was murdered."

Dunn Hearing
A prominently displayed, two-column photo of little Alice lying in her coffin dominated the *Fort Wayne Journal-Gazette*'s front page on Sunday, July 14. The headline read: "Charles Dunn Held for Murder—Alice Cothrell Was Strangled."

The story told of the preliminary hearing held Saturday to ascertain whether the state had gathered sufficient evidence to continue holding Dunn until the grand jury could hear his case in September. The hearing originally was to be held in the office of Justice Harry F. France. However, due to the crowd size, estimated at 1,500, the proceedings were moved to the Allen County courthouse in Fort Wayne. The *Journal-Gazette* reported, "The courtroom was like a sweatbox. ... It is doubtful if any case in recent years has attracted so much attention or excited so much curiosity as the Dunn-Cothrell case."

Once relative order was established, Emrick for the state and Colerick for the defense laid out their cases and examined witnesses. A few contentious moments arose between Emrick and Colerick about questioning Sampleson and Reed. The prosecutor strenuously objected, claiming the testimony of Dunn's hired help would be key to the state's case, prompting Justice France to excuse them from the interrogation.

Of all the evidence entered at Saturday's hearing, Coroner Barnett's testimony proved the most troubling for Dunn's defense. Barnett explained that Dr. Greenwell assisted him with a post mortem at the Cothrells' residence, and shortly after starting, Greenwell pointed out that the girl's neck was swollen and appeared to have been clenched and squeezed.

"I then looked at the neck," Barnett said, "and found it in an indurated condition at the base and flattened at the side of the thyroid cartilage. I called the sheriff's attention to the fact that it looked as though she had been choked."

Colerick asked Barnett if he had been present at the autopsy performed by doctors Rosenthal and Greenawalt three days later. "Yes," Barnett said, adding that the health commissioner, the prosecuting attorney, and the stenographer were also there.

"What was the result of the examination?" Colerick asked. "What did they find?"

"When they opened the thyroid area, they found the tissues, the cartilage, and the muscles all filled with blood. Then, upon removal of the hyoid bone and tongue, they found that the hyoid had been fractured by compression and that the tongue had been bitten."

"Doctor," Colerick said, "from the conditions of that child, what would you say as to her having been dead when she reached the water in the cistern?"

Barnett answered without hesitation. "It is my opinion, absolutely, that she was dead before she was in the water. The water had nothing to do with the cause of death."

As spectators processed the coroner's pronouncement, a wave of gasps and muffled conversation swept through the courtroom.

"Furthermore," Barnett said, "we are positive this finding bears out the claim of the state that Alice Cothrell's death was due to asphyxiation, the result of being choked, and I can see no room for any sort of doubt about it."

Trial Begins

Dunn was indicted for Alice's murder on Tuesday, September 17 and arraigned the following day. He pleaded not guilty. Judge Edward O'Rourke gaveled the opening of Dunn's trial at 10:00 a.m. Tuesday, October 22. Filling the jury panel was the first order of business. After attorneys on both sides—E.V. Emrick and Samuel M. Hench for the prosecution, and Henry Colerick and Sam L. Morris for the defense—questioned some sixty members of the venire, twelve jurors were selected and sworn in Thursday morning.

In the state's opening statement that afternoon, Emrick promised to show that Dunn had met the child near his barn on Tuesday, July 2, enticed her inside, and attempted to assault her. When she tried to scream, he caught her about the neck with such force that he broke the hyoid bone. He then strangled her and concealed her body until dark, when he carried it into the house and dropped it in the cistern. The prosecutor said witnesses for the state would bear out this theory.

He called his first witness—Alice's mother, Sarah Ellen Cothrell. Mrs. Cothrell spoke in a clear, distinct voice as she told the court that her daughter's last day of life started out like any other Tuesday wash day. After breakfast, she and her daughter walked to the Dunn house, three doors down from their own home, for water, which Charles Dunn drew for her. She and Alice returned home and were joined by the older Cothrell daughter, Edna, age fifteen, for their noon meal. Alice left the house shortly after. At about two o'clock, Mrs. Cothrell went back to the Dunn residence for more water. That time, she was alone and drew it herself. Emrick asked if she had closed the covers to the cistern when she finished. "Oh, yes," she said. "I closed the lids myself."

Mrs. Cothrell didn't see Alice again but didn't think anything of it until suppertime at six o'clock. Figuring Alice was visiting the Dunns, Mrs. Cothrell walked back to their house, where she found Charles Dunn sitting on the porch and asked if Alice was there. "No," he told her. "She left long ago."

Mrs. Cothrell described the search for Alice, in which all the neighbors, except Dunn, participated. She emphasized that on Sunday morning, five days after Alice disappeared and six hours before she was pulled from the Dunns' cistern, Dunn had approached Mrs. Cothrell in her garden and barked, "You've been telling stories about me having done something with Alice and putting her in my cistern. I've searched that cistern and she isn't there."

Alice's father, Edwin Cothrell, was next called. Cothrell, who had been employed by Dunn, testified that the day his daughter went missing, he and Del Reed had hauled logs to Fort Wayne for Dunn. Cothrell said he left home early that morning to meet Dunn in the woods north of town. After loading Reed's wagon with logs, the three men headed for the city.

At twelve-thirty that afternoon, Cothrell said, Reed stopped the wagon, and Dunn climbed off and set out on foot down a side road headed for Wallen. Cothrell and Reed continued on in the wagon for Fort Wayne. However, as Cothrell pointed out, a walk to Wallen from the location where Dunn got off the wagon would have put him back home by two o'clock, the time Alice likely disappeared.

On Friday, October 25, Ballou and Noonan recounted convincing Dunn to let them into his house so they could search his cistern. The next day, the testimony of Coroner Barnett and Dr. Greenwell dominated the courtroom.

To the prosecution's delight, Barnett reiterated his previously stated theory that before little Alice was placed in the cistern, she had already died of strangulation. Greenwell agreed. Once those views were stated, Barnett and Greenwell offered another theory, one that the *Fort Wayne Journal-Gazette* noted had been presented in a soft voice "to observe a decent regard for feminine ears."

Each of the doctors laid out the reasons they believed the child had been raped. Or, as the paper delicately phrased it, "There were no other abrasions on the body, except on the margins of the hymen, which was torn on the left lateral border." The story went on to explain, "The mucus membrane, which covers the hymen here, was broken," and such an abrasion was "the direct effect of something that passed through and stretched the hymen, side from side."

Testimony Damages Dunn
A procession of witnesses that included neighbors, the city health commissioner, and law enforcement officers, testified Monday and Tuesday of the following week. They spoke of Alice's disappearance, the search, the condition of her body, and the filthy condition of the water in the cistern. Among the witnesses, Olive Huguenard, one of Dunn's neighbors, testified that in the days following Alice's disappearance, Dunn had visited her home frequently asking for drinking water. The web of guilt woven by witness testimony tightened around Dunn each succeeding day of the trial. But on Tuesday afternoon, October 29, he was immobilized when the prosecutor called the spider, Marie Sampleson, to the stand.

According to the *Fort Wayne Journal*, Sampleson "made a dangerous witness to Dunn, and the effect was stunning to him and his counsel," evidenced by Dunn's "heavily wrinkled brow as her dreadful story was told." But as the *Indianapolis News* reported, "The white-haired old lumber merchant squirmed in his chair while Marie Sampleson told the jury the revolting details of the old man's conduct toward her."

Sampleson testified most of the day for the prosecution. In brief, she told Emrick that Alice Cothrell had arrived at the Dunn house around one o'clock Tuesday afternoon, July 2. Several minutes later, Sampleson saw Alice depart the kitchen, run through the garden to the alley, then turn north toward the horse barn and disappear. Sampleson heard a child's scream shortly after but assumed it had come from children playing outside and went on with her work. A few minutes later, she noticed Dunn standing in the door of the horse barn, and when he came into the house a moment later, he was white and shaky.

Sampleson continued her testimony, stating she had gone to bed around midnight and a short time later, looked out the window and saw Dunn walking toward the barn with a lantern. Curious, she quietly followed at a distance, until Dunn stopped abruptly, turned to her, and said, "What are you doing?" When she told him she wanted to see if Alice was in the barn, Dunn angrily snapped, "There's no use looking here. I've looked and I can't find her." And with that, he turned, entered the barn, and shut the door.

This part of Sampleson's testimony was key to the state's case, theorizing that after Dunn murdered Alice, he hid her body in the barn; and while the town slept, he carried Alice's dead body into the house and slid it into the cistern.

Defense Takes Turn

The next morning, Wednesday, October 30, Henry Colerick and Sam L. Morris, for the defense, took over. Their cross-examination cast a line of questions and accusations that brought to the surface every mistake Sampleson had made during her seventeen years, including having been fired from past jobs for stealing and that she was pregnant without a husband.

The attorneys tried to confuse her, but she held fast to her previous testimony and not once did she contradict herself. The questioning continued until noon. The *Fort Wayne Journal* reported that, "when the ordeal was over, the girl was half carried from the courtroom by Mrs. Stout, matron of the county jail." According to the *Journal*, the defense lost ground.

Del Reed took the stand that afternoon and helped the state's case. He told the court that when he arrived home the evening of July 2, he proceeded directly to the barn to feed and bed the horses. Finding the feed boxes full and the horses bedded, he didn't enter the barn. However, he thought it odd as Dunn had never before performed those chores.

The state rested late that afternoon.

The defense launched its case when court opened Thursday, October 31. In his opening remarks, Colerick said he intended to prove his client was a stalwart of the community, that Alice Cothrell had drowned, that his client had not been attracted to her, she was never sexually assaulted, and no one had laid a hand on her. Furthermore, he would show that Marie Sampleson's testimony was fraught with lies for the purpose of deflecting suspicion that she was Alice's murderer. "[Sampleson's] were the last human eyes to rest on the little child," Colerick dramatically exclaimed, according to the *Indianapolis News*, "and we expect to show the interest she had in ending the life of the little one."

The rest of that day was spent hearing from character witnesses sticking up for what the *Fort Wayne News* termed, "Dunn's good reputation for kindness and humanity." Unfortunately for the defense, much of the testimony was challenged and disproven by the prosecution. Determined to shore up his sagging case, Colerick surprised the state and everyone else in the courtroom on Friday, November 1, when he suddenly announced, "The defendant may take the stand!"

Dunn Takes the Stand

The *Indianapolis News* painted a picture of Dunn seated in the witness chair as a white-haired old man, his arms resting on the sides, and his body bent slightly forward as "he told his story, guided by his attorneys."

During his three hours on the stand, his testimony was riddled with denials as he laid out his whereabouts for virtually every moment, from the day Alice Cothrell went missing through the night her body was pulled from his cistern.

"Did you see Alice at all on Tuesday, July 2?" asked defense attorney Sam Morris.

"I never laid my eyes on her that day," Dunn replied.

Dunn claimed he went looking for Alice that first night and did not say why he fed and bedded his horses for the first time. He recounted his exchange with the Huntertown Regulators when they came to his house to search the cistern; but in Dunn's version of the story, he welcomed the search and invited them into his home.

The defense counsel had Dunn explain that between his house and the barn was an old, abandoned well and an open cistern near his next-door neighbor's house, where Dunn could have conveniently discarded Alice's body had he chosen to. The defense was building a case to show that ignoring these convenient disposal points, in favor of Dunn's own cistern, was absurd.

Near the end of Dunn's testimony, Morris blurted out, "Did you kill Alice Cothrell?"

Dunn responded in his clear, blustering voice, "No, sir, I did not."

Doctors' Diagnosis: Murder

Doctors G.L. Greenawalt and Maurice Rosenthal, who had examined Alice's body at Dunn's request, were called to the stand. Greenawalt testified that although his examination convinced him that the girl had endured no physical or sexual assault, he could not say conclusively that she had drowned. Rosenthal explained that it would be possible for someone to fall into the water fully conscious and drown without taking in a single drop of water. Both doctors were reputable, but they had to admit that their testimony was being paid for by the defense. Furthermore, they hadn't examined the body until three days after it was pulled from the cistern, and during a vigorous cross-examination by Prosecutor Emrick, Rosenthal conceded that he couldn't tell what caused the child's death.

"I might have come to a definite conclusion," he declared, "if I had seen the body immediately after it was taken from the water and before it was embalmed."

Emrick further diminished the defense's case when he advised the court that he possessed a written transcript of the conversation that flowed between Greenawalt and Rosenthal as they performed their post mortem.

"At the time [the transcript] was made," Emrick said, "the two physicians on the stand today agreed with Dr. Barnett on all material points."

When the trial resumed the next morning, Saturday, November 2, Emrick called John Fonner, the stenographer who captured the doctors' conversation in writing. Fonner testified that during the post mortem, Rosenthal had said:

> I used the utmost care in removing the hyoid bone and found it broken. There is also swelling on both sides of the trachea. This must have been produced by pressure from the outside. This could not have been done in the process of embalming, and unless there was pressure during a previous examination, the bone must have been broken before death.

According to Fonner, Greenawalt made a similar statement. With that, rather than cross-examining the witness, the defense rested its case.

Testimony for the prosecution continued Monday morning. The courthouse lobby was full of witnesses, many of them Dunn's neighbors and most of them farmers, who took the stand in quick succession to attest to Dunn's character. As each testified that Dunn's reputation and character were "bad," the old man's cool demeanor thawed and his face puckered. However, after a couple dozen witnesses, the testimony grew monotonous. As the *Fort Wayne News* surmised, "If anyone in Washington Township escaped a subpoena, he must have been overlooked by the deputies."

Closing arguments followed, consuming the rest of Monday and all of Tuesday and Wednesday.

Final Arguments, Finally

The defense maintained that the state failed to show a motive if Dunn had murdered the ten-year-old girl, nor did it produce proof that Dunn had even seen little Alice on that fateful day. Then, grabbing hold of Dunn's wrist, Morris exclaimed, "Do you gentlemen of the jury believe that this hand seized that girl's throat with force enough to break her hyoid bone and leave no mark?"

To the contrary, Morris insisted that the defense could point to one person who *did* have both motive and opportunity.

"Marie Sampleson is confessedly a thief, and worse," he said. "The testimony shows that Marie had a temper. I don't think she meant to push [Alice] into the cistern, but that in pushing her in a fit of anger, [Alice] fell into the cistern."

At 1:30 p.m. on Wednesday, November 6, Samuel M. Hench launched the final closing plea for the prosecution. The *Fort Wayne News* reported that Hench consumed nearly four hours, utilizing his "super abilities" to make a "clear, logical, forcible, and eloquent speech and left no stone unturned." Hench methodically laid oust every element of the state's case: the day Alice went missing, the search, finding her in Dunn's cistern, witness testimony, doctors' findings, the question of rape, and other suspects. Four hours later, Hench finished with this passionate plea for Dunn's conviction, as reported by the *Fort Wayne Morning Journal-Gazette*:

> I say to you that the evidence warrants you finding a verdict of guilty in the first degree. Take all the facts in view, and you will find that Charles Dunn assaulted that girl. He did not rape her, but he was attempting to take liberties with her and she screamed. In that moment of alarm, he strangled her. He killed her as charged.

With that, concluding ten days of testimony and three more for final arguments, the Dunn trial was turned over to the jury at 6:00 p.m. As the *Indianapolis News* summed it up:

> Granting that the state has proven Alice Cothrell was murdered, the jury is confronted with a choice between the testimony of Marie Sampleson and the defendant himself. If *Marie's* story is true, Dunn is surely proven guilty. If *his* story is true, he is as surely innocent.

Verdict

For the next twenty hours, the twelve men were sequestered on the third floor of the Allen County courthouse. Behind locked doors, the men grappled with the trial's monumental mound of testimony, as well as the life-altering decision resting in their hands.

The jury took fourteen ballots. In each of the first thirteen, nine called for conviction, and three for acquittal. On the final vote, the three crossed over and the vote was unanimous. At two o'clock Thursday afternoon, November 7, the bailiff received word from the jury foreman that the verdict had been reached. Word passed quickly throughout the community, and the anxious spectators returned, jamming the courtroom. Dunn, escorted by the sheriff, was among them.

Fifteen minutes later, the jurors filed into the jury box, and the bailiff passed a folded paper to Judge O'Rourke. The judge opened the paper, gave it a quick read, and announced in his booming voice, "Gentlemen, listen to the reading of your verdict." The judge paused, waiting for the jurors' undivided attention.

Satisfied, he recited the words scribbled across the official document in his hands. "We, the jury, find the defendant, Charles Dunn, guilty of murder in the first degree as charged in the indictment. And we fix his punishment as imprisonment during the term of his natural life. – George Zeimmer, foreman."

The judge again looked to the jury. "Is this your verdict?"

"Yes," replied the foreman. An affirmative response from each juror followed.

Brittle stillness permeated the courtroom. The spectators' focus shifted from the jury to the defendant, whose jaws tightened as his chin jutted forward. Certainly, he wasn't pleased, although the telling shift in his typically cool demeanor was subtle. In answer to an inquiry by a *Fort Wayne News* reporter about the verdict, Dunn replied, "It has gone against me, but I will never give up. It ain't my style. I'll fight until I die. All I have to say is that I am an innocent man."

The *News*' story ended with another Dunn quote, one that was perhaps more telling of the heart of the man. It reported that as Dunn proceeded from the courtroom to the elevator, he grumbled, "Well, well, what in h--l could you expect of a G-d d--m jury, anyhow?"

The *News* called the comment an illustration of "the utter callousness of the man."

Papers reported that the jury's decision was swayed in large part by a "slip of the tongue" during testimony. The slip had come from Dunn, himself, while explaining his behavior when the Huntertown Regulators converged at his house demanding to search his cistern. When the prosecutor asked Dunn why he fetched a rake without having been asked to do so, Dunn volunteered, "To rake up the body." And when asked why he stood so close over the opening of the cistern as the men raked it, he explained, "To help lift out the body."

The jurors couldn't understand why Dunn would make such statements, after previously insisting he was positive the girl was not in the cistern. "Strangely enough," the *Indianapolis Journal* stated, "the two lapsus linguae escaped the attention of attorneys and reporters alike during the progress of Dunn's examination."

Epilogue

As soon as the verdict was in, the Allen County sheriff released Del Reed and Marie Sampleson from jail, where they had been held as material witnesses since shortly after Alice's death. While Reed seemingly reintegrated into his unspectacular life, a page one story in the Friday, November 8 edition of the *Fort Wayne News* reported that Sampleson was taken to the county poor farm to live. She was six months pregnant. On February 11, 1902, she delivered a stillborn baby boy and sank into a deep depression, refusing medical treatment and food. She died five days later. The doctor who treated the young woman ascribed her death to a broken heart and nervous collapse. If Sampleson had withheld information about the Cothrell case that could have proved Dunn's innocence, as his attorneys speculated, it died with her.

Within a week of Dunn's guilty verdict, his attorneys filed a motion for a new trial. They claimed their request was based on irregularities in the Sampleson testimony, as well as judicial decisions. Judge O'Rourke, however, overruled their motion.

Dunn remained at the Allen County jail until his formal sentencing on February 3, 1902. Two days later, amid the cheers of a large crowd at the depot, he and Deputy Sheriff John Ryan boarded a Nickel Plate passenger train bound for the state prison in Michigan City. According to the *Fort Wayne Journal-Gazette*, Dunn shook hands and said his goodbyes cheerfully, as if headed for a pleasure trip to the lakes.

Charles Dunn's murder trial ended November 7, 1901, with a guilty verdict that fixed his punishment as life in prison. Dunn's attorneys repeatedly appealed his case to the Indiana Supreme Court until he regained his freedom in late 1909. He lived another twenty-three years, dying in 1932. *Photo courtesy the Indiana State Archives.*

"I am going to stand it like a man," Dunn said to well-wishers. "I do not deserve the punishment I am receiving. I never committed a crime in my life, and I did not commit this one. That is all I have to say."

Dunn's attorneys, Colerick and Morris, did have more to say. Over the next seven years, they appealed repeatedly to the Indiana Supreme Court for new trials. Their first petition was denied, but in January 1904, their second petition was granted, and Dunn was brought back to Fort Wayne to await his new trial. The trial opened May 30, but it, too, ended in a guilty verdict, prompting the defense attorneys to submit a third motion for a new trial. Dunn remained in the Allen County jail until December 31, 1904, when the special judge denied the request and handed down a fresh life sentence. Dunn was sent back to Michigan City that same day.

Morris and Colerick clung to their belief in Dunn's innocence. After their fourth request for a new trial, the court acquiesced, and Dunn was escorted back to the Allen County jail in June of 1906. But after eighteen months with no trial date in sight, Dunn was released on a $5,000 bond. When his case finally was retried in December of 1908, the jury was hung, resulting in a mistrial.

The January 6, 1909, *Fort Wayne Journal-Gazette* reported that the county council refused to make appropriations for further Charles Dunn trials. Nothing more transpired until December 16, 1909, when the state dismissed Dunn's case, and his freedom was at last restored.

The papers reported that Dunn's attorneys had been unshakable in their untested claim that Marie Sampleson, *not* Charles Dunn, was the person responsible for Alice Cothrell's death. Conveniently, Sampleson could not defend herself.

Charles Dunn died in 1932 at the age of ninety-two. Alice Cothrell's death remains a mystery. ❖

10

THE PRIVATE HELL OF HARRIET DINKINS

DATELINE: DELAWARE COUNTY, 1941

> You think, my dears, that I am sinning now in this act. I feel I'd rather eternally burn in hell (if you do burn) than run the risk of my little folks facing the hell I have here on earth.
>
> Harriet Dinkins
> March 17, 1941

For the third straight day, Harriet Dinkins's modest, West Eighth Street house, south of Muncie's downtown, sat empty and still. A note pinned to the front door read, "The family is away and will not be back until Wednesday." But this was Thursday afternoon—March 20, 1941—and two of Harriet's neighbor ladies were itching to know why the note was still in place. As they ascended the steps to the Dinkins's front porch to find out, a noxious odor assaulted their olfactory senses, and when they knocked on the door, nothing but silence greeted them. By then, their innate trouble detectors were flashing red, so the ladies parted ways and scampered home, each mentally rehearsing the phone call they were about to make to the police.

Sleeping Beauties
Muncie patrol officers Bill Dragoo and Ernest "Rusty" Holaday were first to respond. Finding the front and back doors bolted from within, they forced

The Dinkins children—seven-year-old Vivian *(left)*; Leroy, nine; and Rose Marie, eleven—died of asphyxiation the night of March 17, 1941, after their mother, Harriet, tucked them in bed, turned up the gas, and removed the valve. Harriet also died. The deaths were deemed murder-suicide.

the bedroom window open, parted the curtain, and poked their heads into the shadowy room, expecting to appease the nibby neighbors with a simple explanation for the growing mystery. Instead, the scene awaiting them was anything but simple.

Stunned, the officers raced to the back door, kicked it open, and rushed into the kitchen. Although repelled by the deadly gas fumes, Dragoo and Holaday pressed on until they reached the source of the leak—a gas heater wedged into the front corner of the tiny bedroom. They quickly went about shutting off the jets, twice retreating outdoors to refill their lungs with clean, fresh air before they could tend to the more pressing concern, the faulty stove's four victims.

On the opposite side of the room, tucked into a small bed, lay nine-year-old Leroy Dinkins; beside him, in a larger bed, were his sisters, eleven-year-old Rose Marie and seven-year-old Vivian; and stretched out on a nearby davenport was their mother, Harriet, thirty-nine. All were dead.

Throughout the house, rags had been stuffed under doors, and bed sheets hung over windows. A forgotten pan of homemade candy sat spoiled on the kitchen counter, discarded toys littered the house, and a lifeless goldfish had settled at the bottom of its bowl. The only sign of life was Red, the family's beloved feline, hiding under the back porch steps.

Within hours, Delaware County Coroner Gailon Stephens determined that the family had been dead since late Monday night, St. Patrick's Day, or approximately seventy-two hours. Stephens ruled asphyxiation as the cause. While that was alarming enough, the manner of their deaths sent the city reeling. All three of the children had been murdered by their mother, and she had committed suicide. The evidence driving the coroner's verdict could not have been more clear.

Bit off More Than She Could Handle
Exactly when Harriet decided to kill her children and herself remains a mystery, but her extensive preparations prove her acts were not impulsive, having planned the unfathomable down to the last detail. In an apparent effort to diminish any misinterpretation, Harriet left behind a series of nine notes, each written with a pencil on lined paper torn from one of her children's school tablets, explaining her motives, regrets, hopes, and final wishes. Eight of the notes had been designated for specific recipients and contained personal messages. The last, which started "Dear neighbors and friends," was a rambling nine-page tell-all in which Harriet rationalized her insanity as reasoned logic that justified the impending murders as "a gathering up of loose ends."

The page one story of the March 21 *Muncie Morning Star* included numerous excerpts from Harriet's lengthy note. Among them were:

> I'm crying a little. I don't think it's self pity. I'm just tired in mind as well as body. I'll be so glad to rest and know we are all safe. I'm not at all afraid, and I know if my little folks knew all about it, they'd be afraid, but they'd want to go with Mom. …
>
> I've worked hard and always tried to be honest and square. …
>
> That I have failed to do what I wanted is apparently no one's fault. I just bit off more than I could handle. …
>
> When I came to this little house, I said I hoped I'd never have to move again unless it would be in a hearse. All I've asked of life was a chance to earn with my own hands a comfortable living for me and mine. Being a woman,

I couldn't get the wages to do that, but you all know I tried and I'm so proud of these kids. I'm trying now to keep them so they'll not be knocked around and hurt by life. They are grand little people, my kids. ...

How I'll get through these next few hours, I don't know.

Harriet's prolonged narrative included her plans for the children's final hours. "Time draws nigh," she wrote. "Vivian is home from school, and I'm going to make them candy and cook whatever they want me to and play with them 'til bedtime."

Before concluding her exposition, she spelled out her wishes for her family's funeral and burial. She hoped the service could be held at the Eighth Street United Brethren Church, which she and her family had attended the previous Christmas.

And finally, ending the message to her friends and neighbors, she wrote, "Isn't it swell? No financial worries, no wondering if folks like us or not, no mean thing can be said to hurt us, etc. ... The rest of you good neighbors, goodbye and good luck."

Unhappily Ever After
Harriet Zula Mahin Dinkins was, by nature, an unhappy woman. Life was hard in 1941 for a single mother with low-wage skills and an unreliable revenue stream. She was understandably bitter. Her first husband had died, and her second husband, Albert, whom she had divorced, had moved to California.

Harriet and Dallas Albert Dinkins married in 1925. They endured a stormy eleven years that produced three children and an abundance of heartache that didn't stop even after their divorce became final in August 1936. Albert fought for custody of the children, but Harriet contended that her former husband had been cruel, that he had made false accusations about her, and frequently became mad. Albert finally dropped his petition for custody in November, but the bickering hadn't stopped there.

In January 1937, Harriet claimed Albert threatened to kill her. But Albert had no record of breaking the law. In fact, he had run for Center Township Trustee in Delaware County's 1934 Primary and had even been a Boy Scout leader. Albert denied his ex-wife's allegation, but pleaded guilty to assault and battery anyway and paid the $25 fine and $10 court costs. After that, he left Muncie for California. But he never gave up.

After the news of the murder-suicide broke, many people in the Muncie

After writing a nine-page note explaining why she could no longer allow her children to "face the hell I have here on earth," Harriet Dinkins planned and perpetrated the deaths of her three children, and herself, the night of March 17, 1941.

community elevated Harriet to a saint. Sympathizers fabricated a scenario that cast Albert as a ne'er-do-well, who had shirked his breadwinner responsibilities, deserted his family, and left his ex-wife in the lurch. For a while, prior to their divorce, Harriet and Albert had owned and operated a neighborhood grocery store. But after his departure, Harriet claimed that her stigma as a divorced woman forced her to eke out a living doing other people's dirty laundry and cleaning their houses. She even asserted in her letter to friends and neighbors that her ex-husband was to blame for the murderous act she was about to commit. Many of her supporters gleefully believed that as well.

"Don't let my children's father, Dallas A. Dinkins, have anything at all of theirs or mine," Harriet stated. "He hasn't cared if they starved or froze or anything. Ask Mr. H.D. Singer [Albert's former employer] about him if you don't believe me or Miss Horney at the Family Service Bureau. She's been so kind to us."

A "Good Mother"

On Saturday, March 22, exactly as Harriet had requested, the funeral was held at the Eighth Street United Brethren Church, located three doors west of the house in which she and her little "chickadees," as she often called her children, had died. Also, per her wishes, Reverend Raymond E. Gant officiated. Nearly eight hundred attendees—family, friends and neighbors—packed the tiny church to pay their respects. The *Muncie Sunday Star* reported that Rose Marie, Leroy and Vivian appeared "restful in their plush caskets."

During his eulogy, Gant referred to the children as God's messengers, sent to bring news before they flew away. Ignoring the elephant in the room, Gant spoke kindly of Harriet, complimenting her efforts to provide for her family and calling her a "good mother."

"Success," he said, "is measured by our accomplishments and our willingness—the spirit in which we do things."

After singing the last hymn, the mourners—the children's playmates at Harrison Elementary School among them—filed down the aisle to the altar to say goodbye. Afterward, all four bodies were returned to the Potter-Stephens Mortuary at Centennial and Wheeling Avenues to await the arrival of Albert Dinkins, who would be flying back to Indiana from California on Sunday.

Despite the mean-spirited gossip permeating the community about Albert, the funeral home honored his request to delay the burial until Monday to allow him a few moments alone with his children. Albert's plane from San Diego landed at Indianapolis's Weir-Cook Airport Sunday afternoon, and he drove directly to the mortuary. After what surely was a painful hour, he proceeded to his brother's home in Royerton.

Albert returned to Muncie on Monday afternoon for the chilly graveside service in Beech Grove Cemetery. Joining him were several members of his family and approximately two hundred members of the Muncie community. Most in the crowd were strangers to Albert, but that didn't stop the unveiled stares of suspicion and disgust, even in the face of his unbearable bereavement. The majority, however, displayed quiet respect and sympathy.

"As the young minister began reading 'The Lord Is My Shepherd,'" reported the March 25 edition of the *Muncie Morning Star*, "the father began to sob, and William Fields [Harriet's son by her first marriage] placed his hand on the older man's knee. The stepfather's hand closed over it for a moment. While the minister was speaking, the father gazed at the three white caskets before him. Almost imperceptibly, he shook his head in hopeless negation."

At the end of the service, according to the *Star*, when Reverend Gant recited the biblical phrase, "Ashes to ashes ... dust to dust," Albert buried his face in his handkerchief and sobbed.

Reportedly, as Albert was being escorted to his automobile, a woman called out to him from the crowd. "Bertie, they loved you. Remember that." Her kind words prompted Albert's response: "I know. I loved them too. If I could just have had them..." Appearing unable to express the anguish that weighed so heavily on his heart, Albert turned slowly and walked away, looking back one last time before he slid into the passenger seat of his waiting vehicle.

Relief Rejected

The Dinkins family tragedy contained the characteristics of a classic Dickens tale: a poverty-stricken but proud single mother, who unselfishly bore the burden of providing for her beloved children, but ultimately remedied her desperation with the only solution she could fathom.

The distressing story captured the collective heart of the Muncie community. The gossip mongers initially blamed the father, accusing him of abandoning the family. By Monday, however, new rumors began to circulate, claiming the township trustee had cut Harriet off the relief assistance roll.

A *Muncie Evening Press* story, published the day of the funeral, quoted township trustee John Kinnear as saying, "Mrs. Dinkins had never applied for township assistance." According to Kinnear, his assistant had searched their relief files but found nothing for Harriet, and the state's relief investigator covering the south Muncie area "did not even know the woman."

Gertrude N. Horney, director of the local Family Service Bureau, on the other hand, said she knew Harriet quite well. In fact, one of Harriet's suicide notes included a call-out to Horney, specifically noting, "She's been so kind to us." According to Horney, rumors that community agencies had refused aid to the Dinkins family were "unfounded." The family's troubles were not "financial," Horney said, insisting that a number of community service agencies had assisted the family with milk, coal, and rent. As proof of her claim, Horney presented receipts showing that during the previous year, Harriet had received $361.55 from the bureau and payments had continued through March of the current year.

The rumor that Albert Dinkins had refused to help the family, despite Harriet's frequent and desperate pleas, was debunked by a page one story in the March 25 *Muncie Evening Press*. The paper emphasized that its report was "backed up, at least in large part, by those intimately acquainted with the circumstances."

Albert repeatedly attempted to reconcile with his wife, the paper claimed.

Harriet Dinkins's wishes were fulfilled when she was laid to rest in Muncie's Beech Grove Cemetery alongside her children under a large shade tree that has only grown larger and shadier over the passing years.

Although working in distant cities, he returned to Muncie in hopes of retrieving his place as the head of the family. But, quoting Albert, the paper stated that each time he offered to help the family, his ex-wife refused it, claiming she was "getting along all right and did not need any of my money." Furthermore, according to the news story, when Albert could not persuade Harriet to take him back, he attempted to convince the county to take the children in and allow him to support them through their foster homes.

Weeks before the tragedy, Albert secured a well-paying toolmaker's position with Consolidated Airlines of San Diego, California. According to the *Muncie Evening Press*, an emotionally wrought Albert had told their reporter, "If she only had waited another month, even another week, I would have been in a position to help—if she would have let me." Referring to the Family Service Bureau, Albert had nothing but praise. "Miss Horney always tried to help me," he said, "and wished to do everything she could for the children, too."

Summing up Albert's claims, the paper wrote:

> Dinkins was anxious that his side of the story not be published until it had been confirmed from other sources, including his wife's relatives, and said he merely wanted the public to know he was grateful for its kindness to his children while they lived and for their sympathy and consolation after their deaths. He was especially anxious that no word be said which would reflect in any way upon the memory of the woman who had been his wife.

The talk about the Dinkins situation persisted for the next few days, exemplified by *Muncie Evening Press* editorials and a few letters to the editor written in support of the estranged father. The March 26 editorial revealed that the paper's investigation confirmed the veracity of Albert's account. It stated:

> All of [Albert] Dinkins's story cannot well be told, since it now would serve no good purpose to tell it, except further to exonerate him and he does not care about that; but enough is known to dissipate the charges that he did not love his children and would not have cared for them had he been given the opportunity. ... Too many people are made happy by believing the worst.

Epilogue

In one of Harriet Dinkins's final notes, she had written, "If our 'Red' don't go with us, someone please be good to him. He's a good pet, and we love him."

The *Muncie Sunday Star*'s story about the Dinkins family's funeral service reported that shortly after the hearses rolled away, Delaware County Coroner Gailon Stephens accompanied a young man to the Dinkins house. After unlocking the front door, the young man entered. A moment later, he walked out. In his arms, he carried a big, red cat.

The *Star* found some joy that Harriet's wish had been granted.

Pity she hadn't wished the same good fortune for her children. ❖

11

PANDEMONIUM AT WILLIAM REED ELEMENTARY SCHOOL

Dateline: Blackford County, 1960

Decades before Americans mourned the devastating loss of innocent lives in ordinary towns like Uvalde, Texas, and Parkland, Florida, an ordinary town in Indiana had already experienced the horrors inflicted by a deranged gunman on the loose inside one of its schools. Indiana's first deadly school shooting occurred February 2, 1960, at the William Reed Elementary School in the Blackford County seat of Hartford City. Three lives were lost that day, and while no child was injured physically, two classrooms of innocent fifth-graders witnessed the horrifying shooting deaths of their teachers. The nightmare would haunt them for the rest of their lives.

A Hartford City Pillar

The William Reed Elementary School principal, Leonard Redden, was a well-liked, highly regarded Hartford City citizen—a friendly, caring pillar of the community. Quiet and mild-mannered, the forty-four-year-old husband and father taught Sunday School and never uttered an unkind word to anyone. As principal of Hartford City's three elementary schools, he was entrusted with the well-being and education of all kindergarten through sixth-grade students.

But lately, Redden had been acting strange, and his behavior had not gone unnoticed. His wife, Hazel, had known for months that his grip on reality was

Leonard Redden, principal of the William Reed Elementary School of Hartford City, stunned all who knew him when he showed up at the school mid-morning, Tuesday, February 2, 1960, carrying a loaded twelve-gauge shotgun. His first stop was the fifth-grade classroom of Harriett Robson. After he shot her in the chest in full view of her horrified students, he proceeded to Minnie McFerren's classroom, also filled with fifth-graders, and shot her in the face. Redden then hurried outside to his car and drove away. Police found him early that afternoon in a wooded area south of the city, where he had taken his life. *Photos courtesy the Blackford County Historical Society.*

Leonard Redden

deteriorating. His boss, Superintendent E. Phillips Blackburn, as well as other school officials, had noticed it, too. But neither Hazel nor anyone associated with the schools confronted Redden about the obvious. Instead, they waited for him to raise the topic. When he finally did, he was less than twenty-four hours away from a complete mental collapse.

Nightmare on Chestnut Street
On that morning of Tuesday, February 2, Redden didn't care whether the groundhog saw its shadow or retreated to its nest for another six weeks. When Redden arrived at the two-story, yellow-brick school building on East Chestnut Street shortly past ten o'clock, he snatched the loaded twelve-gauge shotgun off the seat beside him, slid out of his 1952 Ford sedan, and stormed inside the school. First stop: Harriett Robson's classroom.

The fifty-two-year-old teacher was seated at an absent student's desk near the coat closet busily grading papers. She didn't appear startled when Redden barged in, until he shouted, "Hang *me*, will you?" When she looked up at him, he pointed the gun at her chest and fired. Robson slumped forward and crumbled onto the floor, landing faceup.

Before Redden pulled the trigger, the roomful of ten- and eleven-year-olds giggled, thinking their gun-toting principal was playing a joke. However, once the gun fired and blood began gushing from their teacher's chest, they shrieked and scattered. The kids' reaction angered Redden, prompting him

Harriett Robson   Minnie McFerren

to turn his shotgun on the kids and direct them to sit back down at their desks.

Once the peace and quiet were restored, Redden walked into the hall and strutted up the ramp to the classroom of another veteran teacher, sixty-two-year-old Minnie McFerren. When he stepped into the room, McFerren was reading poetry to her students. The instant he locked eyes with the teacher, he announced, "If anyone moves, I'll shoot you."

McFerren stared down the barrel of the principal's gun, keenly aware of the threat not only to her, but to her twenty-one pupils as well. "Leonard," she pleaded, "don't shoot!"

That was when, according to the February 3, 1960, *Muncie Evening Press*, Redden "calmly put the gun to her head and pulled the trigger."

The Unraveling

Few people had comprehended the depth of Redden's mental anxieties or his slippery grip on his control switch. According to Hazel, her husband suffered from what she called a "persecution complex" that had originated during World War II, when he was wounded in the South Pacific. Throughout their marriage, Hazel had watched helplessly as his torment waxed and waned, but this time the downward shift in his temperament was dramatic.

She first saw the change the previous April. Redden told her that troubling gossip about him had started to circulate. The rumors accused him of engaging in extramarital conduct, but he swore the innuendos were untrue.

"People are saying you and I aren't getting along," he told Hazel. "They're saying I'm interested romantically in Harriett Robson." Furthermore, he claimed McFerren had fabricated the vile stories to humiliate him.

Hazel knew Leonard wouldn't cheat on her, and she knew Harriett. She was one of Hazel's closest friends. And so was Minnie McFerren. Hazel told her husband to ignore the rumors—if they even existed—and to shake off the worry.

For months, Hazel believed her husband had moved on, but on Saturday of the last weekend of Christmas break, his demeanor darkened again and his talk of the rumors returned. But even worse, he injected violence into the conversation.

"You know," he told her, "during the war, I killed a lot of people I didn't know just because they wore the wrong uniform. ... If this thing keeps up, I'm going to get me a couple of teachers and then myself."

Stunned, Hazel jumped to her feet and rushed to the telephone. She intended to call the doctor, but Redden stopped her. He wouldn't have it. He firmly objected to his wife's interference.

However, after suffering three more weeks of near-debilitating moodiness over the same non-existent rumors, he relented. On the morning of Monday, February 1, he dropped in at Superintendent Blackburn's office. Blackburn later described Redden as "overwrought." When Blackburn asked him what was wrong, Redden replied, "I'm sick. I'm afraid. I want your help."

Blackburn phoned the principal's family doctor, Dean Jackson, on Redden's behalf and arranged an appointment for him that afternoon. During the visit with Jackson, Redden admitted to "mental troubles." In response, the doctor urged his patient to seek psychiatric care. Redden agreed to it, and Jackson called a psychiatrist he knew in Muncie. The psychiatrist agreed to see Redden at two-thirty the following afternoon—Tuesday, February 2. But it wasn't soon enough. That Monday evening, Redden broke down, sobbing uncontrollably and begging Hazel for help.

Hazel comforted her husband the best she could and persuaded him to relax, to go to bed and get some sleep. Once he ascended the stairs to the bedroom, Hazel set to work, searching the house for knives and shotgun shells. And hiding them. After her mission was accomplished, she spent the rest of the night pacing and downing coffee.

The morning of February 2, 1960, Leonard Redden walked into Harriett Robson's fifth-grade classroom and shot her in the chest. This photo of Robson's abandoned classroom, captured shortly after the shooting, shows students' books still open to the day's lessons that had been in progress before Redden entered. *Photo by Arnold McCombs provided courtesy* The News Times *of Hartford City, Indiana.*

Redden rose early that Tuesday and made a covert trip to the hardware store to replenish his supply of shells. From there, he returned home, picked up his gun, and drove to the school.

The Getaway

Maintenance supervisor Silas McCaffrey had been laying a new tile floor in the school's back hallway upstairs near McFerren's door, when he heard the blasts. Observing Redden walk out of McFerren's classroom clenching a shotgun, McCaffrey hurled his crowbar at Redden and knocked the gun from his hands.

Sixth-grade teacher Ralph Grimme, whose classroom was next to McFerren's, bounded into the corridor in time to see Redden retrieve his gun. Redden saw Grimme, too, and Grimme later described the dicey encounter to the *Muncie Star Press*.

"He leveled the gun right at me," he said. "I stood there for a second, then scrambled around the steps and behind the bannister. I could hear him running down the halls. I waited a few minutes, until it was quiet, and then I went into Mrs. McFerren's room."

William E. Reed Elementary School, the site of one of Hartford City's most incomprehensible tragedies, has long since been converted to the Hartford Square apartments.

Outside, music teacher Esther Nesbitt was strolling up the walkway to the school's main entrance, when Redden ran out the door on the west and McCaffrey dashed out the door on the east. Redden spotted Nesbitt and stopped. Raising his shotgun at her, he asked, "Do you want to live?"

"Yes, of course, I do, Mr. Redden," she replied weakly.

"Then get inside the building," he growled.

The young woman hurried toward the front door, and Redden bolted to his car. But when he saw McCaffrey sprinting toward him, he paused and again raised his gun. McCaffrey froze in his tracks.

"Don't shoot me," McCaffrey cried.

Redden shook his head and lowered the gun. "I won't, Si."

McCaffrey remained motionless, watching Redden climb into his car and drive away, heading west toward State Road 3.

Manhunt Ensues

Recovering from the tense moment as a potential target, Grimme charged into McFerren's classroom. What he found surpassed anything he could have imagined. The teacher was lying on the floor a few steps inside the door. Blood was everywhere. The children were terrified and confused. He told them to get out of the building and go straight home.

Darting back into the hallway, he ran down the ramp to Robson's classroom. He also found her lying on the floor covered in blood. He thought at first that she was alive, but when he couldn't locate a pulse, he raced to the school office, picked up a phone, and dialed the police.

Superintendent Blackburn closed all the city schools for the rest of the day and sent the students home. Many of the frightened William Reed Elementary School children had already fled in hysterics, leaving their books and even their winter coats behind.

Local law enforcement agencies launched a manhunt, enlisting help from more than a hundred officers from surrounding counties, as well as the Indiana State Police. They set up roadblocks, flew in aircraft, and canvassed the vicinity.

About 1:00 p.m., a farmer discovered Redden's car abandoned alongside a county road, some five miles south of Hartford City in the northern Delaware County countryside. After that, the search concentrated on the woods in that region. Three hours later, a team of officers found Redden's body sprawled in an isolated wooded tract northeast of Eaton.

According to the *Muncie Evening Press*, Redden had stumbled upon a large wood pile that provided protection from the cold north wind. He stopped there and smoked three cigarettes. He then propped the barrel of his shotgun against his sternum and blew a hole through his chest.

Redden likely died instantly, taking his mindset with him. Thus, no one would ever know his final thoughts about the heinous acts he perpetrated a few hours before, or whether he was remorseful.

Shock Sets in

Blackburn kept all the Hartford City schools closed Wednesday. The school board met in secret and decided to reopen Thursday. No point in dragging this thing out, they figured. They're kids. They'll get over it. Yet, despite the board's dismissive stance, it did make one concession. It swapped the classrooms of the murdered teachers with two other classrooms. Consequently, the students who had watched their teachers gunned down wouldn't have to return to the site of the shooting day after day to relive the horror.

When school opened Thursday, students of the murdered teachers were directed to the auditorium, where Dr. Ralph W. Graham, pastor of the city's Grace Methodist Church, spoke to them and led them in prayer. At the conclusion of the minister's talk, the children proceeded to their new classrooms and resumed their studies.

Due to the school board's sudden implementation of a new policy of silence, members of the press had been forbidden to attend the assembly. Therefore, the content of the clergyman's message was never reported.

"We have decided to make no further comment," Graham said. "You can understand. Children are involved. We want to get back to normalcy, even if we can't forget what happened."

Blackburn told the faculty to carry on as if the two deceased teachers and the principal were simply absent with the flu. "We brought in substitute teachers," Blackburn told the *Muncie Star*, "and we are trying to have normal school. We are not going to talk about what happened Tuesday. The boys and girls are more ready to go on than we are."

A parent, whose eleven-year-old son had watched his teacher die, told a United Press International reporter, "Even little children have to accept reality. I wonder if the real things are any more terrifying than some of the things children see on television."

Blackburn would not say how many of the youngsters whose teachers were killed were staying home from school. "From here on," he insisted, "our schools are going to be out of the spotlight if I have anything to do with it. Our schools are going to be just like schools down in Podunk, Muncie, or Indianapolis."

Time to Move on

School was closed Friday to allow students and teachers to attend the funerals for Robson and McFerren. Redden's was Saturday. Classes were back in session Monday, despite reports that many children weren't coping well.

Due to Blackburn's cavalier dismissal of the shock the murders had inflicted on the young William Reed students, dealing with their psychological well-being was shifted to the parents. Few, if any, of the parents possessed the skills necessary to diagnose, let alone treat the post-traumatic stress awaiting their children.

The vice president of the school's PTA tried quelling her ten-year-old son's fears with sleeping pills prescribed by her doctor. The mother of a boy who watched his teacher take a bullet in the chest bought her son a model ship to assemble, because she felt it was healing to keep his mind and hands busy. Another mother, whose daughter also witnessed Robson's murder, chose to let her little girl sleep with her. "She hadn't done that for years," the woman explained. And still another mother, who had grown annoyed at her son's constant chatter about his teacher's slaughter, declared the topic off limits. "There's a certain romance about horrible things for an eleven-year-old," she said.

In the Redden home, to the contrary, Hazel was determined to shield her children from the horror—and the shame—of their father's rampage.

"I can't give up," she said. "I have my two sons—one in third grade and the other a high school freshman. I know they need me. I'm going to try to hold up for them if I can."

Epilogue

While the school board had taken a tight-lipped approach and refused to comment publicly about the school shootings, much of Hartford City did have something to say about them. The driving force most often cited to explain Redden's violent outbreak was his diminishing mental state. A local attorney complained to an *Indianapolis News* writer that someone should have alerted the police about Redden's strange behavior.

"We don't want to hurt anybody's feelings," the attorney said, "so we don't report to the proper authorities that someone has been acting strangely. This man should have been given medical aid. Now it's too late."

An editorial in the *Hammond Times* titled, "But Nobody Heard Him," took a different approach at spelling out what had gone wrong. The editorial postulated that part of the problem was society's adherence to pseudoscientific mental-health beliefs as old as time, and that mental illness unfairly reflected a negative stigma on an individual or his family.

"Regardless," the editorial emphasized, "the principal had exhibited symptoms of mental illness for days, and possibly weeks, before the tragedy. Unconsciously, he was calling for help. But no one heard him. Until it was too late."

In the final analysis of how a highly regarded, solid member of the community with everything going for him had so unexpectedly and tragically lost his way, perhaps Redden's wife, Hazel, summed it up best: "He was just plain out of his head."

Two William Reed Classmates Bound by Shared Horror

Life-long Hartford City residents Shirley Harter Dollar and Nancy Tatman Lenfestey were ages ten and eleven that February morning in 1960, when Leonard Redden, principal at the William Reed Elementary School, walked into their classrooms—Shirley's on the first floor, Nancy's on the second—toting a shotgun. Unsure of the proper reaction, the girls followed their classmates' lead and laughed. Their levity quickly turned to horror, however, when their fun-loving principal pointed his weapon at their teachers and fired point blank.

Shirley watched as her teacher, Harriett Robson, took the blast from Redden's shotgun in her chest and dropped to the floor. Nancy was only inches from Redden, when he fired into the face of her teacher, Minnie McFerren. Witnessing the brutal murders of their teachers was more than simply an unforgettable memory for the students. It was life-changing.

Shirley and Nancy reunited at the Hartford City Historical Society in January 2023 to take a look back at their shared nightmare. As they compared experiences, they paused frequently to quell a surge of emotions brought on by the rise of an unwelcome memory.

"Each time there's a shooting and it comes on TV," Shirley said, "I'm right back there. It's something I live with every day."

Nancy agreed, adding that she was still bothered by loud noises, such as fireworks. "I am afraid of so many things," she said. "It made me a coward."

Shirley said that even after nearly six decades, explaining why they react as they do to unexpected situations and noises is very difficult.

"I don't really think we're cowards," she said. "I think it's just anything that's sudden. I can't even open a can of biscuits."

Both women remained conflicted by their lingering feelings about their

Former William Reed Elementary School students—Nancy Tatman Lenfestey *(left)* and Shirley Harter Dollar—reunited in Hartford City at the Blackford County Historical Society in January 2023 to share their memories of the shootings of February 2, 1960, a day they called the worst day of their lives.

principal. Both claimed they, like nearly all their classmates, loved him.

"I remember he always had a smile on," said Nancy, "and we'd go, 'Good morning, Mr. Redden.' But that morning, we didn't do that. He didn't have the smile. It was a stern look."

Redden often amused the students by dressing in a funny costume.

"Sometimes in a silly outfit," Shirley said, "just to make our day."

Thus, when Redden entered their rooms that morning, wearing hunting clothes and bearing a shotgun, the kids didn't think anything nefarious about it.

"We were in the middle of our geography reports," Shirley recalled. "I actually remember Miss Robson laughing. Until he pointed that gun at her and said, 'Hang *me*, will you?' Those were his exact words."

Robson had been sitting at the desk of an absent student. When Redden's shot struck the teacher's chest, she fell to the floor, and he ran out of the room, heading for Nancy's classroom.

"We all started screaming and somebody called the police," Shirley said.

The students in Nancy's class had been studying poetry, and that morning, each was prepared to stand and read a poem they had written. Nancy was excited to share her poem and had worn her best Sunday school dress for the occasion.

Her desk was situated next to the room's entrance, and when Redden walked in, he held his gun directly over Nancy as he aimed it at McFerren.

"He told us to be quiet," Nancy said, "and I remember Mrs. McFerren saying, 'Oh, please,' and as she was walking this way, he did it. And her face came off."

Nancy was frozen in shock. Her dress was spattered with her teacher's blood.

"I just sat there," she said. "I couldn't believe my eyes, and then he ran out the door. The next thing I knew, Mr. Grimme came to the door and told us, 'Run like hell. Go home!' It was the first time I'd heard a teacher cuss. I was still sitting there, and [a classmate] pulled me out."

Because Robson's body blocked the entrance to the cloakroom, Shirley and her classmates ran out of the room without their coats. Some lived nearby; others lived up to a mile away.

The temperature in Hartford City that morning was twenty-five degrees.

"When Mom came home at two o'clock," Shirley recollected, "she said, 'Let's go get your coat.' We went back to the school, but of course, they wouldn't let us in."

Throughout the years, each time the women's classmates met, their shared nightmare was always a topic of conversation. Most remain critical of the casual way school administrators brushed aside the effect of the murders on their young students' psychological well-being, Shirley said

"If they had just let us share," Nancy said, "talk it out. We didn't talk about it for a long time. The first time my sister-in-law, who was in Miss Robson's class, and I talked about it, we were married with babies."

"In all the years since it happened," Shirley said, "I've never been as scared as I was that day. I can honestly say, it was the worst thing that's ever happened to me." ❖

PART III
KILLERS: KIDS

12

WHEN MURDER IS CHILD'S PLAY

Dateline: Jay County, 1922

A popular nineteenth-century nursery rhyme—*What Are Little Boys Made of?*—contends that little boys are made of "frogs and snails and puppy dog tails." While the innocent characterization has delighted children for two hundred years, perhaps Mother Goose should have footnoted that some boys are made of "anger and knives and snuffing out lives." Goose fans may deem the perverse portrayal of little boys inappropriate for her brand. Nonetheless, that's what played out in Portland, Indiana, on Friday, June 2, 1922—the day nine-year-old Robert Silvers had a falling out with nine-year-old Bernard Teeter, grabbed a knife, and slit his throat.

Prosperity Special
By three o'clock that sunny Friday afternoon, scores of Jay County people had assembled along the Grand Rapids & Indiana railroad track at Votaw Street near downtown Portland. They had flocked there to cheer the Prosperity Special, a historic, mile-long train of twenty newly built locomotives, as it steamed through town on its way to Richmond.

Amid the multitude of train enthusiasts was Bernie Teeter. Bernie had been nonchalantly leaning on a light pole and gazing across the tracks at his mother, until Bobby Silvers suddenly tore through the crowd and lunged at him. Clenching a knife in his raised fist, Bobby screamed, "Now, you see what

I got," and rammed the four-inch blade straight into Bernie's throat, slicing the jugular, severing an artery, and penetrating the apex of his right lung. Stunned, Bernie wrapped his tiny hands around his neck as blood gushed from the gaping hole. Gasping for air, he stumbled into the crowd, gurgling a barely discernible, "Mama." Bobby's eyes bulged at the sight. Panicking, he tossed the knife aside and ran away.

The *Indianapolis News* reported that Bernie's mother, Golda, had witnessed the brutal attack and frantically shoved her way through the throng of people and hastened across the tracks. The second she reached Bernie's side, his strength gave out, and he crumbled to the ground unconscious. Golda cradled her mortally wounded child and begged for help. Pastor W.E. Hogan of Portland's Methodist Episcopal Church heard the woman's cries and rushed to her aid. Taking the boy in his arms, he led Golda to his car and sped to the Jay County Hospital. A team of doctors and nurses worked feverishly to save the young boy's life, but the cut to his jugular was too deep. Bernie bled to death within the hour.

Badgered, Bullied, and Browbeaten
Bobby and Bernie may not have been chums, but as Lincoln Elementary School classmates, they were well-acquainted. Earlier on the day of Bernie's murder, according to several area newspapers, the two boys had engaged in a heated argument over who was the rightful owner of the baseball glove in Bernie's possession. The bitter verbal exchange ended when Bobby stomped away for home, crept into the kitchen, and snatched one of his mother's paring knives.

After the fatal assault, Portland Police Chief Harry Huey and Officer Harry Woods paid a visit to the Silvers's house and found Bobby hiding under his bed. They coaxed him out and took him to police headquarters. When Bobby learned Bernie was dead, he broke down and wept bitterly. He hadn't meant to hurt Bernie, he said. Bobby later told authorities that Bernie and his older brother, Walter, had often picked fights with him, and on that day, the Teeter boys had threatened to throw Bobby onto the tracks in front of the oncoming Prosperity Special. From Bobby's perspective, he was merely defending himself.

By evening, Bobby had been charged with first-degree murder under a tentative affidavit and locked in a jail cell. The Saturday, June 3 edition of Fort Wayne's *News-Sentinel* reported that throughout the ordeal, the fright-

Robert Silvers was only nine years old when, on June 2, 1922, he stabbed his nine-year-old schoolmate, Bernie Teeters, in the throat and killed him.

ened little boy sobbed incessantly and clung to his mother. While he expressed hope that Bernie's family could forgive him, Bobby's parents, Charles and Fannie Silvers, said they would gladly let him pay the penalty for taking the life of his playmate.

"We have tried every means to make our son behave," said Bobby's father. "We even tried to have him admitted to the boys' reformatory."

Pint-Sized Crime and Punishment

During his first night in jail, Bobby was released from his cell and permitted to cuddle with his mother in a comfortable area of the sheriff's office. Saturday morning, the Silvers family learned that their attorney had conferred with the Jay Circuit Court judge and the Jay County prosecutor about the unusual circumstances of the case, particularly the perpetrator's young age. The meeting resulted in a reduction of the charge against their son from murder one to involuntary manslaughter.

A few hours later, however, when Bobby appeared for arraignment in the Jay County Juvenile Court before Circuit Court Judge E.E. McGriff, the

The Prosperity Special was nearly a half-mile long as it hauled twenty Baldwin steam locomotives from Eddystone, Pennsylvania, to Los Angeles, California, in May and June of 1922. It was called the "most remarkable single train of locomotives ever hauled across the country." As the Prosperity Special rolled through Portland, Indiana, on June 2 that year, a huge crowd lined the tracks to cheer it on, just as the crowd had done when the train arrived at the depot in Riverside, California, pictured above.

Silverses were told that the charge had again been changed, that time to *voluntary* manslaughter. Bobby's attorney advised him to plead guilty, which he did, but Bobby also insisted that he had only meant to hit Bernie, not to stab him, and certainly had no thoughts of killing him.

"I told Bernard to stand back," Bobby told the court. "He did not and I struck him. I intended to hit him in the jaw."

The judge acknowledged Bobby's statement and postponed the sentencing until Monday, June 5. When court convened that morning, curious spectators filled the room, but when Bobby shuffled in—accompanied by his mother, his father, and his aged grandfather—stillness enveloped the room. The members of the Silvers family were visibly nervous, and Fannie cried into her handkerchief.

When Judge McGriff called Bobby to the witness stand, according to the *Muncie Evening Press*, the boy looked too young and innocent "to be accused of so great a crime."

The well-behaved youth slid onto the chair and sat quietly, while Jay County Prosecutor A.H. Williamson explained the charge being leveled in the State of Indiana v. Robert Silvers case.

"He's at the age of unaccountability now," the prosecutor said of Bobby. "However, he should be placed in a boys' school of correction until he's twenty-one years old."

Williamson was followed by Bobby's attorney, Malcolm Skinner. After a brief consultation with Charles Silvers, Skinner entered a guilty plea on Bobby's behalf. After that, according to the June 5, 1922, *Muncie Evening Press:*

> Judge McGriff leaned far out over his desk, looked Bobbie Silvers squarely in the eyes, and said, "Robert, do you know that you have killed another little boy?"
> Bobbie shook his head.
> "And that the other little boy is at home now in a casket?"
> Again Bobbie shook his head. That was all.

Several newspapers speculated about Bobby's culpability and outside influences that may have driven him to murder, regardless of whether it was intentional or accidental. According to the *Muncie Sunday Star*, Bobby had been in trouble many times for minor misdemeanors, and a few days before the fatal stabbing, the city's deputy postmaster had taken a knife from Bobby for threatening to use it on a boy. Charles and Fannie referred to their son as "incorrigible," and one of their neighbors called him "the terror of the neighborhood."

Cowboy Bob
The *Indianapolis News* theorized that Bobby's foray into the dark side followed a head injury suffered in an automobile accident. The *News* wrote, "Since that time, [Bobby] is said to have been afflicted with kleptomania and has been in much trouble as a result. For some time, he had been practicing climbing porch poles and taking out screen windows, the police say. The dead boy had never been in any trouble."

Was it a case of "mental haziness," as the *News* suggested, related to a recent head injury? Or was the driving force behind the boy's violent act linked to his fondness for "Wild West moving pictures," as his parents claimed?

"Bob always attended Wild West moving pictures," Fannie told the *Muncie Evening Press* reporter, "and Friday [the day he killed Bernie], he was playing cowboy with his little brother. I saw him put several knives in his belt, and I took them away from him for his own safety. After that, when I was out of sight, I guess he slipped into the kitchen and took a paring knife."

Fort Wayne's *News-Sentinel* reported that Bobby had been examined by a local physician to determine why he was prone to violence, or "meanness," as his parents termed it. However, the doctor found a mentally sound, above-average nine-year-old.

Following the June 5 hearing, despite a state law that prohibited committing children under age ten to the Indiana Boys' School at Plainfield, McGriff sentenced Bobby to a minimum of two years at the school with the recommendation he remain there until reaching his twenty-first birthday.

Jay County Sheriff James Badders prepared to take Bobby to the Plainfield facility the following morning, as the court ordered.

Boys' School a No-Go
A hitch in the Silvers sentence arose Tuesday morning, June 6, when the boys' school superintendent, Charles McGonagle, informed McGriff that admitting nine-year-old Robert Silvers to the school was not possible until he turned ten the following May. McGonagle had no flexibility in the law, but suggested Jay County authorities hold the boy for a year and then commit him to the school. Or they could subject the boy to a psychological evaluation, and if doctors determined he was mentally ill, they could admit him to a mental hospital until he was old enough for the boys' school.

In response to the obstacles to Bobby's sentence, McGriff and Williamson sent Governor Warren McCray a petition, requesting that he order the superintendent of the boys' school to take the Silvers boy into custody, despite his age. No other resolutions were considered.

The governor was out of town. In his stead, Indiana Attorney General U.S. Lesh responded to McGriff, suggesting he commit the boy to the county jail until he was old enough to transfer to the Indiana Boys' School. Legally, the judge couldn't do that. McGriff's only other idea was sending Bobby to the private boys' and girls' school at Whiting, Indiana. If that fell through, he didn't know what else he could do but release the boy.

Things finally started to gel on Friday, June 9, one week after Bernie Teeter's murder. That morning, Bobby, his father, and his attorney, Malcolm Skinner, traveled to Indianapolis to sit down with the governor and attorney general. Skinner believed if McCray and Lesh could meet the boy, they might be more inclined to resolve the dilemma over his age. The attorney was correct. After the meeting, the governor ordered that Bobby be sent to the boys' school in Plainfield for one year, with the understanding that, at the end of that time, he would be returned to the Jay Circuit Court to be sentenced for manslaughter and returned to the school until he reached his twenty-first birthday.

When the foursome came home from Indianapolis, they returned Bobby to the jail, where he remained until Wednesday, June 14, when Sheriff Badders transported him to Plainfield.

One month later, on July 13, Fannie Silvers received a letter from Governor McCray's private secretary, Adah Bush. She had recently visited Bobby at the Plainfield school and wrote to his mother to tell her, "Robert has been classified as 'the baby of the school,' and he appears much improved since undergoing an operation for the removal of his adenoids and tonsils." Bush also reported that Bobby was looking forward to a visit with his parents.

Merry Christmas

On Thursday, December 21, six months after entering the Indiana Boys' School, Bobby walked out, and his waiting parents took him home. It was a gift from the governor, who had commuted Judge McGriff's sentence.

"Send that boy back to his folks for a Christmas present," the governor declared.

McGriff, Williamson, and McGonagle fully supported Governor McCray's decision. In a message to the governor, McGonagle wrote:

> The Binet-Simon mental test indicates that [Robert] has a normal mind for a boy of his years, and I do not believe it probable that a normal nine-year-old boy would commit a wilful murder. I believe that the ends of justice will be attained if you will grant the prayer of this boy's father and approve the recommendation of Judge McGriff and the prosecuting attorney.

And so it was. The youngest person to be committed to a penal institution in Indiana for murder was free. A Fort Wayne *News-Sentinel* editorial expressed that the action taken by the Jay County court was "ridiculous and absurd." It stated, "Had the youngster been treated to a good spanking and a stern admonition, it is likely that much more good would have been accomplished."

The *Indianapolis Star* argued that Bobby Silvers's deed called for punishment, but justice would not have been served by detaining him. "The governor's mercy is of the quality that 'blesseth him that gives and him that takes,'" the *Star* wrote, "and is an act which typifies the spirit of Christmas."

A week later, the *Star* ran a brief item reporting that Bobby had written the governor a thank-you letter, which included this prophetic statement: "My greatest hope is that someday when I become a man, I shall be able to repay you for your goodness in releasing me from the boys' school."

Epilogue

The life of the Silvers family was never the same after the death of Bernie Teeter. While Charles and Fannie were overjoyed to have their son home, their joy was short-lived. Returning to Portland was one thing, but returning to normal was impossible. With Bobby back, the community steered clear. People looked at him with suspicion. What responsible parent would risk allowing their child anywhere near him?

In time, the Silvers family moved to Dayton, Ohio, and settled in. Growing up there, Robert occasionally found himself in trouble with the police—nothing major, but enough to plant doubt that he would ever prove worthy of the gift bestowed upon him by Indiana's governor.

By the late 1940s, Robert was running a Dayton dry cleaning service and, by all measures, had become a productive member of society. But that changed in 1953, when he became a member of a six-man burglary ring that perpetrated numerous break-ins throughout the Dayton area. In late July of that year, the men were busted. Although Robert consistently denied taking any part in the crimes, he was tried, convicted, and sentenced to five-to-thirty years at the Ohio State Penitentiary.

In 1962, after his release, forty-nine-year-old Robert Silvers took a bride and started over. When cancer claimed his life in 1984, his obituary in the *Dayton Daily News* described a successful, stable family man—a husband, father, and grandfather. It may have taken a bit longer than he expected in late 1922, when he vowed to repay Governor McCray's kindness, but Robert Silvers had, indeed, paid his bill in full. ❖

13

THE MOTHER GOOSE MURDER TRIAL

DATELINE: STARKE COUNTY, 1920

I have made a scientific examination of Cecil Burkett for the *Richmond* [Indiana] *Item*. I am convinced that he could plan and execute a murder, but that he would not. ... I found Cecil to be fully normal mentally and morally—exactly like the average normal boy of his age. ... But we still must consider whether he can have a fair trial. He cannot. He should be tried by a jury of his peers—equals. But will the twelve men who hear his story, and the stories of the other child witnesses in this case, be his peers? They will not. ... No child, whatever the evidence, should be brought to bar as an adult, to be tried before adults. ... Why then should he be tried by adults for his life? Why should he stand to lose his life on the words of adults who cannot understand him?

Dr. Harold N. Moyer
Criminologist and Alienist
February 10, 1921

The news ricocheted from household to household throughout Ora, the tiny Starke County village, on that Thanksgiving Day of 1920: A bullet had ripped through the abdomen of seven-year-old Benny Slavin. Despite prayers and round-the-clock medical care at the hospital in nearby Winamac, thirty hours later, Benny was dead. At first, folks believed he had been shot accidentally. But before he passed, he uttered four words that at once put Ora on the map, sowed seeds of rancor, and cast a net of suspicion over the eleven-year-old boy next door.

"Mother," Benny had said, "Cecil Burkett shot me."

The roots of bitterness were soon creeping into every crevice of the close-knit community, inserting a wedge of hate that pitted friend against friend, neighbor against neighbor. Some blamed Benny for carelessly handling a loaded rifle; others claimed Cecil deliberately pulled the trigger.

A Not-So-Grand Grand Jury Decision

Two months later, on January 27, 1921, the *South Bend Tribune* carried a brief story headlined "Jurors Indict Child for Capital Offense." The story reported that the Starke County Grand Jury had charged Cecil Burkett with first-degree murder for the shooting death of his neighbor, Benny Slavin. Cecil's trial was scheduled for March, and were it to result in a guilty verdict, he would face life in prison or execution.

The public was outraged and implored Starke County Prosecutor James A. Dilts to refer the case to juvenile court. But Dilts dug in, pointing out that juvenile courts did not consider murder a form of delinquency, regardless of the perpetrator's tender age. Until the trial, however, by special dispensation, Cecil was "at liberty on bond of $10,000," provided by his father.

Inexplicably, newspapers around Indiana were slow to embrace the historic significance of the indictment. Aside from the few that printed brief items containing the barest of facts, the majority of news outlets waited two weeks or more before picking up on the unprecedented case and what it could mean to the moral evolution of justice.

The Moyer Report

Finally, the February 10 edition of the *Streator* (Illinois) *Daily Press* allocated several inches to the story, including a two-column-wide photo of Cecil. The coverage featured a detailed report by a former Chicago health commissioner, Dr. Harold N. Moyer, who argued why it was wrong for adults to try a child for murder.

The sixty-two-year-old doctor had devoted a great deal of his career to studying criminology and the human brain, particularly that of prison and asylum inmates. Moyer had recently examined Cecil Burkett's brain, basing his approach on the Binet-Simon Intelligence Scales, precursor to the modern IQ test, to ascertain if plotting a murder was in Cecil's makeup; and if it were,

Lena Slavin *(left)* and Anna Burkett *(right)*—mothers of seven-year-old Benny Slavin *(lower left)* and his accused killer, eleven-year-old Cecil Burkett *(lower right)*—remained strong throughout the unthinkable, tragic ordeal.

whether he could pull one off.

Bottom line, Moyer determined that Cecil was a "normal boy," who displayed no sign of innate cruelty or criminality and clearly understood the difference between right and wrong. Moyer's report made it clear that no child, regardless of the crime or the evidence, should be tried in an adult court; nor should a child be judged by a jury of adults.

Thanks to the Moyer report, the Burkett-Slavin case started to receive the attention it deserved coast to coast. Among the papers carrying an in-depth report of the Starke County Grand Jury's historic indictment was the February 12 edition of the *Richmond* (Indiana) *Item*. The paper included Cecil's compelling account, in his own words, of Benny's accidental shooting, as well as the prosecutor's version based on witness statements.

He Said, He Said

Cecil told the grand jury that earlier on Thanksgiving afternoon, he and his friend, Frederick Schermann, had been shooting at sparrows with his rifle. When they began cleaning straw out of a birdhouse, Cecil propped the gun against the house.

"I was taking some of the straw into the house to burn," he said. "I had not seen Benny, and I couldn't see the gun from where I was walking."

He then heard a gunshot ring out, he said, and it was immediately followed by a yell.

"I ran around the corner of the house," he explained. "Benny was running, and the gun was on the ground."

Unaware Benny had been shot, Cecil took the gun with his armload of straw into the house. No sooner had he stepped inside than he heard Mrs. Slavin yelling from somewhere across the yard.

"So I found my mother, and we went out right away," Cecil said. "I think Benny picked up the gun and was dragging it away, when the trigger got caught in some weeds and fired."

Regarding local talk suggesting animosity had developed between the two boys, Cecil denied it, stating firmly, "I didn't have any quarrel with Benny."

Anna Burkett validated her son's account of the shooting, but the Slavins rejected it. According to the *Richmond Item*, during Benny's waning hours of life, he twice told his mother that Cecil had shot him.

Starke County Prosecutor Dilts countered Cecil's testimony with stories gleaned from statements by the children who had been playing in the Burkett and Slavin yards when the gun went off. Corroborating Benny's claim, the Slavin's six-year-old daughter, Elsie, told her parents she had witnessed Cecil step up to her brother and shoot him with a rifle. The gun barrel was so close to Benny, she said, that when Cecil pulled the trigger, a spark flew out and set her brother's sweater on fire. She also told them Cecil had threatened to shoot her, too.

Dilts also maintained that Cecil, his brother, Alfred, and their friend, Frederick Schermann, were playing in the Burkett backyard, while Benny and Elsie were playing in the Slavin yard.

"There were bad feelings between the two lads," Dilts told the jurors, claiming that Cecil teased Benny and tried to get him to come over to the Burketts' backyard. Benny's stubborn refusal prompted Cecil to take a new tack, Dilts said.

"He retrieved his kite," Dilts asserted, "and showed it to Benny, taunting him, 'If you want it, come and get it.'"

Benny couldn't resist and eagerly stepped into Cecil's yard with his hands outstretched.

"With that," Dilts continued, "Cecil reopened the old squabble."

The prosecutor then claimed that Cecil grabbed his father's .22 caliber rifle and shot Benny "in cold blood."

"I have also been told that he pointed the weapon at Benny's sister," Dilts said.

The prosecutor's words didn't sit well with Cecil. They compelled him to speak up in his own defense. "I didn't do it," he protested, "and I'm not afraid to go to trial. How can they kill me for killing a boy I didn't kill?"

Benny's father dismissed Cecil's profession of innocence.

"Cecil killed Benny, and he did it purposely," Harry Slavin passionately proclaimed before the grand jury, according to the *Richmond Item*. "He ought to hang for it, and I'm going to see that he does."

The Burketts' attorney, W.J. Reed, swore that he would "go to bat for Cecil" on the evidence. "The boy is telling the truth," Reed insisted, "and the facts will free him."

Cecil's trial date was set for March, but it was later moved to Tuesday, April 5. In the interim, details and updates about the Ora case would dominate the daily news nationwide.

Woof of the Warp

In the weeks leading up to the trial, reporters flocked to Ora looking for tips related to the case that could be expanded into sensationalized stories that would sell papers. They sought out county officials, residents and, better yet, members of the Burkett and Slavin families for emotionally provocative quotes to fill their pages.

On April 2, Benny's father told a *Richmond Item* reporter, "In a little place like Ora, there is no peace among neighbors. And my boy is dead. ... There is just one punishment for crime, and it must fit the crime—an eye for an eye, a life for a life."

The Richmond paper reported that there was no consensus on what had actually happened that fateful November day. "Opinion rends the town in twain," the paper artfully asserted, although generally, the public was troubled by the prospect of executing a child.

Clearly, the Slavins wanted justice for their son, even if the cost was the life of another young boy. But, aside from the Slavins, almost no one wanted Cecil to pay with his life, even if the jury deemed him guilty.

Many aspects of the Burkett trial were disturbing. For example, Indiana would be the first state to try a child for first-degree murder. Further, the court officials who would prosecute, defend, and pass judgment on the boy were adults. And yet, the testimony of the witnesses, most of whom would be children no older than the defendant himself, would surely weigh heavily on the conscience of the jurors as they decided the defendant's fate and the penalty awaiting him.

The *Richmond Item* explained the dichotomy this way: "Grownups will testify, too, but their testimony will serve only as the woof through which is woven the warp of testimony. Upon the design of this fabric, Cecil Burkett will die, go to prison, or be set free."

The adults to be called as witnesses included the boys' teachers, parents, grandparents, and neighbors. The value of the adults' contribution to the court record was unclear, however, since none of them had been present at the Burkett home when the shooting occurred. The only witnesses to the activities leading up to the shooting, as well as the shooting itself, were children.

As the trial date approached, the public's anticipation expanded. But unexpectedly on April 4, the day before the trial was to begin, news broke that the trial would be delayed again. Prosecutor Dilts was suffering from a serious case of tonsillitis, necessitating the postponement to late May.

There was an upside to the delay, however. It would allow Cecil to complete the spring term at his school.

Kiddie Court

Tuesday, May 31 finally arrived, and the long-awaited trial at the Starke Circuit Court in Knox was in session. As the *Indianapolis Star* pointed out, the case was without parallel in Indiana history and was already attracting nationwide interest.

Under the direction of Judge William C. Pentecost, day one kicked off with its first order of business—selection of the jury. By mid-afternoon, quicker than expected, the twelve-man panel had been picked from a venire of forty-five prospective jurors. They were sworn in by the end of the day.

The following morning, June 1, Prosecutor Dilts called his first witness

—Cecil's eleven-year-old buddy, Frederick Schermann, who had been playing with Cecil in the Burketts' backyard the day of the shooting.

Outfitted in homespun knickerbockers and a faded blue shirt, Freddie clutched his crumpled cap as he approached the bench, stepped to the witness stand, and slid onto the wooden chair. Freddie nervously chewed his lower lip as Dilts instructed him to tell the jury what he had seen the day Benny Slavin was shot. Freddie gave a nod, and through taut, colorless lips, spoke in a tone barely above a whisper.

"We were playing in the Burketts' backyard last Thanksgiving," Freddie said slowly. "We wanted to go huntin'. So Al Burkett, Cecil's brother, got a shotgun, and we popped at some birds but didn't hit any."

The gang came back to the Burkett yard, Freddie said, and Cecil took the gun.

"He pointed it right at Elsie, Benny's sister," Freddie continued, "and Cecil said, 'You better run or I'll shoot you,' and Elsie ran."

Freddie said he put his hand on Cecil's shoulder and asked if the gun was cocked.

"Was it?" Dilts asked.

Freddie nodded. "Cecil said, 'Bet your boots it is.'"

"What did you do then?" Dilts asked.

Freddie said he climbed a ladder to the birdhouse and began to clean it out. Within minutes, he heard the old gun "go pop."

"And there went Cecil running around the corner of the house with the gun in his hand," he said, "and I heard Alfred [Cecil's brother] say, 'Now you'll get it.'"

Freddie said that as he descended the ladder, he saw Benny dart down the hill toward the Slavin home holding his burning sweater away from the wound in his left side. He assumed Benny's mother heard the screams, he said, because she ran outside and started smothering the flames.

When the prosecution introduced Benny's burned clothing as evidence, Mrs. Slavin turned her head away.

In wrapping up Freddie's testimony, Dilts asked him if there had been friction between Cecil and Benny.

"Yes, sir," said Freddie. "I saw Cecil slap Benny's face once, and another time I saw him throw big rocks at him in the school yard."

Defense attorney W.J. Reed followed with a tough cross-examination but failed to shake Freddie's story. Although, as the *Indianapolis News*

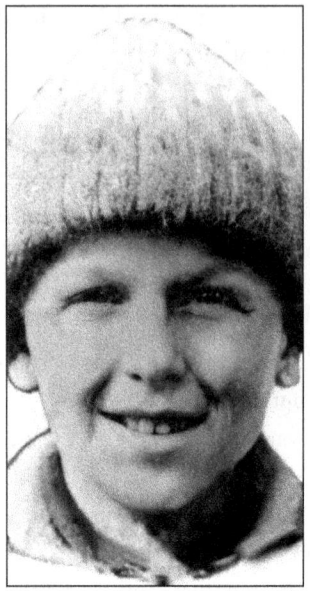 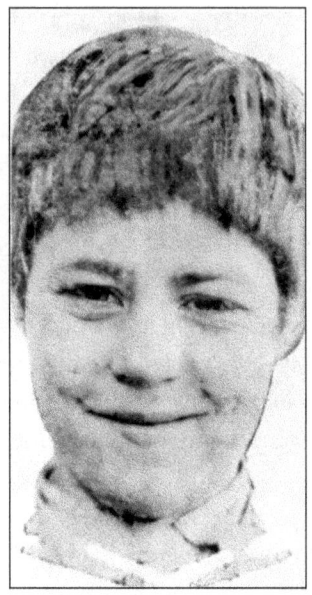

Frederick Schermann *(left)*, age eleven, Cecil Burkett's good friend, and Cecil's nine-year-old brother, Alfred *(right)*, were playing in the Burkett yard at the time Benny Slavin was shot. For that reason, Freddie and Alfred were among the trial's most important witnesses.

reported, Reed's questioning did yield one new important detail: Freddie conceded that he had not seen Cecil deliberately point the gun at Benny when it fired.

Anna Burkett sat stiffly with her son at the defense table. Unsmiling, she glanced often at Cecil with her sad, dark eyes. Cecil too appeared tense and unmoved as his former friend swore on a bible that Cecil killed the little kid next door.

Still, Cecil remained resolute that he was innocent. In fact, that very morning as court convened, Cecil had assured several newspapermen within earshot, "I ain't afraid. I ain't done nothing. I didn't shoot Benny."

Cecil followed Freddie on the stand. The last witness of the day, Cecil was neatly dressed in a suit, and his unruffled, poised demeanor surprised the spectators that packed the courtroom. The *South Bend Tribune* described Cecil as "calm throughout, much more so than any previous witness." The paper also noted that "he answered Prosecutor Dilts's questions promptly and appeared bent on being accurate in every statement." The story Cecil told the court was nearly identical to the version he told the grand jury in January,

Accused murderer, eleven-year-old Cecil Burkett, calmly testified in his own behalf for nearly an hour during his trial. According to reports, when Cecil was cross-examined by the prosecution, his account of the shooting was unshakable.

insisting that the rifle had gone off accidentally.

The *Seattle* (Washington) *Star* reported that during his testimony, Cecil produced a crumpled map he had drawn with a pencil stub. "See," he said, displaying his sketch, "Freddie Schermann was up on the ladder taking straw out of the birdhouse, and I was below, carrying it away." Pointing to a different area on his map, Cecil added, "Benny was over here by the side of the house playing with a gun. I heard a shot and saw Benny stagger down the hill. And that's all I know."

Cecil was on the stand for about an hour, and according to the *South Bend Tribune*, he made a strong impression on the jurors. Even the prosecutor complimented Cecil's performance on the stand, saying, "Cecil made an excellent witness for himself."

"I Brung It"

Alfred Burkett, Cecil's nine-year-old brother, was the first witness on Thursday, June 2, day three of the trial. Alfred hoped his testimony would absolve his big brother of Benny Slavin's death.

"I brung the gun from the house," he muttered between his sobs, according to the *Los Angeles* (California) *Herald*. "Mamma said we shouldn't take the gun, but Freddie Schermann wanted to shoot sparrows, so I brung it."

In an effort to clarify Freddie's claim that Alfred had told Cecil, "Now you'll get it," after Benny was shot, Alfred explained that he had directed the remark at Benny, not Cecil. "I meant Benny was going to get in trouble for playing with the gun," Alfred said.

When the defense attorney asked his witness to tell the court about the shooting, Alfred replied, "There was a shot, and then Benny ran down the hill."

Dilts countered Alfred's testimony by calling Benny's mother, Lena Slavin, to the stand. She emphasized to the court that her son had told her, "Cecil shot me."

Winding up the testimony were Cecil's mother, the doctor who attended Benny when he was taken to the Winamac hospital, a nurse, two neighbors, and two of Cecil's sisters.

The Rumble

State and defense attorneys made their closing arguments shortly after the noon recess. Rather than insisting on the death penalty, the prosecution asked the jurors to return a verdict of manslaughter and permit Judge Pentecost to fix Cecil's punishment as incarceration at the Indiana Boys' School at Plainfield until he reached the age of twenty-one. Conversely, the defense asked for acquittal, insisting that Cecil was innocent and that the evidence against him was entirely circumstantial.

Pentecost turned the case over to the jury at about 4:00 p.m., instructing each member to take the defendant's age into consideration when determining if he was capable of committing first-degree murder. Or, as the *South Bend Tribune* reported, the judge entrusted "twelve grizzled men with the fate of a lad of eleven years."

The jury spent the next nineteen hours wrangling over Cecil's fate. According to the *Los Angeles Herald*, throughout the night, crowds paced the courtroom and the grounds outside the courthouse listening to the jurors argue. "Often the debate in the jury waxed so loud and venomous that it could be heard more than half a block away," wrote the *Herald*.

Emphasizing the dramatics, the story continued:

> The scene had the highly dramatic accompaniment of a windstorm which whistled through the straggling branches of the trees in the courthouse yard. Heat lightning flashed outside and thunder claps shook the building.
>
> Those in the courthouse could plainly hear the argument, and it seemed that most of the time, all the jurors were talking at once.
>
> "We haven't all agreed yet that this eleven-year-old boy is guilty," someone bellowed.
>
> Shortly after this, the angry tones of one man arose in a speech which other jurors applauded.
>
> While the jury argued, the lights of the town went out, and through pitch darkness there still came the rumble of the arguing jurors.

When court reconvened the next morning, Friday, June 3, as the *Princeton Clarion-News* noted, "The red-eyed, bedraggled jurymen, who tried to decide the fate of Cecil, reported to Judge Pentecost that they failed to agree."

Cecil would eventually learn he had come within one vote of conviction. The first ballot ended with a tie—six for manslaughter and six for acquittal. But when the jury finally conceded to an impasse, eleven of them stood firm for conviction, while the twelfth held fast for acquittal.

The judge dismissed the jury, saying he was uncertain whether Cecil would stand trial again. The judge's pronouncement wasn't what Benny's father wanted to hear.

"He killed my boy," Harry Slavin hissed. "We will prosecute until justice is done. I demand another trial."

Prosecutor Dilts assured Slavin that he wasn't finished and promised to retry the Burkett case during the October court term.

Cecil displayed no visible emotion when the jury failed to convict him. "It's been awful, cooped up here all the time," he said. "I'll be glad to get out, and I hope I won't have to come back here."

A reporter asked Cecil's mother, Anna, what she had in mind for her son when they returned home. "He takes care of most of the plowing," she said, "and there will be pickles to take care of."

When the Burkett family finally piled into their battered automobile to return home, Anna told the *Indianapolis Star*, "I wish we didn't have to go back to Ora. I am just about at the end of my string. They call us..." She paused for a beat, prompting her thirteen-year-old daughter, Edna, to pick up her mother's statement.

"...murderers," Edna said through her sobs. "In Ora, they call us murderers. We are just hated, all for nothing. Cecil never killed Benny, but people believe he did, and it's awful for us."

"Aw, come on," Cecil whined. "Let's go home. I'm tired."

Epilogue
Within days, letters to the editor protesting the retrial of Cecil Burkett began appearing in newspapers throughout the state. A major point of contention was treating a juvenile like a hardened criminal. As a letter in the *News-Sentinel* of Fort Wayne put it, "If [guilty of first-degree murder] had been the verdict of the 'Mother Goose' jury at Knox, an eleven-year-old stripling would have been placed in the same category with Gene Geary, Sam Cardenella, and Carl Wanderer," all executed murderers of their day.

When October rolled around, Judge Pentecost threw a wet blanket on the prosecutor's plan to retry Cecil. As reported by the October 12, 1921, *Indianapolis Times*, "When state's attorney Dilts entered court to have a date set for the second arraignment of the lad, the judge intimated that the case had gone far enough. The prosecutor then officially announced that he would not call the case at this term of court. He added that he wasn't certain the case would be called at the January term."

And that was that.

"It is believed," wrote the *South Bend News-Times*, "other than the marks of memory on the mind of the lad and in the minds of those who know the story, the case has passed into history."

For the most part, it had. But in November of 1986, the *Indianapolis Star* resurrected the "Mother Goose Murder" case when it ran a story featuring seventy-seven-year-old Cecil Burkett. He still lived in Ora.

By age fourteen, Burkett had become a "spiker" for the Erie Lackawanna Railroad, he told the *Star*. He worked for the EL until he retired as a track foreman thirty-five years later. In the meantime, he had married and raised nine children. The *Star* reporter asked Burkett what he remembered about that long-ago Thanksgiving, when little Benny Slavin took a bullet. Without hesitation, Burkett replied, "Not a damn thing."

Perhaps not, but Burkett's close encounter with the death penalty had sown his unique perspective on the topic. An outspoken opponent, he was a firm believer that convicted killers should be spared because people can only contribute to society while they are alive.

The *Star*'s story noted Burkett's surprise that Indiana still allowed execution of children as young as ten. It was "crazy" when he was a kid, he said, and "It's still crazy."

Indiana had the lowest death-penalty age in the nation until 1987, when Indiana State Representative Earline S. Rogers of Gary introduced a successful bill that raised the state's minimum execution age from ten to sixteen. It has since been raised to eighteen.

Cecil Burkett died quietly in 1989 at a nursing home in Knox. He was a testament to a well-lived, long life that almost wasn't. He is buried in Ora. ❖

14

THE SAGA OF SORORICIDE CHARLES MESSEL

DATELINE: VANDERBURGH COUNTY, 1911

> I meant to do it. I was so mad at her, I hardly knew what I was doing. She told me I was as guilty as Father. I didn't try to aim at her head. I just pointed it at her and fired. Then I ran to her and picked her up and asked her where the bullet hit. I was sorry I had done it as soon as I saw the blood.
>
> Charles Messel
Per the Evansville Journal
February 2, 1911

The Evansville papers broke the news on Friday, February 3, 1911, that eleven-year-old Fern Messel had taken a bullet in the head at ten-thirty Thursday night and was dead within minutes. The shooter was her seventeen-year-old brother, Charles. Other circumstances surrounding little Fern's death were not yet known, yet a lack of verifiable facts didn't hinder the local media from spinning it as a murder most foul. Whether the shooting was deliberate or accidental, only Charles could say, and what he said kept changing.

Another Mess for the Messels
A series of unfortunate events had plagued the Messel family for months. Clark, the father of the five Messel kids—Claude, fifteen; Henry, seven; Orphia, five; Charles, and Fern—was a lazy drunk; and their mother, America, was a terminal patient at the Boehne Tuberculosis Farm. The children were frail, on

their own, and living in squalor on Canal Street.

On Wednesday, February 1, the day before the fatal shooting, the police hauled forty-year-old Clark Messel to jail and locked him up on a charge of, as the media politely phrased it, "ruining" his daughter, Fern. Thursday evening, all the Messel kids were home, and their teenage neighbors, Bessie and John Logsdon, were visiting. Fern wanted to write a letter to her grandmother, but because her handwriting was sloppy, she asked Bessie to pen it for her. According to Bessie, as Fern was dictating the missive, Charles heard her say he was as guilty as her pa, and he immediately bolted across the room and slapped his sister across the face. In his anger, he stomped out of the room, returning a moment later with a rifle clutched in his hands. After that, Bessie said, everything happened quickly. Charles aimed the gun, it fired, and Fern dropped to the floor. By Friday, Charles, too, was in jail.

According to the *Evansville Press*, Charles told Evansville Police Chief George L. Covey and Chief of Detectives Ed Ossenberg that he and Fern had quarreled all evening. His temper flared when Fern taunted him, saying that he would soon be in a jail cell, exactly like their father. But when she said he was as guilty as their father for her "ruination," Charles's temper exploded and so did his rifle. Once he realized what he had done, however, he cradled his dying sister in his arms and sobbed inconsolably. When the police arrived, he admitted he had shot her.

"Lust and murderous anger had done the tiny girl her last wrong," mused the *Evansville Journal* in its Friday coverage of the breaking news story, which included a sidebar about the Messel children that described Charles as "undersized and ill-nourished," his skin an "unhealthy white," and his eyes "pale and tired."

Charles was arraigned for the murder on Saturday, February 4. When the judge asked if he was pleading guilty or not guilty, Charles hesitantly answered, "Not guilty." Later that day, a reporter for the *Evansville Press* called on Charles at the jail and asked why he had killed his sister. According to the reporter, Charles shambled to his feet, and with nervous, shifting eyes, peered through the bars for almost a minute, as if organizing his thoughts and searching for the right words. When he finally spoke, his tone was laced with fear and sorrow.

"I didn't tell the police I intended to kill Fern," he said slowly. "I told them I pointed the gun at her and pulled the trigger. I didn't know the gun was loaded. I never put no shell in it."

Newspapers ran this drawing of father and son, Clark and Charles Messel, on February 4, 1911, after Charles shot and killed his eleven-year-old sister, Fern, for accusing him of "ruining" her, exactly as she had claimed their father had done.

Reunited and Indicted

The two Messels were indicted the following Monday. When brought into the courtroom to answer for their respective charges of rape and murder, even though they had not been together for several days, both kept their heads down and avoided eye contact. The *Evansville Courier* described the behavior of the father and son as trance-like, seemingly "unable to realize the enormity of their crimes." After both entered pleas of not guilty, the elder Messel's attorney, Ernest J. Crenshaw, agreed to represent Charles as well. Clark's trial was set for Thursday, February 16. Charles's was set for Wednesday, March 8.

When Clark's trial opened, many of the spectators seated in the crowded courtroom were women, who, according to the *Evansville Press*, seemed undisturbed by the straight-to-the-point questions or the "nakedness of the language." Despite Clark Messel's desperate denials that he had sexually assaulted his daughter, the jury found him guilty and fixed the sentence to life in the Indiana State Penitentiary in Michigan City.

The *Press* described the father and son's final farewell on Monday, February 20 not as a tender moment of reflection and regret, but rather a simple, unemotional bidding of "goodbye and good luck."

Nothing about the family's tragedies was shared with Mrs. Messel as she fought for her life at the tuberculosis farm. "There is no chance for recovery," said one of her doctors, "and the probabilities are, she will go to her grave without knowing the terrible events that have occurred since she was removed from her home to the farm." Sadly, as predicted, America Amelia Messel died the following Saturday, February 25, believing her family was safe and thriving at home. Her body was interred in Evansville's Oak Hill Cemetery next to her daughter, Fern.

A Change of Venue

As Charles's trial date approached, his attorney's doubts grew that a Vanderburgh County jury could reach an impartial decision. Consequently, the trial was moved to neighboring Warrick County with a new start date of Friday, March 17.

When the scheduled day arrived, Judge R.A. Roberts called the courtroom to order at 8:00 a.m., and jury selection lasted until noon. Following a meal break, opening statements were made by Vanderburgh County Deputy Prosecutor William LeMasters and defense attorney E.J. Crenshaw. The first witnesses called by the prosecution were Vanderburgh County Coroner Dr. E.C. Macer and Dr. J.N. Baughman, both of whom had examined Fern's body. Each confirmed that the girl had been sexually assaulted and explained the upward trajectory of the bullet that killed her.

Police Chief Convoy took the stand and denied cursing or using threats of a mob to get Messel to confess to shooting his sister. Chief of Detectives Ossenberg, who had been with Covey when Messel allegedly made his confession, verified the chief's statements.

The day's final witness was Claude Messel, Charles' fifteen-year-old brother. Claude described Charles as a loving, caring big brother and swore that the shooting of his sister was accidental. The *Evansville Courier* concluded that Claude had been a good witness for Charles.

A Star Is Born

The state concluded its case shortly before noon on Saturday, March 18. After the lunch break, Crenshaw took charge, laying out his case and arguing the shooting was purely accidental. He then called his star witness, Charles, to the stand.

According to the *Evansville Journal-News*, when Crenshaw asked Charles about the events leading to his sister's shooting death, Charles was uncustomarily cool and clear-spoken. He explained that he and his brother, Claude, had clashed intensely for most of the evening, but the bickering stopped when Claude threatened to shoot Charles with the Flobert rifle in the closet. The moment was tense, but Claude immediately relented. He hadn't really wanted to hurt his big brother.

"I held him until he cried," Charles said. "Then he went out, and I got the gun and hid it under the pillow on the bed."

He admitted to slapping Fern, but added, "I was not mad, and she did not cry."

Shortly after that, one of the younger children had grown sleepy and was ready to crawl into bed. Charles escorted the child to the bedroom and snatched the rifle from under the pillow.

"I saw it was cocked," he said, "and snapped the hammer."

"Was that when the gun went off?" asked Crenshaw.

"Yes," replied Charles, growing emotional. "I had stood facing the kitchen doorway when it went off. I cried out and ran to my sister. I couldn't realize that I had shot her. Then [the police] took me away, and some men in plain clothes—there was three or four of them—told me I would be better off dead, that I ought to be hung, and that I would be lucky if a mob did not get me that night."

"That must have terrified you," Crenshaw said, empathy glazing his words.

Charles looked away and nodded.

A Flobert Fumble

Crenshaw stepped to the defense table, grasped the Flobert by the barrel, and carried it back to the witness stand. Holding the weapon in front of Charles, Crenshaw asked, "Is this the gun that killed your sister?"

Charles timidly answered, "Yes," and studied the attorney with obvious puzzlement.

"It's all right, Charles," Crenshaw said. "I would like you to demonstrate how you handled this rifle before it went off.

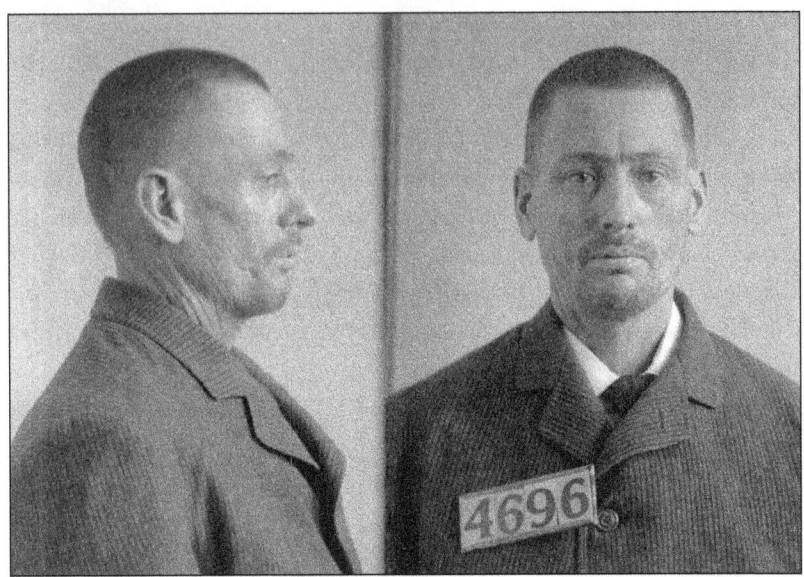

The Messel children's father, Clark, was convicted for raping his minor daughter, Fern, and sentenced to life in the Indiana State Prison in Michigan City. After serving eight years, however, the Indiana State Board of Pardons determined that, because the evidence against him was entirely circumstantial, due to his daughter's unfortunate death, his conviction had been unfair. The state, therefore, pardoned Messel in May of 1919. *Photo courtesy the Indiana State Archives.*

Charles took the gun from Crenshaw and, according to the *Journal-News*, he cocked the hammer and pointed the muzzle in the direction of the jury.

"What were you doing when it fired?" Crenshaw said.

"I was only looking at it," Charles said. "I didn't mean to shoot Fern."

"What caused the gun to fire?" Crenshaw said.

"I don't know," Charles insisted. "It was an accident."

Crenshaw asked Charles why he confessed to Chief Covey if the shooting had indeed been accidental.

Without hesitation, Charles answered, "He asked if I killed my sister to protect Father and told me he didn't want any lies. He said, 'You killed your sister on purpose, and I know you did. You tell me the truth and nothing else.'" Charles's eyes clouded with tears, and he wiped them away with his fists. "He scared me," he continued, "and I just came out and said, 'yes' to everything he asked. They scared me and made me cry."

Cross-Examination

Crenshaw cross-examined Chief Covey in an effort to discredit his earlier testimony claiming Charles had confessed to the murder. Asked why he would frighten the boy with threats of a lynch mob, Covey denied the insinuations, insisting he had merely asked tough questions designed to reveal the truth.

"I asked him if he killed his sister to keep her from testifying against their father," Covey said, "and he admitted that he did and immediately declared he was sorry."

Covey's story was corroborated by Chief of Detectives Ed Ossenberg. In addition, a motorcycle officer, Andy Friedle, testified that Charles admitted to him that he had assaulted his sister twice.

Charles's defense was eroding with each witness, but Crenshaw had already prepared an argument he was certain would prove Charles had not shot his sister deliberately.

He reminded the jury that Charles stood five-feet, four-inches tall, and Fern had been one foot shorter. Accordingly, Crenshaw underscored that if Charles had shot her intentionally, the bullet would have taken a downward trajectory through her body. But clearly, as the doctors who examined the girl's body testified, the bullet had coursed upward from its point of entry.

"If Charles had meant to shoot his sister," the attorney declared, "he would have raised the rifle to his shoulder and taken aim, and the bullet could not have ranged upward. Therefore, Fern's death was indisputably a tragic accident."

Crenshaw's logic was insightful, but whether he had convinced the jury of his client's innocence was yet to be known. Judge Roberts sent the case to the jury late Saturday afternoon with instructions to return a sealed verdict to be opened in court on Monday.

And the Verdict Is …
The jury reached an agreement at 1:00 a.m. Sunday, and Roberts unsealed and read the verdict aloud to a packed courtroom Monday morning. "We the jury," he said, "find the defendant guilty of manslaughter."

The outcome had taken the spectators, as well as the attorneys, by surprise. The very nature of the crime, combined with the age of the victim and the perception of the boy's guilt, convinced those following the trial that the jury would return a verdict of life in prison. The manslaughter finding, carrying a penalty of two to twenty-one years, could only be attributed to the jury's sympathy for the Messel family's plight, as well as lingering doubts that the shooting had been intentional.

While the spectators' gasps were still sucking the air out of the courtroom, something even more unanticipated happened. Crenshaw bolted from his chair and cried out to the judge, "Give this boy a chance!"

Heads whirled in the direction of the defense attorney who was about to deliver what may have been the most impassioned argument of his legal career—imploring the judge to give the boy a parole.

> Your honor has seen him and knows that such a boy as this—pale, sickly, and undersized, fed with few of the finer emotions of life, insensible to much that makes the children of the better classes more accountable for what they do—has needed a home more than anything else. And I offer him the advantage of my own home. Into my house will I take him and rear him as I would my own child.

Crenshaw's soliloquy went on for another minute and a half during which he suggested that a life of dignity in a good home would surely mold Charles into a "citizen of whom no ill can be said." He also reminded the judge that the boy's poor health could not possibly improve in the confines of prison.

> Give him the air of outdoors, give him the freedom of a free man's house, to regain his strength. ... I appeal to your honor to save him, to take what is left here of a human life, to change it and reform it, to award it to the outdoors, and to turn the tide of a soul from hate to respect, from the depths to the heights.

The crowd had listened intently, and the moment Crenshaw sat down, the courtroom echoed with rousing applause, foot stomping, and cheers. The judge pounded his gavel as he bellowed, "This is no place for such a demonstration."

A Deleterious Effect

Vanderburgh County Prosecutor O.R. Luhring vowed to fight "vigorously" against a parole, reported the *Evansville Journal-News*, which quoted him saying, "Twelve men, after hearing a strong presentation of the facts here, have shown unmistakably just what their wish is. They have found Messel guilty and the law should take its course."

Luhring sanctimoniously claimed that allowing Charles to live with Crenshaw would have a "deleterious effect on the whole community," adding "the punishment accorded young Messel is mild, and he should be made to suffer it."

Attorney Ernest J. Crenshaw represented Charles Messel at his trial for the shooting death of his younger sister, Fern. Immediately after the jury found Charles guilty of manslaughter, Crenshaw pleaded with the court to give the boy a second chance by allowing him to make his home with Crenshaw and his wife. Although the Vanderburgh County prosecutor strenuously objected, the judge granted Crenshaw's request.

The next day, Tuesday, March 21, Judge Roberts granted the request, awarding Crenshaw guardianship of Charles until the sentence was satisfied. Roberts noted that his landmark decision had been influenced by the nine members of the jury who had advocated for the boy's parole.

Epilogue
"The boy is beside himself with sober joy at the thought that he has an opportunity to show he is not all bad," Crenshaw said, "even though he did accidentally shoot and kill his sister."

Crenshaw's wife, Sadie, fully supported the addition to the family. "I was entirely in sympathy with my husband," she told the *Evansville Courier*, "and I'm glad to have the boy with us here. I want to treat him as I would my own child. You know, I have no children, so all my interests will be in Charlie."

Five years later, the January 31, 1917, *Evansville Press* reported that Charles had kept his promises and "made good." After making his home with the Crenshaws for four years, he moved to the central part of the state to live on his uncle's farm. "He is doing fine," Crenshaw said.

Charles lived an honorable life, including service in the U.S. Army during World War I, and never forgot those who had given him a second chance in his darkest hours.

Charles died December 30, 1970, in Evansville at the age of seventy-seven. He is buried in Evansville's Oak Hill Cemetery not far from his sister, mother, and brother Claude, who died in 1917 at age twenty-two at the Boehne Tuberculosis Farm, where his mother had died six years earlier. Clark Messel was paroled on May 21, 1919. He died in 1943 in Vincennes. ❖

15

REMEMBERING NELLIE MAYNARD, THE GIRL ON FIRE; AND ROSIE PERKINS, THE GIRL WHO STRUCK THE MATCH

DATELINE: MADISON COUNTY, 1904

Yellow-orange blades of fire flared as they voraciously ravaged the tiny body of eight-year-old Nellie Maynard, frantically screaming for help as she stumbled along the quiet, tree-lined street on Alexandria's northwest side. Charity Morris heard Nellie's cries and raced from her house to the distressed child's side. Charity snuffed out the flames with her shawl, but they had already reduced the pretty, fair-haired little girl's skin to a leathery dark-brown. Three days later, on Tuesday, December 6, 1904, Nellie died.

Impromptu Inquest

The funeral was planned for the following Thursday afternoon, but Madison County Coroner Charles Trueblood ordered Nellie's parents, Walter and Bertha Maynard, to delay the burial to allow time for an informal inquest. Trueblood, Prosecutor Albert Vestal, and Alexandria Town Marshal John Mountain visited the Maynard home the morning of the funeral to question members of the family and friends. According to the *Anderson Morning Herald*:

> The remains were resting in a handsome white coffin, and in the lifeless arms of the child reposed a big doll, which had been the companion of the girl during life. The scene was a heartrending one, and as the witnesses were called before the coroner one by one, they burst into tears as the figure in the small casket met their gaze.

Bertha Maynard told the law enforcement officials that she originally expected her daughter to recover, so she had not yet pressed her to explain how the flames started. But as the hours passed and the little girl's condition worsened, Bertha grew desperate for the truth. A few hours before Nellie's passing on Tuesday morning, Bertha gently asked her daughter what had caused the fire. Despite the brave child's diminishing strength and increasing pain, she began to speak.

Nellie's Story
Barely above a whisper, Nellie described playing with the Perkins children—Elda, ten; John, twelve; and Rosie, fourteen—at their Canal Street house that frigid Saturday afternoon. Their mother, Malinda Perkins, had gone to town, and without adult supervision, her children had become rowdy and out of control.

Nellie said one of the boys touched her inappropriately and, according to the *Elwood Call-Leader*, "began making approaches that were repugnant even to her immature sensibilities." Nellie fought the boy off, and once it became apparent she was capable of holding her own, Rosie started tormenting her verbally. And when verbal harassment seemed insufficient to Rosie, she lit a match and set fire to Nellie's dress. Exacerbating her heinous deed, Rosie shoved the child into a closet and locked the door. In a matter of seconds, however, Mrs. Perkins returned home, and to avoid a spanking, Rosie opened the closet door, freeing the terrified little girl to run away while an expanding, smoldering fire devoured her clothing.

The Perkins Kids Speak
The police first talked with the Perkins kids on the day of the tragic event. Initially, Rosie and her brothers claimed Nellie's clothing had caught a spark as she played near the stove. The law enforcement officers did not believe the children's story, and on Friday, after assessing the testimony of the funeral attendees, and particularly Nellie's deathbed statement, the Alexandria police rounded up and arrested the entire Perkins family—the kids for murder, and their mother and her boyfriend for adultery.

The kids were questioned at the Alexandria city jail, and the *Anderson Morning Herald* reported that, "Great crowds swarmed the little room used for the police station and curiously watched the children huddled together in a corner, sobbing piteously."

Eight-year-old Nellie Maynard *(top photo)* of Alexandria, died there on December 6, 1904, three days after fourteen-year-old Rosie Perkins *(lower photo)* set Nellie's dress on fire and shoved her in a closet.

Coroner Trueblood spoke with the boys, and neither John nor Elda admitted to participating in the torching. Both said they had been ice skating at a nearby pond when the fire erupted. Their stories were debunked, however, by witnesses who had observed the boys outside the Perkins house, sneaking away after Nellie was seen enveloped by fire. Still, the boys stubbornly insisted they were innocent, claiming the witnesses were lying.

Rosie, too, denied responsibility and appeared unaware of, or indifferent to, the consequences of her act. Because of Nellie's statement, the officials dismissed Rosie's denial and took her to the Anderson police headquarters to

Madison County Prosecutor Albert Vestal *(left)* rejected the coroner's wish to charge Rosie Perkins with murder and instead charged her with incorrigibility. Judge John F. McClure *(right)* agreed and sentenced Rosie to the Industrial School for Girls at Indianapolis, where she would remain until reaching the age of twenty-one.

undergo a rigid interrogation by Anderson Police Chief Mark Robbins and the county probation officer, Anna DeWeese.

Confession

At first, Rosie maintained her innocence, but with little effort, Robbins and DeWeese wore her down. Once they penetrated the girl's wall of fear and won her trust, she confessed.

The Perkins girl said Nellie had been sitting on her lap, and, just in play, she set fire to a piece of paper and dropped it onto the little girl's dress.

"Not to hurt her!" Rosie exclaimed. "I only wanted to see if she would be afraid of the flames."

She hadn't expected the garment to ignite so rapidly, Rosie explained, and realizing what she had done, she grew fearful of what her mother would do to her. Tears formed in Rosie's eyes as she said, "I swear I meant no harm, but my mother would have killed me if she had known the truth. So I didn't tell."

DeWeese took Rosie's undisciplined upbringing into consideration. Rosie's mother had left her husband, the children's biological father, Hampton Perkins, the previous March for a deadbeat named John Hogan, who deserted his wife and three children without giving them a cent. Mrs. Perkins's life choices had deprived her children of sound judgment, as well as a basic understanding of socially accepted behavior and a sense of right and wrong.

Sickened by Rosie's home life, DeWeese submitted a report to the court, stating that the Perkins's family history "shows a state of depravity bordering on the degenerate" and "any sense of decency and morality is sadly lacking."

The lack of normalcy persuaded DeWeese to accept the girl's explanation of the fire as truthful, and in her expert opinion, she believed that when Rosie Perkins dropped the lit piece of paper onto Nellie Maynard's lap, no crime had been intended. Consequently, DeWeese recommended the court impose a lenient punishment on Rosie.

The Brothers' Resolution

Coroner Trueblood disagreed. He advocated for charging Rosie with murder and holding her at the county jail in Anderson to await action by the grand jury.

"The evidence secured is conclusive," asserted the *Morning Herald*. "If the deathbed statement of the Maynard girl can be accepted without question, there can be no doubt that a fiendish crime was committed."

The *Morning Herald* also printed Prosecutor Vestal's statement regarding the legal punishment of children who murder:

> A girl or boy fourteen years of age can be prosecuted and punished for murder the same as a full-grown man or woman. If they are adjudged guilty, their punishment may be fixed at life imprisonment. In the case of a girl fourteen years of age, on conviction, she would be taken to the Girl's Industrial Training School at Indianapolis until she was twenty-one years of age, when she would be removed to the Women's Prison.

The next day, December 10, according to the *Morning Herald*, John and Elda Perkins underwent a "scrubbing process with a brush and plenty of soap and water and were transformed into bright, healthy-looking children." The brothers then stood before Madison Circuit Court Judge John F. McClure, who sentenced them to the Indiana Boys' School at Plainfield until they reached age twenty-one.

Rosie's Resolution

A newly disclosed report on Rosie's intellectual limitations and the moral depravity of her family convinced Prosecutor Vestal to reject the coroner's desire to charge her with murder.

The Industrial School for Girls at Indianapolis housed two strikingly different types of girls. One area was for girls under age fifteen who were sentenced there for incorrigible conduct, and the other area was for girls over age fifteen as punishment for criminal behavior.

Therefore, on Tuesday, December 13, Vestal charged Rosie with incorrigibility. Judge McClure quickly deliberated the evidence, along with the recommendations of the police chief and the county probation officer. McClure, likewise, concluded Rosie Perkins had contributed to Nellie Maynard's death through carelessness, rather than a willful desire to end her life. The judge sentenced Rosie to the Industrial School for Girls at Indianapolis, where she would remain until her twenty-first birthday.

Epilogue
With that, the Nellie Maynard case, which the *Elwood Call-Leader* referred to as Madison County's "last and saddest death" of 1904, came to a close. And yet, the hearts of Nellie's loved ones were irreparably broken and their lives forever changed. Rosie's life was forever changed, as well, with a chance to turn it around in a safe, structured environment. However, what became of Rosie after she left the state institution has been lost to time. ❖

PART IV
KILLERS: WOMEN

16

ROCK-A-BYE-BYE, BABY: THE UNSPEAKABLE CRIME OF NORA MOSHER

DATELINE: HUNTINGTON COUNTY, 1907

The waxing gibbous moon of April 27, 1907, cast a tranquil glow over the Huntington County hamlet of Makin, while a chilly breeze wafted through Nora Mosher's open bedroom window and swept across her weary body writhing in pain. She hadn't expected childbirth to be easy, but the hours-long, torturous ordeal had become unbearable. When, at last, Nora's beautiful, healthy baby girl emerged into the world, rather than welcoming her bundle of joy with a tender embrace, Nora bashed in the newborn's skull and stashed its tiny corpse in the coal hod.

A Family Affair
Nora, the thirty-eight-year-old, divorced daughter of Dorman "D.A." and Rosa Mosher, lived with them and her younger brother, Emery, and his wife, Pearl, in a three-room farmhouse on Bracken Road. Nora, like all the Moshers, led a quiet, private life that conveyed an appearance of simple earthiness. The gossip-starved nosy parkers who lived nearby thought otherwise, however. Consequently, Nora's life, along with her family's, was uprooted and ripped apart the morning of Wednesday, May 1, 1907, when the Huntington County prosecutor, accompanied by the sheriff, the coroner, a local doctor, and a stenographer, came calling. When the men climbed out of their buggy

and approached the Moshers' yard gate, D.A. stopped them.

"Morning, fellers," Mosher said, projecting a tinge of uneasiness. "What can I do for you?"

Coroner Dr. Frank Morgan stepped forward. "Morning, D.A.," he said. "We've heard from your neighbors that your daughter gave birth a few days ago, but nobody's seen hide nor hair of a baby. Naturally, folks are getting suspicious."

Mosher, a long-established oddball, winced but said nothing. In light of the growing mystery of his daughter's missing baby, neighbors had him pegged as its father.

"We need to take a look around," Sheriff George Mahoney said, "and we need to have a talk with Nora."

"And the family, too," the prosecutor, George M. Eberhart, added. "Mind if we come in?"

The men followed Mosher to the front door and stepped inside. Mosher called the family to the front room, and the officials began asking questions. Straightaway, Nora admitted she had delivered a child four days before.

"I was in a great deal of pain," she explained, "so Emery fetched Doc Fry. But by the time he got here, the baby was born and already dead."

Once Nora confirmed that the baby had died, Mahoney asked the question the county officials wanted most to know. "Where's the body?"

An Unlikely Grave

Nora answered the question, her father begged for leniency, and the sheriff asked for a shovel. The party then proceeded to the chicken coop, where Mosher pointed to a wooden barrel in the southeast corner. It was there, he said, under the barrel that he had buried the baby.

Mahoney and Eberhart rolled the barrel aside and swept away the rubbish under it. They spent considerable time shoveling through the ground and scooping out loose dirt by hand, until they hit a flat rock about a foot long. Several inches below it, they found the baby, its body naked, without so much as a towel or even a newspaper wrapped around it.

Disgusted by the Moshers' lack of humanity, Mahoney turned the tiny corpse over to the coroner and continued his inquiry with D.A. and Nora.

The next day, Coroner Morgan, assisted by three doctors, conducted a post mortem of the infant's remains. The skull was crushed on both sides, and when they removed the bone fragments, they found vessels in the brain ruptured. In addition, the baby's right side and its left leg bore deep cuts, both sides of the throat were bruised, and one arm and both legs were broken. According to Morgan, the nine-pound baby girl had been fully physically developed at birth. Furthermore, the doctors tested the lungs and agreed that at the time of birth, the child had been perfectly healthy and capable of sustaining life.

Huntington's May 2, 1907, *Evening Herald* reported that the infant's death was "said to be due to the fracture of the skull, though whether this was caused by violence or accident, no statement is made. Other marks seem to indicate violence." The next day, the *Daily News-Democrat*, also of Huntington, ran the coroner's verdict, which stated:

> I find the circumstantial evidence points toward Nora Mosher and her father, D.A. Mosher, as being the parties charged with the cause of the death of the child, and I recommend that the grand jury be called immediately and take the proper steps in the investigation of the child's death, and that Nora Mosher and D.A. Mosher be placed under the custody of the circuit court of Huntington County.
>
> — Coroner Frank B. Morgan

Arrested and Jailed

Two days later, Saturday, May 4, Deputy Sheriff Thomas Van Antwerp and Huntington businessman C.E. Wintrode visited the Mosher farm, where they arrested D.A. The *Daily News-Democrat* reported that Mosher uttered not a word of protest and went peacefully. Nora, however, grew hysterical. Protesting her father's arrest, she screamed and tore out her hair.

"It was me," she exclaimed, accepting the blame for the infanticide. "It was all my fault. Take *me* instead."

The deputy brushed past the woman, ignoring her outburst.

"Do you intend to come back for me?" she cried.

With that, Van Antwerp paused and looked back at her. "To my knowledge," he grumbled, "no warrant for your arrest has yet been issued. But that could change."

Van Antwerp resumed his walk to the buggy, climbed in alongside Wintrode and Mosher, and headed directly to the Huntington County jail.

According to the *Daily News-Democrat*, Mosher was not an offensive man, and no one had accused him of being a bad neighbor. "The worst features of his life have been connected with affairs of his own family," the newspaper stated, "and in this, he seems to have gone the limit."

The grand jury convened several days later, and on the afternoon of Friday, May 17, D.A. and Nora Mosher were indicted for murder in the first degree. The indictments charged that D.A. and Nora:

> [D]id purposely and with premeditated malice, kill and murder one infant female child, name unknown, born to said Nora Mosher, by then and there unlawfully, feloniously and purposely and with premeditated malice striking, beating, cutting, and choking said infant female child on the head, body, and person, and then mortally wounding said child.

The next day, Nora was arrested, joining her father at the county jail, where they would remain until they were tried.

Postpartum Filicide

Judge S.E. Cook gaveled in the first day of D.A.'s murder trial on Tuesday, June 11. The first witness to take the stand was Dr. C.W. Fry, called by the prosecution. Fry testified that he had been awakened in the predawn hours of April 27 by Emery Mosher, who told him that his sister had given birth and needed medical attention. Fry rushed to the Mosher home and found her alone in the bedroom. She was not well.

"Did you see the infant?" asked Prosecutor Eberhart.

"Not until she pointed to the corner behind me," Fry said. "I turned and saw the child lying on a paper on the floor."

"Was the child alive?" said Eberhart.

"The body was cold," Fry said. "Miss Mosher told me the baby was born dead, which I accepted as the truth, until I performed a cursory examination."

"What did you find?"

"The lines of the head were broken, but the lungs had been inflated."

Eberhart asked Fry if he thought the child was born alive. Fry replied, "There was every reason to believe that it was."

Huntington County Coroner Morgan next took the stand. He spoke of the visit at the Mosher home on May 1 and confirmed Fry's description of the baby's body. Morgan said the various tests made during the post mortem showed that prior to the infant's death, its heart and lungs had been healthy and strong.

"Furthermore," Morgan stated, casting doubt on D.A.'s innocence, "in the opinion of all the physicians present at the autopsy, the child had come to its

Thirty-eight-year-old Nora Mosher of Makin was indicted for the murder of her newborn baby in May 1907. Her trial, held the following October, resulted in a guilty verdict for manslaughter.

death by some external violence."

Highlighting day two of the trial was the sensational testimony by Nora's ex-husband, John Dial. The couple had married in 1891, but they divorced in 1901, he said, after hard times forced them to reside at the crowded Mosher farmhouse for a short time in 1900. The arrangement had not been the best, he noted, but he and Nora tried to make it work. He explained that during those waning days of the marriage, he became aware of his wife's unacceptable behavior.

"I rose one morning," he explained, "and went to the woodhouse for kindling. I left my wife lying in her bed and D.A. in his bed."

"They were in the same bedroom?" Eberhart asked.

"Yes," Dial said, "in different beds, but they were so close that the foot ends touched."

Eberhart harrumphed and muttered, "Uh-huh." He glared at the defendant, and asked, "When you returned with the kindling, were they still in their separate beds?"

"Oh, no," Dial said. "I found them together in a compromising position."

"Did you say anything?" asked the prosecutor.

"No, I did not. I left the house, and aside from coming back the next day for my team and farm implements, I never returned."

As intended, Dial's unsavory claim suggested that D.A. may have had a reason for killing the infant, and once spectators grasped the insinuation, gasps erupted throughout the crowded courtroom. Attorneys for the defense immediately objected, and for the next hour and a half, strenuously argued the inadmissibility of the evidence. Judge Cook ultimately overruled the objection, thus providing the prosecution with a viable motive for murder.

By the end of the trial's second day, Wednesday, June 12, the state had hit its mark concerning the who, why, and how of Baby Mosher's murder, all of which pointed to D.A. While those shameful revelations were devastating for the Moshers, an even more crushing blow was coming.

At 12:30 p.m. Thursday, D.A.'s son, Emery, age thirty-three, took a stroll down the old Fort Wayne Road, placed a revolver to his forehead, and pulled the trigger. The circumstances that had driven Emery Mosher to commit such an egregious act were never disclosed, leaving townspeople to speculate whether his suicide had been linked to the murder of his niece. Many asked if he had known that his sister had taken the stand just two hours earlier and turned the case upside down by confessing that she, not her father, was the infant's killer.

Agree to Disagree

As the *Evening Herald* reported, "Nora Mosher, a little, faded woman, dressed in black with weak mouth and flabby face, took the stand. Between tears and over a perfect volley of objections to the questions asked by [defense attorney] John S. Branyan, most of which were overruled," she told the story of the baby's birth and death. Nora blamed the pregnancy on her former fiancé, James Fulton. The two met in December of 1905 and became engaged to marry shortly after. Nora claimed she told no one about her condition until the night of the baby's birth. At that time, because of strained relations with her sister-in-law and her mother's declining health, she chose to deliver her baby alone.

"I was beside myself with anguish and pain," she told the court. "My mind was pretty near wild, and in my despair, I struck the child's head with my fist."

"Was the infant alive at that point?" asked her attorney.

Nora shrugged and lowered her eyes. "It did not move, and I did not see it breathe."

"What did you do next?"

"I called for my father," she replied. "He wrapped the child in a cloth and put it in the coal hod in the corner of the room."

According to the *Evening Herald*, the judge declared a recess and sent the jury out of the courtroom. The news report noted that, "Somehow, the story did not seem to impress many, although it was pathetic enough in confessions of depravity, if nothing more."

The next day, Friday, June 14, James Fulton was called to the witness stand, and Nora dissolved into an unrestrained, tearful fit. Fulton admitted to having kept company with Nora but denied "improper relations." He also denied a promise of marriage, or, as he insisted, "At least there was never anything said about it to me."

After Fulton's testimony, both sides rested their case. Describing the spectators' response, the *Daily News-Democrat* wrote, "It seemed as if a hush fell over the audience as they realized that the most important criminal case in the county for years was closed."

Each side was allotted two-and-a-half hours to deliver their final arguments, and at 9:32 p.m., Judge Cook laid out the jury's instructions. With that, the jury began its deliberation. At eleven o'clock Saturday morning, the jury sent word that it had reached a decision. After the jurors returned to the courtroom, the judge asked foreman J.A. Leonhardt if they had reached a verdict. In response, Leonhardt rose and stated, "Your Honor, we have come to a conclusion."

Judge Cook frowned and asked, "A conclusion?"

"Yes," Leonhardt replied. "We, the jury, agree to disagree."

The judge quickly rejected the jury's childish attempt to slough off its responsibility and sent the men back to the jury room. However, at five-twenty that evening, the jury admitted that it was hung. The vote count had remained unmoved from the first ballot—six for acquittal and six for conviction.

Judge Cook called the jurors back to the courtroom and discharged them. A new trial for D.A. Mosher would be scheduled for the fall term. Nora's would follow.

Temporary Insanity Denied

D.A.'s retrial kicked off at 11:45 a.m. Monday, October 7, and went to the jury at 6:00 p.m. Thursday, October 10. In between, virtually no new evidence was introduced. Thus, not surprisingly, after the jury deliberated for sixty-six hours, it again admitted that it was hung, and the judge again discharged it. A third trial would eventually be necessary, but for the present, all eyes shifted to Nora.

Her trial opened on Monday, October 21 with a plea of temporary insanity, and her defense counsel asked that she be acquitted. The state at once requested that the plea be denied, which it ultimately was.

The day's *Daily News-Democrat* noted that the defendant "manifested more emotion this morning than she has shown at any time during the tragic circumstances, which have brought such grief to the Mosher family." Nearly all the testimony that followed over the next four days was recycled from D.A.'s previous trials. On Thursday, October 24, however, the most damning statements came from Emery Mosher's widow, Pearl, who testified that her sister-in-law had shown no inclination of insanity, neither before nor after the birth of the child. The defense objected, of course, but Judge Cook overruled it.

Nora took the stand in her own defense and recited the same story she told at her father's trials, that she had struck the baby as soon as it was born. But this time, she accepted no responsibility for her heinous act, claiming stress had driven her to it.

The case went to the jury Friday night. Unlike the juries for D.A.'s trials, Nora's jury reached its verdict within fifteen hours.

'We, the jury ...'

The jurors filed into the courtroom at 1:45 p.m., Saturday, October 26, and the foreman handed a sealed envelope to the judge. According to Saturday's *Evening Herald*, "The defendant watched every motion with an impassive face the color of chalk and eyes that seemed dead to all else."

The judge withdrew the sheet of paper from the envelope, glanced at the handwritten verdict, and read aloud, "We, the jury in the above cause, do find the defendant guilty of manslaughter."

As the judge announced the verdict, Nora gazed at him blankly, revealing no understanding that the jury had dismissed her plea of temporary insanity and instead declared her responsible for her baby's murder.

Manslaughter carried a penalty of two to twenty-one years in prison, and on Wednesday, November 13, Nora and Sheriff Mahoney boarded a train destined for the women's prison in Indianapolis.

Reporting on the departure, the *Daily News-Democrat* surmised, "Nora

Nora Mosher was sentenced to serve two to twenty-one years at the Indiana Women's Prison on October 26, 1907, following her manslaughter conviction for the murder of her newborn baby. After serving two-and-a-half years, Nora was granted a parole.

Mosher does not look forward with any fear to going to prison, her only care being of her aged mother, who is left alone."

Epilogue
Nora's father remained in the county jail awaiting his still-unscheduled third trial for murder, while her confused, broken-spirited mother, Rosa, roomed at a local boarding house. The hours ticked by slowly for all of them, until the news broke the following March that D.A. Mosher's third trial for the murder of his daughter's newborn baby had been scheduled.

That trial opened Wednesday, March 25, 1908, and strategies for the defense, as well as the prosecution, deviated little from D.A.'s two previous trials. Even Nora, who was brought from Indianapolis as a witness, gave basically the same testimony, admitting that she alone had killed the child. The case went to the jury Friday evening and in less than three hours, it returned a not-guilty verdict, acquitting D.A. Mosher.

The murder of Nora Mosher's baby ruined the lives of every member of the Mosher family. Emery committed suicide; his wife, Pearl, was outcast by everyone she knew; Rosa's health was deteriorating, and D.A. was scorned by the community until Dr. C.W. Fry found him lying dead in his garden on May 4, 1910.

When Nora returned to Huntington to bury her father, the state granted her parole, allowing her to care for her mother. Nora had served two-and-a-half years in prison.

Nora married former Huntington Fire Chief Charles Delvin in August 1912. Thirteen years later, the couple moved to Benton Harbor, Michigan, where Nora died of cancer of the uterus on September 7, 1945. Charles died the following year.

The identity of Baby Mosher's father, as well as the truth behind its birth and death, remains a mystery. ❖

17

THE PROSECUTION OF ALICE LAWSON: THE 'HUMAN ICICLE'

Dateline: Tippecanoe County, 1906

Alice Cooper Lawson hadn't set out to shoot, let alone kill, her husband, Charles, that Friday evening at his downtown-Lafayette saloon. She had wanted only to bring him home so he could eat his supper and sober up. Unfortunately, he wasn't receptive to his wife's wishes, and to his irrevocable detriment, he picked up a two-pound glass mug from the bar and hurled it at her. The instant the lethal beer glass whizzed past Alice's head and shattered against the wall, Charles's fate was sealed.

What Happened
Seven months later, seated on the witness stand in the Tippecanoe County courtroom, Alice calmly recounted the events of Friday, September 21, 1906, that had led her to shoot and kill her husband. She explained that at around 5:30 p.m. on that terrible day, accompanied by her twelve-year-old daughter, Ethel, she entered her husband's saloon to drop off his freshly laundered aprons, as well as his Smith & Wesson revolver. Charles was standing at the far end of the bar, but the instant Alice saw him, she knew he was drunk again.

He saw her approaching and grumbled, "What do you want?"

She told him she wanted to take him home. He hadn't been home for two nights.

He gulped a shot of whiskey and asked, "Do you know what I'm going to do to you?" She didn't answer. After a beat, he said, "I'm tired of you. I hate and despise you!" Then he pulled a wad of dollar bills from his pants pocket and shook it at her. "I've got all kinds of money, enough to get out of this town."

Alice only shrugged.

Her blasè attitude added to Charles's anger, and he bellowed, "I'm going to kill you!"

Alice again asked her husband to come home for supper.

"I'll never come home with you," he said as he grabbed a glass beer mug off the bar and pitched it at her. The mug soared past her head and smashed into a framed picture on the wall behind her, spewing shards of glass in all directions. Missing the target stoked Charles's anger, prompting him to pick up a heavier, thicker, deadlier glass mug.

Alice realized the situation had gotten out of hand and bolted for the front door. But Charles outpaced her and jumped into her path, gripping the beer glass as he would a deadly weapon. Intending to throw the glass, he raised it above his head but did not notice Alice withdraw the loaded Smith & Wesson from her handbag.

"Put down the glass, Charles," she warned, "or I swear, I'll shoot."

He stepped toward her, narrowing the space between them to a few feet. Alice pointed the gun at her crazed husband and warned him again. When he didn't back off, she fired two shots, neither hitting him. Charles lunged at her, but she sprinted out of his reach and fired again. She resumed running and almost made it to the front door, when she stumbled. Charles stood over her, and she fired twice more.

Righting herself, she glanced at her defeated, wounded husband as she called out to her daughter, "Ethel, honey, come on. Let's go." The two walked out of the saloon, making their way up Columbia Street to the police station, where Alice would give herself up.

A Demon in the Rough

Alice was born February 13, 1873, in Fairbury, Illinois, and was two, when she and her widowed mother, Sarah, moved to Lafayette. Sarah met and married Anderson Vick in 1877, providing a stepfather for her daughter. Before reaching the age of fourteen, Alice had dropped out of school and gone to work at the Thomas Baker Laundry. Charles also worked there; and although he was ten years Alice's senior, the two fell in love and married the next year, 1888.

Alice Cooper Lawson *(left)* shot and killed her abusive husband, Charles, on September 21, 1906, in his downtown Lafayette tavern as their twelve-year-old daughter, Ethel *(above)* stood by.

The marriage produced three children, two of whom died, leaving only Ethel, born in 1894.

Charles had opened the Lawson Saloon at 428 Columbia Street in 1893, and he and the family lived in the apartment upstairs. He was a successful proprietor. Although, as his business prospered and grew, his lust for liquor grew too.

According to the *Lafayette Daily Courier*, Charles was a good-natured, honest, generous man, who helped his friends in time of need. When Charles was sober, he was a king among men; but when he was drunk, he was a "vicious, brutal, and dangerous demon." Thus, the Lawsons' marriage suffered as Charles increasingly became verbally and physically abusive to Alice, often knocking her down and kicking her, and throwing dishes, stove lids, knives, lamps, and beer mugs at her. He also frequently belittled her in front of others, calling her names, even threatening to kill her.

Claims Shooting Justified

Several people in the area heard the shots, prompting two men to dash to the saloon. They found Charles still standing, but barely, as blood flowed from his right hand, his left shoulder, and a wound in his chest just north of his heart. As the men approached Charles, he collapsed. One of them, a doctor, set to work on Charles, while the other summoned an ambulance. The wagon arrived quickly, but Charles's injuries were excessive, and he expired en route to the hospital.

Within the hour, Lafayette Police Superintendent Charles H. Powell broke the news to Alice that her husband had died. At first, she refused to believe Powell's claim, but even after accepting it, she remained cool as she was arrested. Little Ethel clung to her mother and wept hysterically when strangers pulled her away to be transported to an unknown destination, where she would be assigned to temporary caretakers.

The next day's edition of the *Daily Courier* called Alice "Tippecanoe County's first murderess," reporting her claim that "He had it coming!"

The State v. Alice Lawson

Three weeks later, the Tippecanoe County Grand Jury indicted Alice for first-degree murder, and her trial was scheduled for April. Her attorney asked the court to consider bail for his client, but because Tippecanoe County Prosecutor Daniel Flanagan objected, Judge Richard P. DeHart denied the request.

On the first day of the trial, Monday, April 15, 1907, Alice entered the courtroom accompanied by Sheriff Jack Ray, her attorneys John J. McHugh and State Senator William R. Wood, and little Ethel. According to the *Daily Courier*, "all eyes were riveted on the powerfully built woman in black, who sat facing the jury, sad-faced but not dejected, an expression of determination being readily traced in her firm mouth and calm, stern glance."

At the stroke of ten o'clock, Judge DeHart called for order, and Alice was called before the bar while Prosecutor Flanagan read the indictment. The judge asked for her plea, and in a strong, clear voice, she replied, "Not guilty."

Alice returned to her seat and selection of the jury commenced. The last juror was selected Wednesday afternoon, and the twelve-man panel was sworn in. With that bit of business completed, the trial was off and running.

Flanagan rounded out day three of the trial with his opening statement, laying out a vivid overview of the case. The prosecutor drove home the state's position that the victim was "not blessed with much intellect, and although sometimes intoxicated, Charles Lawson was a man of good impulses and generosity," thus implying that Lawson's only culpability in his murder was his failure to keep the little wife in line. Consequently, the prosecutor lamented, Mrs. Lawson was wholly at fault for the "most cold-blooded and dastardly murder that ever stained the records of [Tippecanoe] county."

Witnesses for the Prosecution

Word of the trial's sensational nature had spread overnight, demonstrated by the size of the crowd squeezed into the courtroom on Thursday morning, April 18, or as the *Daily Courier* reported, the courtroom was "packed to suffocation." With the clack of the judge's gavel, the court's business was brought to order, and act one of the Lawson Show was underway.

Spectators were riveted to their seats by a series of state's witnesses, each relaying stories of Alice's alleged extramarital affairs, disregard for her domestic duties, excessive whiskey and beer consumption, overbearing temper, resentment toward her husband's entrepreneurial success, and maternal neglect of little Ethel.

Among the prosecution's final witnesses was Police Superintendent Powell, who recounted his conversation with Alice when she arrived at the station after the shooting to turn herself in.

"I asked her why she killed her husband," Powell said, "and she replied, 'My God, I don't know.' So I asked her where she got the revolver, and she told me, 'I heard he was at Vester's saloon with Honey Buckshot, and I took the revolver with me to my husband's saloon.'"

A clarification of Honey Buckshot's identity was unnecessary. She was already well known as one of the city's "working girls."

The prosecution called witnesses through Tuesday, April 23, each testifying to what they saw at the Lawson Saloon the previous September 21, before and after Charles died by a bullet fired by his wife. For the first time since the trial began eight days before, Alice Lawson lost control of her restrained, stoic demeanor and wept. Her momentary breakdown occurred while a witness described a scene at Folckemer's Mortuary, when Alice looked down at her dead husband and moaned, "Oh my darling man, why did I do it?"

That afternoon, prosecuting attorney Flanagan announced, "The state rests."

The Defense Takes Its Turn

The next day, Wednesday, April 24, John F. McHugh delivered the opening statement for the defense. While the state sought to show the shooting as premeditated, the defense would endeavor to dismantle that theory at every turn. The attorney insisted that his client, Alice Lawson, had acted in self-defense after her husband weaponized a massive beer mug by throwing it at her head.

"Gentlemen of the jury," said McHugh, according to the *Daily Courier*, "under her plea of not guilty, we will show you that when Alice Lawson acted on the twenty-first day of September, a man weighing 220 pounds and standing five-feet, six inches tall, rushed at her with a beer glass weighing exactly one pound and fourteen ounces." At that point, McHugh paused to display a glass mug exactly like the one Charles had pitched at his wife. "At that moment," McHugh continued, "a shot was fired."

Detailing Charles Lawson's drunkenness and habitual cruelty to his wife, the counselor explained, "For several days prior to the regrettable tragedy, Lawson was in a state of intoxication. The Tuesday before, Lawson drove his wife and daughter out of the house with a knife, and on the Wednesday before the shooting, Charles yelled at Alice, 'I'm so tired of looking at you, I will kill you!'"

As McHugh wrapped up his opening statement, he dramatically asserted, "Mr. Lawson was advancing aggressively toward his wife and was only two feet from her when she fired the fatal shots. Alice Lawson did not have to retreat. She was justified in standing her ground!"

Alice Takes the Stand

The next morning, scores of women who expected the defendant to take the stand crammed the courtroom. Their anticipation was fulfilled when the stoic, pale-faced woman in black stepped to the witness chair, placed her hand on a bible, and swore to tell the truth, so help her God.

Under the gentle guidance of McHugh and smiles of encouragement from Ethel, Alice initially spoke with pride about life with Charles—of their mutual love and of their early struggles with poverty. But as she told of his downward spiral into alcoholism, she began sobbing like a child. After taking a moment to regain her composure, she recalled incidents that illustrated the marriage's descent into darkness.

"When Charles went into the saloon business, his drink habit grew," Alice said. "He was a good man when sober, but ugly and quarrelsome when he was drunk."

Alice described a number of examples of abuse to which her late husband had subjected her.

"When Ethel was three," Alice began, "she accidentally cut her hand. Charles came home drunk, and blamed me for the cut, so he knocked me down and kicked me. Another time, Ethel had the croup, and he choked me for letting her get sick. And once, when Ethel and I were in bed, Charles came home from the saloon and threw a cuspidor at us." After pausing to dab her wet eyes with a hankie, Alice quietly said, "He threatened to kill me many times."

In addition to painting a picture for the jury of her miserable home life and the abuse she endured, Alice corroborated the defense's opening statement concerning various incidents and actions that occurred the day she shot her husband. Her testimony continued until court was adjourned that afternoon.

Alice Takes the Stand Again

At 11:00 a.m. Friday, April 26, prosecuting attorney Flanagan recalled Alice to the stand for redirect. With her unshakable self-control intact, she calmly answered questions obviously designed to negate her credibility, expose flaws in her previous testimony, and prove that her husband's death was a premeditated, cold-blooded murder.

When Flanagan accused the defendant of shooting her husband as punishment for his alleged tryst with Honey Buckshot, Alice adamantly denied harboring jealousy of Miss Buckshot and reiterated her claim that she had taken the gun to the saloon to lock it in the safe.

Alice remained on the stand until Judge DeHart adjourned court at four o'clock. The prosecution's cross-examination resumed at 10:00 a.m. Monday, April 29. For two hours, Flanagan's co-counselor, Charles Haywood, cited alleged inconsistencies in the defendant's testimony and maintained that none of the stories of her husband's cruelty had been corroborated.

Previously, during direct examination by the defense, Alice had convincingly described a toxic situation of domestic abuse, which was not uncommon in 1906, or any other time in history. And yet, the prosecution disregarded the defense's sympathetic approach, instead casting Alice as a "human icicle," devoid of grief and remorse. And worse, it painted her as a cold-hearted killer.

"Is it not a fact that you pursued your husband in the saloon with your pistol drawn," Haywood blustered, waggling his finger at Alice, "and then, when you had him cornered, you shot him to death?"

She responded with an emphatic, "No."

Haywood then asked, "Is it not a fact that you went to the saloon that afternoon for the purpose of provoking a quarrel and killing your husband?"

"No sir!" was her reply.

With that, Haywood announced, "That's all," and sat down.

Final Arguments

Closing arguments began Wednesday, May 1, with Prosecutor Flanagan calling for Alice's conviction, often referring to her as a cold, lying, selfish murderess, while portraying her husband as a genuinely good man with "a heart as big as his body" and one pitiable fault—"an appetite for drink."

Arguments by the defense started Friday, with Wood and McHugh taking their turns at asserting their client's innocence, thus calling for her release.

"We want no compromise!" Wood proclaimed. "Either hang this woman or send her out into the world to do the best she can for herself and her daughter."

Through the day, Wood kept pulling back the curtain to his client's hard, unhappy life, allowing the jurors to see Alice Lawson in a true light that nullified the false picture painted of her by the prosecution.

"Mrs. Lawson is not being tried because she is a 'human icicle,' as the state termed it," Wood said. "If we were trying her for that, we would go back to the time when her love had been chilled by the fiendish action of the man who swore to love and protect her all his life."

McHugh mesmerized the jury on Monday, May 6, as he argued for Alice's freedom. Concluding his powerful, persuasive plea, he implored, "You, gentlemen, carry the dignity and power of a sovereign. ... Your responsibility involves the fate of Alice Cooper Lawson. May God in his wisdom direct and control you, for without the will of the Creator, not a sparrow falleth."

Haywood followed on Tuesday, wrapping up the state's case on Wednesday with one final declaration that Charles Lawson was "not a brute" and Alice was a "thoroughly bad woman." He then landed the apogee of his case when, with a sweeping gesture toward Alice, he proclaimed, "This woman is guilty. Her hands are dripping with the lifeblood of her husband. God forbid there is a man on this jury who would feel he could not convict a woman simply because of her sex. Do your duty, gentlemen. Do not let this crime go unavenged."

With that, the summary arguments were complete, and Alice Lawson's fate rested in the jury's hands.

Verdict Comes Quickly

The jury cast seven ballots before reaching agreement a few minutes past midnight. The men filed back into the courtroom shortly past eight o'clock the next morning, Thursday, May 9, and the bailiff announced the verdict: "We, the jury, find the defendant, Alice Lawson, guilty of murder in the second degree as charged in the indictment, and that she be imprisoned in the Indiana Women's Prison for life."

From her place at the defense table, Alice Lawson sat frozen as she processed her fate. Nothing on her face revealed the emotion that was surely coursing through her veins. After a long moment, she whispered a few words to her counsel, rose, and walked out of the courtroom, escorted by Sheriff Ray. The defense had expected the jury to acquit, and when reporters stopped Alice for a comment, she told them, "I was bitterly disappointed. I thought the jury would believe my story."

The defense counselors had thirty days to file a motion for a new trial, but when they returned to Judge DeHart's courtroom on Tuesday, June 11, he denied the motion. Looking to Alice, the judge asked if she wished to make a statement before her sentence was passed, and she replied, "No." DeHart then sharply declared that the remainder of her life would be spent in prison.

Alice was pleased when Sheriff Ray decided to drive her to Indianapolis because she had never ridden in an automobile. On Friday morning, June 14, moments before she was about to depart Lafayette forever, she and her daughter, who was living with her grandparents, engaged in a sad farewell on the lawn of the Tippecanoe County jail. Yet, while little Ethel wrapped her arms around her mother and sobbed bitterly, Alice remained unflappable. As the *Daily Courier* reported, "Mrs. Lawson stepped briskly across the front yard of the jail with no grief or remorse to be seen on her countenance. This remarkable creature went to prison with a smile on her face, nothing but composure and indifference depicted there."

Epilogue

Two-and-a-half-years later, Oscar R. McKay, pastor of the First Baptist Church of Lafayette, and State Senator William Wood, who served as Alice's attorney during the trial, spearheaded a miracle. The two men sought to secure Alice's freedom after learning from the prison that she had undergone a reformation of character and was ready to begin life anew. During the summer of 1910, the pastor circulated a petition asking the State of Indiana to issue Alice a parole and obtained scores of signatures.

According to the *Daily Courier*, on September 28, 1910, McKay and Wood appeared before the State Parole Board and made eloquent pleas on her behalf.

Wood explained that the crime for which Alice Lawson had been convicted should have been deemed manslaughter, rather than second-degree murder, an error even the jury had since regretted. Wood then showed the parole board the signatories to the petition. They included every juror, the judge, the prosecutor, the assistant prosecutor, and every other individual connected with the case.

Two weeks later, Indiana Governor Thomas Riley Marshall paroled Alice. When she left the women's prison, she moved into a little house on Wyoming Street in Indianapolis with Ethel, who had blossomed into a beautiful seventeen-year-old woman.

Governor Samuel Ralston granted Alice a full pardon in December of 1914, and the following year, she married the love of her life, David W. Rubins. Alice and David enjoyed their life together until his death in 1943. Alice followed him in 1947.

In the final analysis, once Alice Cooper Lawson Rubins—the woman mocked as a "human icicle"—felt safe enough to warm her heart to love, she at last found the happiness she had always deserved. ❖

18

THE GLASGO FIASCO

Dateline: Clay County, 1907

Rose Glasgo showed up unannounced at the Sheridan Brick Works on Brazil, Indiana's north side to confront her estranged husband, Edward. On that late summer afternoon in September of 1907, Rose had but one thought on her mind—reconciliation or ending it. If only she hadn't stashed that revolver in her parasol, perhaps Edward wouldn't have even thought of killing himself.

Surprise Visit
Happiness had eluded Edward and Rose from their first day as husband and wife. The childhood friends became engaged in 1902, while Edward was in medical school at Indianapolis, but four years passed before they finally tied the knot. Although Edward was the son of wealthy, highly respected physician Thomas Asbury Glasgo of Brazil, he frequently begged Rose to bail him out of whatever wily situation he had gotten himself into. She, the daughter of noted Terre Haute doctor Wallace Purcell, was a school teacher whose low wages barely supported her. Yet, she always came through for Edward.

Even on the evening of May 29, 1906, the day before their wedding, Edward asked Rose to scrape together $150 to cover the check he had forged to pay off his bar bill and gambling debt. He promised it would be his last shameful blunder and vowed that as Rose's husband, he would turn a new leaf.

Predictably, the responsibilities associated with marriage did not alleviate Edward's reckless pattern, and in the fall of that year, the couple separated.

The following spring, he filed for divorce.

On Thursday, September 5, 1907, Rose, along with Charles Whitlock, a young attorney with whom she had been acquainted for years, boarded the eastbound Interurban in Terre Haute for the sixteen-mile ride to Brazil. Upon their arrival, they rented a rig and drove to the Sheridan Brick Works, where Edward was employed. At Rose's request, the bookkeeper summoned an unsuspecting Edward to the front office. The unscheduled reunion did not go well. Rose insisted they get back together, and when Edward refused, they began to quarrel.

"Excuse me," said Whitlock, stepping in to mitigate the rising tension. "Let's calm down, shall we? This might be a discussion best had outside."

The three exited the building, and after a brief negotiation, Rose and Edward climbed into the horse-drawn buggy and headed for town, leaving Whitlock to return to the train station on foot. The buggy hadn't proceeded for more than a block when three shots rang out in rapid succession. Whitlock bolted to the rig.

"I saw Glasgo lying limp in the buggy," Whitlock told the *Brazil Daily Times* reporter. "Blood was streaming from two bullet wounds on the left side of his head."

Mortal Wounds

Whitlock raced to the nearest house for help. Doctors Gifford, Young, and Hollingsworth responded and found Rose calmly seated in the buggy, cradling her husband's mortally wounded head. Rose had sustained a mild wound to her left breast, but Edward was beyond help. When he expired, Whitlock drove Rose to the home of her brother, Charles Purcell, where she was later arrested and taken to the Clay County jail. She reportedly refused to discuss the shooting with anyone, not even the sheriff, but she had told Whitlock and the physicians that it was her husband who had done the shooting.

Almost immediately, gossip concerning Edward's death began wending its way through the community. The talk was not favorable to Rose. Most townspeople believed she had deliberately fired the two bullets into Edward's skull, before accidentally releasing a third one, which merely grazed her breast. Even worse for Rose, the murderous scenario was not based only on uninformed rumors.

"The theory that Glasgo tried to kill his wife and then committed suicide is refuted by the physicians who examined the wounds in Glasgo's head," stated

Rose Glasgo was arrested for the shooting death of her husband, Edward, in Brazil on September 5, 1907. She was held at the Clay County jail until her trial in November. When the jury found her not guilty, the courtroom broke out in cheers. Glasgo made history as the first female tried for murder in Clay County.

the *Daily Times*. "They contend that it would have been almost impossible for him to have held the revolver to his own head and inflicted the wounds in such a manner."

Locked in a jail cell, Rose was heartbroken, stunned, confused, and scared. She had wanted only to save her marriage when she met with Edward that afternoon. She had never imagined that her well-meaning, hopeful intentions could go so horribly wrong and send her hurtling into such a dark place. As she awaited her arraignment in the light of a new day, she feared that her husband's tragic ending would be the lubricant that threatened her slippery grip on her self-preservation.

Historic Indictment

Rose was escorted to the Clay County courtroom at two o'clock Friday afternoon. Accompanying her were attorneys Albert Payne and B.C. Craig, who entered a not-guilty plea for their client. She was bound over to the Clay Circuit

Court without bail.

As the *Daily Times* noted, among the locals who firmly believed that Rose had murdered her husband was Dr. Eli Glasgo, Edward's brother.

"Ed was not in the habit of carrying a revolver," Eli reportedly said, "and it would have been impossible for him to conceal a gun in the clothes he wore to work."

The defense attorneys, to the contrary, intended to prove that regardless of who brought the gun, the culprit who pulled the trigger was Edward. Such was the scenario laid out in Rose's statement to the court, which read:

> I brought the revolver with the intention of using it on myself. It was lying in the bottom of the buggy. Glasgo picked it up and fired one shot at me and the other two shots into his own head. Glasgo made threats to kill me and then himself before the shots were fired.

What Payne and Craig needed most was a witness who could testify to having seen Edward fire the revolver. Without one, Rose's innocence would be difficult for them to establish.

Edward's funeral was held Sunday, September 8, at his parents' home. According to the *Indianapolis Star*, because so many mourners attended, there was standing room only.

The Clay County Grand Jury indicted Rose on October 18, charging her with murder in the first degree. The trial was scheduled to start Monday, November 4. In the county's eighty-two-year history, Rose would be the first woman tried for murder.

Order in the Court

Scores of curiosity seekers, the majority of them women, were squeezed into the courtroom when Judge John Rawley gaveled in the opening of the Glasgo trial. Attorneys John E. Lamb and A.W. Knight joined Payne and Craig for the defense. For the state were Clay County Prosecutor J.P. Hughes, his deputy, S.W. Lee, and George A. Knight of McNutt & Shattuck.

Seated at the state's table were Edward's somber parents. Across the aisle sat Rose, attired in a simple black suit. Her four attorneys were seated beside her, along with her sixty-year-old mother, Rachel, whom the *Daily Times* referred to as "aged."

Jury selection, the first order of business, was completed by eleven o'clock, and after a break for lunch, the trial got underway. Prosecutor Hughes delivered the opening statement. After laying out an overview of the Glasgos' miserable marriage, he turned his attention to the events of September 5 that led to Edward's death, from Rose's trip to the brick plant until her arrest afterward at her brother's house.

"At all times," Hughes proclaimed, "Mrs. Glasgo was cool and collected, notwithstanding the fact that her husband was in the buggy by her side dying."

Furthermore, Hughes said, throughout the Glasgos' marriage, Rose had frequently threatened to take Edward's life. Hughes concluded his opening statement with a vow that the state would prove the defendant deliberately killed her husband.

The moment Hughes took his seat, defense attorney John Lamb stood and began laying out his case, which, he implored, would decisively prove his client's innocence. Lamb admitted that on the day Rose surprised Edward at the Sheridan Brick Works, she had brought a revolver but intended it only as a last resort to end her own life, not Edward's. After the shooting incident, Lamb said, she told Whitlock that she no longer cared to live.

The attorney insisted that if his client bore guilt of any sort, it was her practice to pay Edward's foolish debts, even at her own detriment. "The only crime Mrs. Glasgo committed," he said, "was falling in love with a worthless man."

Lamb mesmerized the courtroom for more than two hours, during which he frequently paused to wipe a tear from his eye. A number of attorneys who visited the courtroom as spectators told the *Daily Times* that Lamb's address was the most forcible argument they had ever heard in an opening statement.

The defense was counting on that momentum as a force too powerful for the prosecution to overcome.

Ineffective Prosecution

Perhaps the most newsworthy aspect of the trial's second day was the size of the crowd jammed into the Clay County courthouse, while another five hundred people waited on the lawn. The *Daily Times* described the scene as "something of a society affair." Women far outnumbered men, and as the newspaper noted, "The ladies came dressed to the height of fashion, adding a pleasing appearance to the otherwise sober scene."

The paper also claimed it was the largest assembly in the building's thirty-year history, despite the county commissioners having condemned it. And yet, no public official advocated for moving the trial to a safer venue or

The Glasgo trial was held here, in the condemned Clay County courthouse, located in Brazil.

for limiting the number of spectators.

The prosecution called a string of underwhelming witnesses, who did little to help the state's case. Arguably, the strongest testimonies for the state were delivered by doctors Gifford, Young, and Hollingsworth, who had rushed to aid Glasgo after the shooting. The doctors agreed that the first bullet entering Edward Glasgo's temple would likely have caused instant unconsciousness. Thus, they contended, he could not have fired both shots to his brain.

The state rested Tuesday afternoon, November 5, without calling a single witness who could decisively establish Rose Glasgo's guilt. Commenting on the prosecution's weak case, defense attorney Lamb told the *Daily Times* he was greatly surprised and believed all the more that his client would be acquitted.

Defense Takes Its Turn

The defense opened its case and finished the day with a cavalcade of witnesses —all of them relatives, friends, and co-workers—who validated Rose's upstanding character.

When court resumed Wednesday, November 6, Lamb called his star witness, Rose Glasgo. As she rose from her seat at the defense table and stepped to the stand, a rumble of chatter emanated from the gallery and rippled through the courtroom. Rose kept the spectators transfixed all morning.

During those hours, the jury learned that she was born in 1880 on a farm near Reelsville, a tiny community eight miles northeast of Brazil in Putnam County. She and Edward had been mere children when they met. Over the years, their friendship deepened to love, and they became engaged in 1902. They were often separated due to Edward's studies in Indianapolis, but after they finally tied the knot on May 30, 1906, the newlyweds settled in Terre Haute. However, the union was not without challenges. Edward's drinking had gotten out of hand, and to support it, he often turned to Rose for money, usually asking for sums exceeding her resources.

Between convulsive sobs, Rose told the court of Edward's trip to Florida after having written her a letter explaining his intent to seek a divorce. She was devastated. She was desperate to get to him, to convince him to come home with her, to save their marriage. To finance the railway fare to Pensacola, Florida, where Edward was living, she sold her silverware, raising $25. Forty-eight hours later, he broke down in her arms, tearfully vowing his love for her and confessing that his parents had paid for his trip to Florida and forced him to send the letter.

Rose wanted to get him back to Terre Haute, but Edward was penniless yet again. Rose had no choice but to wire her family for help. They sent her $75, more than enough to bring Edward home. Within weeks, however, Edward's father had again convinced him to leave the marriage.

"How did you respond?" asked Lamb.

"I told Edward that even though I loved him with all my heart," Rose said, her eyes overflowing with tears, "that if he did not love me, I could give him up."

"And how did your husband respond to that?" asked her attorney.

Dabbing at her eyes with her embroidered handkerchief, Rose said, "He looked at his father and explained, 'But, Father, I love Rose, and I want to live with her.'"

But that didn't happen. Edward moved back to his parents' home in Brazil, leaving Rose to live alone in their apartment in Terre Haute. Within a matter of weeks, Rose had grown distraught about the breakup. Out of sheer desperation, she made a decision. She would talk with Edward face-to-face, far from the prying eyes of his father, and together, she and her husband would, once and for all, make up or break up. Prior to the meeting with Edward, Rose had consulted with Whitlock concerning a divorce, and he offered to accompany her to Brazil.

Lamb asked her where Edward had obtained the gun.

"You must understand," she said, "I was deeply in love with Edward, and I believed life without him would not be worth living."

"And the gun?" Lamb reiterated, reminding the courtroom of the question at hand.

"It was mine," Rose replied tersely. "I had hidden it inside my parasol. If Edward refused to take me back, I was going to use it to kill myself."

Several spectators gasped. Rose closed her eyes, allowing several seconds to pass before she continued.

The Pistol Route to Hell

"And he did refuse," she said, staring at the moist hankie in her hands. "He told me he no longer wanted to care for me. That's when I opened my parasol to get the gun, but it fell on the buggy's floor. Before I could reach it, Edward grabbed it and bragged, 'I always liked the pistol route. We will go to hell together.'"

Rose closed her eyes and inhaled deeply in an effort to regain her composure.

"Take your time, Mrs. Glasgo," Lamb said gently, obviously aware of the impact her next words would have on the jury, as well as the trial's outcome. "When you are ready, tell us what happened next."

Rose looked at Lamb, nodded, and in a measured tone, continued her testimony.

"That's when Edward shot me," she said. "The wound wasn't serious, mind you, but blood was spreading across the front of my dress, making it appear much worse than it was. I believe he was as stunned as I was and thought I would die. It all happened so quickly."

Rose's voice quivered, and she again paused. After restoring control over her imploding emotions, she carefully explained the haunting moment of Edward's passing.

"Before I could stop him," she said in barely a whisper, "he pointed the gun at his head and fired two bullets into his brain."

Rose stepped down from the witness stand shortly before noon. As she returned to her seat at the defense table, she scanned the spectators' faces. Few dry eyes stared back at her.

After a thirty-minute break for lunch, Rose returned to the stand for a vigorous cross-examination by the determined prosecutorial team. However, according to the *Daily Times*:

All the trickery and wisdom of skilled attorneys were brought into play to confuse and contradict the frail little woman, who was battling for her life and liberty, but she was not shaken in a single point but stuck closely to her first statement, which was summed up in a few words: "I love my husband. I did not kill him but wanted to kill myself."

Jury in a Hurry

The state failed miserably at breaking the defendant. The state's attorneys, obviously realizing the futility of their effort, gave up, and the county's deputy prosecutor, J.P. Hughes, delivered a short, lackluster closing argument.

John Lamb, for the defense, also delivered a brief final argument, but it was nothing short of masterful, noted the *Daily Times*. Lamb stated simply that Rose Glasgo's innocence had been so clearly proven, "it would be an insult to her to go over the story again." With that, he took his seat.

Shortly before 6:00 p.m., Judge Rawley turned the case over to the jury. The courtroom should have cleared, but numerous optimistic spectators, court officials, the attorneys, and Rose remained seated. She was confident of an acquittal. Her optimism spiked when she learned that after deliberating for just forty minutes, the jury reached its decision.

When the jurors returned to the courtroom, the foreman handed Judge Rawley a folded sheet of paper. The judge opened the paper and read the handwritten verdict aloud: "We, the jury, find the defendant, Rose Glasgo, not guilty."

Cheers and applause echoed throughout the courthouse. The jurors shook Rose's hand, and spectators gathered around her. Although she had spent sixty days locked in a jail cell, she insisted on returning to the jail to thank the inmates, the sheriff, and his wife for their many kindnesses. Following that, with tears rolling down her cheeks, she boarded the Interurban and headed home to Terre Haute.

Epilogue

The outcome of the trial came as no surprise to Lamb, who believed he could have won without questioning a single witness. "As far as I'm concerned," he told the *Daily Times*, "I could have closed the case when the state rested."

What he couldn't have won, however, was Rose's reprieve from the anguish and psychological damage that her marriage, Edward's death, her incarceration, and the trial had imposed on her.

Rose's foray into the public limelight was as unintended as it had been short-lived. The indicted darling of Clay County, first woman tried there for murder, and beneficiary of a rapid, record-setting jury deliberation, Rose was absolved of all guilt and set free to resume her life.

And yet, the balance of her life was lost to the ages, except for three recorded milestones: Two months after Rose's acquittal, she suffered an emotional breakdown and required hospitalization; in 1912, she married thirty-nine-year-old Charles V. Wilson, who died seven years later; and lastly, she met her own death on December 4, 1935, at the Central State Hospital for the Insane in Indianapolis.

In the wake of a lifetime of despair, Rose may have embraced death as the long-awaited release from her dark and tortured existence. And who's to say that hadn't been Edward's wish for her all along? ❖

19

THE CONTEMPTIBLE CRIMES OF CLARA CARL: INDIANA'S FEMALE BLUEBEARD

DATELINE: HANCOCK COUNTY, 1920 AND 1921

Robert M. Gibson died March 18, 1920, in Huntsville, Missouri, at the age of forty-two. His obituary in the *Moberly (Missouri) Evening Democrat*, described him as a man of excellent attainments and strict integrity. Seventeen months later, on August 6, 1921, forty-three-year-old Frank E. Carl died in Greenfield, Indiana. Frank's death notice in the *Greenfield Daily Reporter* referred to him as cheerful and hard-working. Both men had been perfectly healthy before contracting an illness that caused their sudden and unexpected demise— Gibson allegedly succumbing to complications of influenza, and Carl allegedly dying of dysentery. Could it have been coincidental that, at the time of their deaths, both men had been married to Clara Green?

Two Times a Widow
Clara Green Gibson Carl was a dour, matronly enigma. Like many wives of her time, she was defined by her husbands' achievements. Thus, Clara's personal aspirations and outlook on life were largely a mystery. Until they weren't.

Clara was born in Perry County, Ohio, in 1880 and married Robert Gibson on March 14, 1908, in Covington, Kentucky. At that time, she resided in the tiny Hancock County, Indiana, burg of Cleveland, and he in Rushville, twenty-one miles to the southeast. Robert was an academic, graduating from Ohio

University in 1895, serving as a teacher and school superintendent, and later as a journalist. Throughout the Gibsons' twelve-year marriage, Robert's work took him to communities in Indiana, Ohio, Kansas, and Missouri, where he researched and authored local history books.

In early 1920, Robert started a new history project in Huntsville, Missouri. Clara remained in Greenfield, where she and Robert maintained a home west of town on the National Road (later renamed U.S. Highway 40). In mid-March, she traveled to Huntsville to visit her husband. Shortly after her arrival, Robert became violently ill and suffered a fatal stroke. Clara accompanied his body to his hometown, Nelsonville, Ohio, for burial, and then returned to Greenfield.

Six months after Robert's death, on September 14, 1920, she married Frank Carl in Indianapolis, and the happy couple settled into Clara's Greenfield home. Frank, another writer of history, was a native of Hiawatha, Kansas. How he and Clara met was not made clear, but, according to Frank's close friends, it was love at first sight.

The Carls' marriage was not without problems, however. According to the November 1, 1920, *Greenfield Daily Reporter*, Clara had filed for divorce in late October. Apparently, as with many newlyweds, the Carls only needed a little time to adjust. A few weeks later, they reconciled, and in late April 1921, they expanded their family and welcomed Frank's eighty-five-year-old father, Alonzo, into their home from Hiawatha.

Alonzo had barely adjusted to his new digs, when on June 2, he suddenly died, reportedly due to heart trouble. Even more alarming, just two months after that, Frank died. His passing was also sudden.

Frank's funeral was held the next day, Sunday, August 7, at the Greenfield home. Immediately after, Clara accompanied her husband's body on the journey back to Hiawatha, Kansas, for burial in the family plot near his parents. Upon her return to Greenfield, she quietly went about living her life, attracting no undue attention from the townsfolk and keeping her name off the front page of the local papers. Her inglorious obscurity would be short-lived.

Anonymous Tipster

Shortly after Frank's death, the prosecuting attorney of Nemaha County, Kansas, R.M. Emery, received an anonymous letter postmarked "Greenfield" asserting that Clara Carl had poisoned both Alonzo and Frank Carl with arsenic. Emery forwarded the letter to Hancock County Prosecutor Waldo Ging. Consequently, the lead story in the January 12, 1922, *Hancock Democrat*

Clara Green Gibson Carl, Hancock County's notorious "Black Widow" killer, poisoned two husbands and a father-in-law. During her trial for the murder of husband number two, Frank Carl, Hancock County Prosecutor Waldo Ging called her "an arch demon, a feminine bluebeard, a guilty wretch, rotten to the core, and a degenerate murderess."

revealed that after a secret investigation, the Hancock County Grand Jury had asked the Kansas State Board of Health to exhume the bodies of Alonzo and Frank Carl from their graves in Hiawatha and to ship them to Indianapolis for analysis.

The *Indianapolis Star* reported on Sunday, January 29, that the state chemist had analyzed both men's stomachs. According to Ging, enough arsenic was found in the elder Carl's stomach "to have killed a dozen men," resulting in Clara's immediate indictment and arrest for the murder of her father-in-law.

The next day, the grand jury issued a second indictment charging Clara with the arsenic poisoning of her husband, Frank. The *Star* reported that the second indictment included the Hancock County prosecutor's intent to have the body of Clara's first husband, Robert Gibson, exhumed and transported to Indianapolis. Gibson also died suddenly and unexpectedly. Ging recognized a pattern.

Murder for Money
According to the *Hancock Democrat*, Prosecutor Ging had been working on the case since Frank's death the past August and considered the Carl murders the most heinous crimes ever committed in Hancock County. Furthermore,

Ging speculated the men's deaths had been "carefully planned and skillfully carried out" with the goal of inheriting Frank Carl's life insurance money, reported to be as much as $2,000, and his property, which included a large amount of real estate he inherited after his father's death.

When Clara was arrested, bail was denied. Thus, over the following weeks, as she sat in her jail cell, she frequently was subjected to questions by the prosecutor, law enforcement, and reporters. But she was steadfast in her refusal to talk to them, exactly as her legal defense team of Omer S. Jackson and John B. Hinchman instructed. People acquainted with her, however, had no such restraint.

"She never neighbored much with people," said an unnamed source, as reported by the *Greenfield Daily Reporter*. "She was just different from the rest of us."

Another called her nervous and high-strung after witnessing her break down in tears in a Greenfield retail shop.

Several others recalled Clara as caring and kind, and the Kansas mortician who oversaw Robert Gibson's funeral reportedly said, "If Clara Carl is a double murderess, I say she is accomplished in acting the part of a widow whose sorrow is deep and could never be healed."

Meanwhile, the Greenfield newspaper noted that sightseers were arriving from as far as one hundred miles away just to look at Clara's house. Many of them snapped pictures with their Brownie cameras, and even more collected souvenirs, carrying away anything not nailed down.

The Plot Thickens

In mid-March, Ging returned to Greenfield from a trip to Nelsonville, Ohio, where he'd been looking for evidence that Clara's first husband also had died from poisoning. Gibson's body was exhumed, and his vital organs were removed and sent to a chemist in Indianapolis for analysis. Within a few days, Ging received the results. His suspicions were confirmed. Gibson's stomach was full of arsenic, just as Alonzo and Frank Carl's had been.

Clara's trial for the murder of her second husband was set for March 21, 1922. As the date approached, Ging was preparing to also introduce evidence related to the murders of her father-in-law and first husband.

The people of Greenfield and Rushville were growing excited about the trial, thanks in part to the sensationalized news coverage touting Clara as a "modern, female Bluebeard. Clara scoffed at the designation and maintained her

The Carl house—where the murders of Clara's husband, Frank, and her father-in-law, Alonzo, occurred—was located on the outskirts of the small Hancock County town of Philadelphia, near Greenfield, on the old National Road. Clara and her first husband, Robert Gibson, had purchased the home a few years after they married in 1908.

innocence. Reportedly, she was confident her legal counsel would portray her for what she claimed to be: a loving wife, a devoted daughter-in-law, and the victim of a ruthless, power-hungry prosecutor.

When Tuesday, March 21 arrived and Judge Jonas P. Walker gaveled court into session, John Hinchman, Clara's attorney, approached the bench and asked for a change of venue, claiming that his client could not have a fair trial in Hancock County due to prejudice against her. Within the week, Judge Walker sustained the motion and sent the case to neighboring Shelby County, where it would be tried in Shelbyville. Only eighteen miles separated Greenfield from Shelbyville, which ensured that curious Hancock County people would make the daily trek to watch Clara's trial, which would begin May 22.

Clara would be defended by Hinchman, Omer Jackson, Ed K. Adams, and Charles Tindall. Hancock County Prosecutor Ging would be assisted by Greenfield attorney Charles Cook and Shelby County Prosecutor Elmer Bassett.

Clara was transferred to the Shelby County jail on April 4. With her, she brought a suitcase crammed full of clothing and beauty supplies. Her room was twice the size of the one she had occupied at the Hancock County jail. It also was equipped with four windows, a bath, comfortable chairs, and reading

Sketches of Indiana's "Female Bluebeard," Clara Carl, and two of her three murder victims—husbands Robert M. Gibson *(left)* and Frank E. Carl *(right)*—sensationalized the front pages of newspapers coast-to-coast once her trial started in May of 1922.

materials. Once she unpacked and arranged her room, she settled in, projecting the pious demeanor of a woman wrongly accused.

Order in the Court

On Monday morning, May 22, 1922, Clara's unwavering insistence of innocence electrified the courtroom, when Shelby County Judge Alonzo Blair called the first day of her trial to order. Jury selection was the first item of business, and by noon, based on potential jurors' views of the death penalty—both in favor and opposed—at least thirty members of the panel had been excused. By day's end, however, the attorneys had reached an agreement and selected their twelve-man jury composed largely of area farmers.

The next item of business, Clara's plea of not guilty, included an explanation that her indictment was the product of "idle gossip."

On day two, Tuesday, May 23, the state wasted no time getting to the point of its case, calling its first witness, Rhoda Loehr, clerk at Early Drugs in Greenfield. Loehr testified that she had sold five-cents worth of arsenic to Clara on the last Saturday of July of 1921, seven days before Frank Carl's untimely death.

The prosecution took the opportunity to explain that an ounce of arsenic was composed of 480 grains, and an ounce of arsenic sold for ten cents at Early Drugs. Thus, the five-cents worth of arsenic purchased by Clara contained 240 grains of arsenic.

"What did Mrs. Carl say when she bought the arsenic?" Prosecutor Bassett asked Loehr.

"Something concerning a cat in her chicken house," she replied with a shrug.

Loehr was followed by William D. McAbee, the Indianapolis chemist that had analyzed Frank Carl's liver, stomach and kidneys. McAbee told the court Carl's organs contained 5.81 grains of arsenic, far more than enough to cause his death. In fact, he noted, one or two grains could be considered a fatal dose.

The prosecution's point had been made: If two grains were enough to kill a man, why did Clara buy 240 to kill a kitty?

In the coming days, the prosecution called Bert B. Beatty, secretary of the Modern Woodmen Lodge No. 644 of Seneca, Kansas, issuer of Frank's $2,000 life insurance policy. Beatty testified that Frank's policy originally listed his father, Alonzo, as the beneficiary; but after a little persuasion from Frank's new wife, that changed.

"Tell the court how that change came about," Prosecutor Ging said.

Beatty cleared his throat and fidgeted with the knot in his tie. "Back in March of 1921, Mrs. Carl came to me and asked if the beneficiary on her husband's policy could be changed."

"And," Ging gently prodded, "could it?"

"Yes," Beatty said, "but I told Mrs. Carl that Frank's consent and signature were necessary."

"Did Frank agree to that?" Ging asked.

Beatty nodded with a sigh. "A few days later," he explained, "Frank and Clara came to see me. And yes, he signed the application, but not without complaining that he guessed he had to."

For the next several days, Beatty said, while the transfer of the policy was under consideration by the head officers at Rock Island, Illinois, Clara visited him every single day and frequently phoned him.

"Mrs. Carl appeared very anxious to have the policy changed," Beatty testified.

"Again, this happened when?" Ging prompted.

"March of '21," Beatty repeated.

The timing was paramount, as the defense no doubt noted, considering that Alonzo moved in with his son and daughter-in-law in April, and in June, he died.

Until the fourth day of the trial, May 25, neither side had referenced the deaths of Alonzo Carl or Robert Gibson. The state's attempt to introduce evidence about their deaths resulted in a fiery objection from the defense. With that, Judge Blair ordered the jury to vacate the room. He then asked Prosecutor Ging to explain how he would present the similarities of the three deaths.

After a short break, the judge announced his ruling on the defense team's objection. He warned the prosecution that unless it could connect the defendant to the death of Alonzo, he would instruct the jury to ignore all testimony related to him. In addition, because Robert Gibson's death was separate from the deaths of Frank and Alonzo Carl, the court would not allow testimony about Gibson.

According to the May 25, 1922, *Indianapolis News*, the ruling was not a hard blow to the state, and as Ging told the paper, "The testimony concerning the death of Alonzo Carl will not materially strengthen the case against Clara Carl."

However, that did not deter the prosecution from calling William McAbee back to the stand two days later. That time, he testified that 27.75 grains of arsenic had been found in the vital organs of the senior Carl. "With 27.75 grains," McAfee said, "the jury in this case could be killed and there would be enough left over for the judge."

The *Rushville Republican* called McAfee's testimony, "One of the most damaging bits of evidence against the alleged feminine Bluebeard."

The state wrapped up its case shortly after.

Defense Rolls the Dice

Clara's team took charge on Monday, May 29, day seven of the trial, and began introducing evidence intended to prove her innocence. The *Rushville*

Republican called it "the dice of fate."

Going in, their strategy had been to show that Clara was not responsible for the arsenic found in the intestines of Frank Carl, nor in those of Alonzo Carl or Robert Gibson. Unfortunately for Clara, the prosecution had out-strategized the defense by having already introduced evidence showing that not only had she possessed sufficient arsenic at the time of Frank's death, she also had the motive and means to administer it.

The courtroom, filled almost to the point of suffocation, heard Clara's side of the case from her own lips on Thursday, June 1.

Taking the witness stand, Clara met the state's charges in a manner that suggested she had prepared well for the role she was playing in the greatest drama of her life. Her testimony was generously sprinkled with noncommittal answers, such as "I don't remember" and "I can't recall," when Prosecutor Bassett asked her to confirm damaging testimony about herself.

The trial dragged on for a few more hours as attorneys cross-examined character witnesses and bickered about Clara's loyalty to her dead second husband, although the state's evidence of Clara's guilt was solid.

During the prosecution's closing summary on Friday, June 2, Ging called Clara "a lady Bluebeard," "an arch demon," and "a degenerate murderess," as she listened with a hankie pressed over her face. But when Ging referred to her as a "latter-day Messalina," Clara peeked out from behind her handkerchief and wrinkled her brow, conveying the impression that she was unaware that Messalina, third wife of Roman Emperor Claudius, was known as the queen of deviant sexual indiscretions.

The defense followed, emphasizing the principle of reasonable doubt, while blaming Clara's arrest on Ging, whom they portrayed as an overzealous, ambitious prosecuting attorney. Clara broke down in loud sobs as her attorney bellowed, "Whether Mrs. Carl is guilty or innocent, she is a woman entitled to decent treatment, which she did not receive from Prosecutor Ging."

Bassett made the final plea for the state in a "quiet and easy manner," according to the *Hancock Democrat*. He accused Clara of committing murder out of a lust for money. He urged the jury to find her guilty of murder in the first degree but did not ask for the death penalty. However, as the paper explained, "Mr. Bassett said, 'If you men feel that you are justified in rendering the death penalty, you should not hesitate to do so.'"

Before handing the case over to the jury, Judge Blair instructed, "If you believe beyond a reasonable doubt that the defendant purposely killed

Hancock County Prosecutor Waldo Ging was only thirty years old when he prosecuted Clara Carl's case. His success earned high praise from the legal community throughout Indiana. Although he had a bright future in elected office, when he finished his term at the end of 1924, Ging resumed his Greenfield-based private practice of Ging, Free, and Brand.

Frank Carl with a wickedness or depravity of heart toward the deceased, and the killing was determined beforehand—even a moment before the fatal act was done—then the defendant is guilty of murder in the first degree."

Life for Death

The case went to the jury at 4:11 p.m. Friday, and the jurymen spent the night deliberating. At 7:30 a.m. Saturday, the foreman sent word to the court that a verdict had been reached. Within the hour, Shelby County Sheriff Ray Sexton escorted Clara into the courtroom to learn her fate. Although her attorneys had tried their best to dismantle the state's case, they ultimately failed. In the end, the prosecution prevailed. Clara was found guilty of murder in the second degree and sentenced to life in prison.

The *Indiana Daily Times* wrote that upon hearing the verdict, Clara suddenly turned white and fell back, nearly tumbling out of her chair. She appeared dazed and required the assistance of the sheriff's wife as they departed the courtroom. Back in the comfort of her cell, she teetered on the edge of hysteria, demanding constant attention.

The *Indianapolis News* reported that no previous Indiana case had presented a stronger line of circumstantial evidence, which was one reason Clara's attorneys filed a motion for a new trial. The request was denied, and Clara was transported to the Indiana Women's Prison in Indianapolis on June 12, 1922.

Leapin' Liberty

A few weeks later, the *Greenfield Daily Reporter* let their readers know that Clara had settled into prison as a dressmaker and was being touted as "a model prisoner." Clara next made news in November, when the *Indianapolis News* reported that she would attempt to obtain a complete pardon. According to the *News*, the citizens of Hancock County found the notion "cause for indignation." The story also quoted Prosecutor Ging, who pledged, "I will never approve of any proposition to have Mrs. Carl released from prison, either by parole or pardon."

More than three years passed without further newspaper stories reminding Hancock County of its "female Bluebeard." That changed on October 3, 1925, the evening Clara shinnied up a wooden plank propped against the eight-foot prison wall and jumped to freedom. For the next week, she made banner headlines throughout Indiana and much of the nation.

She had been a trusty, which earned her the enviable task of feeding the prison chickens. On the day she scaled the prison wall, Clara had been feeding chickens with another prisoner, Nellie Collins, who was also serving a life term for poisoning her husband. Although Mrs. Collins did not witness the escape, she reported it to a prison officer once she realized Clara was missing.

Greenfield officials feared Clara would head home to fulfill her promise to harm the county prosecutor. Instead, bypassing her old homestead, she thumbed rides, rode traction cars, and hiked halfway across Ohio to link up with her sister in Columbus. It was there on the evening of Saturday, October 10 that two Columbus police officers noticed a disheveled woman walking through the Interurban station. One of them picked up a newspaper and saw Clara's photo on the front page.

"We want you, Clara," one of the officers told her as they approached.

"I knew you'd get me," she said, "but I thought if I tried, I might have been able to get away before you could pick me up."

Clara was returned to the Indiana Women's Prison the next day. "She was extremely tired and worn out," said a prison spokesperson. "In addition, her feet were cracked and bleeding, and she was hardly able to walk." As punishment, she permanently lost her trusty status, and for three months, she lost liberties, such as letter writing, receiving visitors, and socializing with prisoners.

Nine years went by before Clara's name again appeared in newsprint. It was March 22, 1934, when a few Indiana newspapers reported that a petition for Clara's clemency had been denied by the state clemency commission. A large part of the commission's decision was due to Waldo Ging's refusal to recommend clemency.

Epilogue

Thirty-year-old Ging reaped high praise from throughout Hancock County for his success in the Carl case, the *Indiana Daily Times* calling it "one of the strongest circumstantial cases in the history of the state." And as the *Hancock Democrat* opined, "Mr. Ging has proven himself a capable lawyer, an efficient officer, anxious to serve the people, and with it all, he is a very sincere young man." After completing his four-year term as prosecutor at the conclusion of 1924, Ging did not seek re-election, choosing to return to private practice. He died in Greenfield in 1971 at age seventy-nine.

As for Clara, her persistence ultimately paid off. At age fifty-six, she was in declining health, and although she had served only fifteen years of her life sentence, on May 26, 1937, Indiana Governor M. Clifford Townsend granted her parole. She was released a few days later.

Indiana's "female Bluebeard" died on March 3, 1962, in Canton, Ohio, at the age of eighty-five. How Clara Green Gibson Carl spent the twenty-five years between her release from prison and her death remain a mystery. ❖

20

CORNBREAD TO DEATHBED: THE DELICIOUS REVENGE OF NELLIE COLLINS

DATELINE: WHITE COUNTY, 1924

Nellie and Aaron Collins of Monticello had been married for thirty-two miserable years, and Nellie was sick and tired of her husband's angry outbursts, name calling, physical abuse, and perpetually hateful disposition. She would have left him years before, but because of his bad heart, she resolved to simply wait it out. She would have, too, had it not been for two recent developments—a kind offer from a male acquaintance and another harsh beating from Aaron. Consequently, for her husband's noon dinner on Thursday, March 6, 1924, Nellie carefully prepared his favorite meal: steak, gravy, and a pan of cornbread seasoned with arsenic. By five o'clock the next morning, Aaron was dead. And Nellie was free. But not for long.

A Rapid Decline
Sixty-two year-old Aaron Collins had been working his job as Monticello's park custodian on that fateful Thursday. At around 10:30 a.m., he came home for dinner, and Nellie, age fifty-two, surprised him with a fresh pan of the cornbread he was so fond of. She had been feeling out of sorts and went to bed, leaving Aaron to scarf down his meal alone. He had barely finished, when he called out to her for help. He told her his stomach was on fire and hurt like the devil.

Nellie summoned the family doctor, Homer B. Gable. Upon his arrival,

After thirty-two years of marriage to a cruel, abusive man, Nellie Collins wanted out. So, on March 6, 1924, she whipped up a pan of tasty cornbread, seasoned it generously with arsenic, and served it to her husband with his noon dinner. His death was the solution to one problem, but it opened the cupboard door to many new ones.

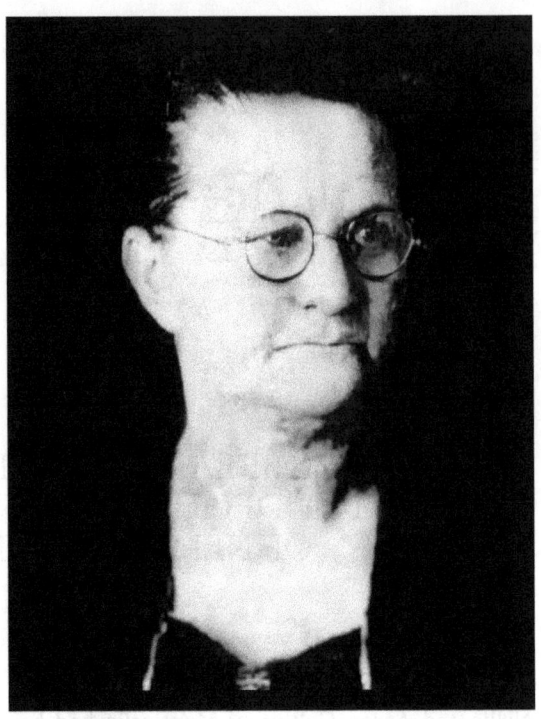

he found Aaron stretched out on the living room sofa writhing in pain.

"I've been sick before," he told the doctor, "but I've never had anything like this. I don't think I can live through it."

Suspecting that Aaron had ingested some sort of toxic substance, Gable administered a stomach wash of mustard water. Aaron felt better within minutes and complained to Gable that his wife's cornbread had tasted bitter.

"I knew it as soon as I ate the first bite," he lamented.

Aaron appeared to be out of danger, so Gable packed his doctor's bag and returned to his office. Responding to a request from Nellie that evening, the doctor visited Aaron again. His pulse was weak, and Nellie said he had vomited a great deal of blood. Alarmed by Aaron's deteriorated condition, Gable treated him as best he could and went home, only to return at three o'clock Friday morning.

By then, Aaron was barely conscious, his breathing shallow. Mustering his dwindling strength, he whispered, "Doc, am I going to get well?" Gable shook his head. "I'm sorry, Aaron," he said, "but it's doubtful." Aaron groaned. His eyelids closed. "Everything is turning dark," he mumbled, barely audible.

Within seconds, he lapsed into a deep sleep from which he never woke.

During those final hours, a number of concerned neighbors dropped in to show Nellie their support. A few quietly confirmed Gable's suspicion of foul play, and at least one advised him of Nellie's adulterous affair with a man from Northern Indiana. Accordingly, Gable notified the coroner and recommended an autopsy.

Led a Dog's Life

White County Coroner H.L. Miller, with the assistance of doctors Guy R. Coffin and Howard Turner, performed the autopsy later that Friday and sent portions of Aaron Collins's liver, kidneys, and stomach to the State Board of Health in Indianapolis. At noon Sunday, March 9, the state board informed the coroner that Aaron's liver had contained "enough arsenic to kill several men." Aaron was buried that afternoon, and Nellie was arrested shortly after.

At the Monticello city jail, Sheriff Clark Myers confronted Nellie with the State Board of Health's findings and suggested she explain how arsenic had entered her husband's body. Nellie assured Myers she didn't know. She maintained her innocence of wrongdoing for hours, until Coroner Miller stepped in and pleaded with her to free herself of the burden and tell the truth. With that, Nellie began to tremble and through her quivering lips, cried out, "All right! Yes, I did it! I poisoned him!"

Once she started to talk, the truth flowed as she laid out the entire murder scenario in concise, graphic detail.

"I made a pan of cornbread for Aaron," she said, "and added about a half-teaspoon of the white powder to the ingredients. I baked the cornbread and gave it to him for his noonday meal."

When the sheriff asked why she did it, Nellie explained, "Because he treated me very cruelly, and because a Mr. Clarence Bell of Indiana Harbor told me that if I came to him, he would always be kind and would provide for me."

As she spoke, the prosecutor's stenographer scribbled down her words in shorthand. The notes were immediately transcribed and typed up as a written confession, which Nellie signed. She was then charged.

A restful night's sleep in her jail cell restored Nellie's composure. When she awoke Monday morning, she spoke far more calmly about the murder. She told the sheriff she had led a dog's life. Her husband had abused her for years, often struck her, and threatened many times to kill her. He had a gun, and she feared he would use it on her. She felt that killing him was her only way out.

With regard to Clarence Bell, whom authorities suspected had influenced Nellie's murderous act, she had met him the previous year at a Lafayette hospital, where her son was being treated for an injury.

"Mr. Bell had been very kind to my son," she told Sheriff Myers, "and always courteous to me. He told me if I decided to leave my husband, he would help me find work in Indiana Harbor. It was an offer I couldn't refuse."

Nellie confirmed Bell had written her letters, but emphasized they were quite proper. In fact, she said, the letters were so proper, she had allowed her children to read them.

The White County Grand Jury convened Monday afternoon to launch an investigation. The *Evening Journal* reported that the jury questioned "a large number of witnesses." Many Monticello residents insisted that the grand jury give Nellie "a square deal," and several neighbors disclosed they had first-hand knowledge of the physical brutality Aaron had inflicted on her. One neighbor, in particular, testified that Nellie had come to his home seeking protection on six occasions. Nevertheless, the grand jury recognized that murder is never an answer, and on Friday, March 14, it indicted Nellie Collins for first-degree murder.

Arrest and Relaxation

Nellie was arraigned the next day by Circuit Court Judge Benjamin F. Carr. George Kassabaum, her attorney, proclaimed that when the act was committed, his client was of unsound mind and, therefore, not guilty.

When Carr asked for Nellie's plea, she responded simply and firmly, "Not guilty, Your Honor." The judge set the trial for early May.

Following the arraignment, Nellie gathered her belongings, bid her friends at the city jail goodbye, and was transported to the Cass County jail in Logansport to await her trial.

According to the *Indianapolis Star*, never had an alleged murderer amassed more sympathy than Nellie Collins. During her confinement at the Monticello jail, the staff had elevated her to a favorite-aunt status. In fact, Monticello Police Chief Orville Rothrock was so certain she would not try to escape, he declined to lock her cell. Nellie appreciated the stress-free change of pace and told the *Star*'s reporter, "I've had more peace and pleasure right here in this jail in the last few days than I ever had in my thirty-two years of married life."

The *Star* described Nellie as a stout woman with a pleasant, round face and "very blue eyes" that observed the world through a pair of old-fashioned spectacles. "She looks exactly like the pictures of mothers in the movies or on the covers of those 'mother songs,'" the *Star* wrote, elucidating, "but her hair is hardly gray at all."

Even while incarcerated at the Cass County jail, Nellie maintained a connection with her Monticello supporters. Her letter to them appeared on page one of the March 20 *Monticello Evening Journal*. It started:

> Just a line or two to let my Monticello friends know that I am well and happy and enjoying life more than I have in the last thirty-two years, even confined in my cell in the Cass County jail. Mr. Bowyer, the sheriff, and Mr. Vaughn, the manager, are very kind to me.

And on it went, reassuring her perceived followers that she was content and hopeful, and asking for letters from home, copies of the *Evening Journal*, and books. The *Journal* printed another letter from Nellie on April 12. In it, she noted that her jail cell door was never locked, and she was spending a good part of her time cooking, cleaning, washing, and ironing. She asked the readers to remember her in their prayers, and she signed off, "I am still your friend, Mrs. Nellie Collins."

In less than a month, Nellie would be back in Monticello, fighting for her freedom in a White County courtroom.

Court in Session
Judge Carr called the court to order at 9:00 a.m. Monday, May 12, 1924. George Kassabaum and Ralph McClurg represented Nellie, while White County Prosecutor Glenn R. Slenker and Special Deputy Prosecutor John A. Rothrock represented the state.

Slenker made the opening statement, explaining in detail what the state expected to prove, and aligning the facts of the case with the findings of the autopsy and the defendant's confession.

For the defense, Kassabaum pledged to prove beyond a reasonable doubt that Nellie Collins was not guilty. Because her husband's emotional and physical abuse had pushed her to the point of distraction, on the day the crime was committed, the attorney claimed, she was distraught beyond the point of sanity. He followed with a list of Aaron Collins's worst abusive acts.

"The defense will prove," Kassabaum said, "that one of the favorite diversions of Aaron Collins was to sit down and whet a butcher knife, saying grimly to his wife, 'I'm going to cut your throat with this.'"

Slenker's first witness for the state was Dr. Gable, who testified to Aaron Collins's deterioration from the first house call the afternoon of March 6 until his death at around five o'clock the next morning. Recalling that Collins had complained about the cornbread, Gable said when he asked Mrs. Collins what she had done with it, she told him she burned it. Consequently, the doctor refused to sign the death certificate.

"And why was that?" asked Slenker.

"Because I thought Mr. Collins died under peculiar circumstances," Gable replied, "and in fairness and justice to Mrs. Collins, a complete investigation should be made."

Kids Say the Darndest Things
Four of Nettie's seven children were next called as witnesses. First among them was twenty-seven-year-old Fred, who recalled hearing his mother say she'd like to kill her husband. He denied taking her seriously until March 9, when she told him, "Yes, I did it, but I was driven to it." The next witness was twenty-year-old Myrtle Collins Mullendore, who told of a letter she had read. It was to her mother from Clarence Bell promising to care for her if she would come to Hammond. It was signed, "Goodbye, darling, your true friend." Also helpful to the prosecution's case, Myrtle said her mother told her that she had indeed poisoned the cornbread. Goldie, age seventeen, followed her sister on the stand and testified, "Mother said she didn't know what she was doing when she did it." And the last Collins kid to inadvertently persecute their mother was thirty-one-year-old Harry. He stated his mother had divulged to him, too, that she poisoned his father but didn't know whether she could get by with it.

The defense waived cross-examination of each of the Collins children. Perhaps, they were deferring to the wishes of their client.

Doctors Coffin and Turner next took a turn on the witness stand. Each spoke of the autopsy they conducted and what it revealed.

The trial continued into the evening and concluded with the testimony of Coroner Miller. In addition to explaining the findings received from the state chemist's office, Miller told of conversations he and Nellie had shared concerning the abuse she suffered from her husband. He said Nellie also spoke of a man in Northern Indiana who had written to her twice and whom she intended to see again.

The next morning, Tuesday, May 13, the state called James Boze, Nellie's brother-in-law. Boze testified that Nellie had told him about a rendezvous with Clarence Bell of Indiana Harbor on Decoration Day at the Perrigo Hotel in Monticello. Until Boze took the stand, Nellie had maintained a strikingly calm demeanor. But the unsavory insinuations drawn from Boze's story rattled her equilibrium. Her eyes grew watery, and she put her hand to her mouth to stifle her sobs.

Busted

Moments after Boze stepped away from the stand, Kassabaum and McClurg conferred with their client. Her brother-in-law's testimony had taken them by surprise, as Nellie had assured them that her friendship with Clarence Bell had been purely platonic. The attorneys then asked Judge Carr for a recess until the afternoon. When court resumed at two-thirty, they made a motion to have the trial withdrawn from the jury and changed Nellie's plea to guilty.

Awaiting her sentence, Nellie displayed her customary poise and dignity with her arms folded across her chest and staring straight ahead. Only her quick breathing and the jiggling of her foot betrayed her anxiety.

Silence echoed throughout the crowded courtroom as Judge Carr pronounced Nellie's sentence: life in the Indiana Women's Prison. Immediately, Nellie's friends surrounded her, embracing her, wishing her well, and telling her goodbye. She remained unruffled and assured them that admitting her guilt "was the best thing to do."

The next day, Wednesday, May 14, Nellie, Sheriff Myers, and jail attendant Martha Ward boarded the noon train bound for Indianapolis. Only Nellie's children, Goldie and Harry, came to the depot to bid her farewell. Despite leaving her life behind, Nellie maintained her signature composure, and as the *Evening Journal* noted, "The imperturbable calm, which has made [Nellie Collins] one of the most extraordinary characters in the history of the county, continued to the end. She boarded the train without shedding a tear."

Epilogue

Nellie Collins walked through the doors of the women's prison without a backward glance, and for the next seventeen months, no newspaper spent a single drop of ink on her. When Nellie's name next appeared in newsprint, it was in connection with fellow inmate Clara Carl's escape.

The October 6, 1925, edition of Monticello's *Evening Journal* reported that Nellie had "played a leading part in attempting to thwart the escape." Carl, a trusty serving a life sentence for poisoning her husband, had been feeding chickens with Nellie inside a walled enclosure on the facility's grounds. The two engaged in one brief conversation about their incarceration, according to the *Journal*. Carl had told Nellie, "You know I have no business being here," and Nellie responded, "I don't belong here either, but I am, and I can't help it."

Carl covertly moved on to the lower end of the yard, and when no one was looking, she climbed over the prison wall and bolted. Once Nellie realized Clara was gone, she reported her companion's disappearance to a guard. While Nellie's admirable, quick action prompted officials to launch a timely search for the escapee, it garnered no reward for Nellie.

However, on May 31, 1939—with the recommendations of Benjamin F. Carr, the judge at Nellie's murder trial, and Marion Gallup, head of the Indiana Women's Prison—Indiana Governor M. Clifford Townsend granted Nellie's parole. Thus, at the age of sixty-six, she returned to her Monticello home on South Maple Street to quietly live out the balance of her life and ponder what might have been had she not opened that bottle of arsenic.

Five years later, the love and happiness Nellie had longed for came calling in the embodiment of seventy-one-year-old Monticello widower William Greer, and the two married September 2, 1944. The Greers were joyfully inseparable until February 20, 1950, when William's heart gave out, again making Nellie a widow. This time, however, her cornbread was not to blame. William was buried in Monticello's Riverview Cemetery. In October of 1955, Nellie joined him. ❖

BIBLIOGRAPHY

PART 1: VICTIMS / WOMEN
Chapter 1—Dorothy Poore: The Girl in the Dresser Drawer

"Girl's Body Found in Hotel." *The Indianapolis Star.* July 19, 1954.
"Fine Girl Had Reason to Fear City." *The Indianapolis Star.* July 19, 1954.
"Body of Local Teen Is Found in Indianapolis Hotel–Police Search for Missing Man in Case." *The Daily Clintonian.* July 19, 1954
"3 Identify Killer Suspect: 2 at Hotel and Cabbie Pick Photo." *The Indianapolis Star.* July 20, 1954
"Dorothy Poore Not a Playgirl, Claim Two Detectives Today." *The Daily Clintonian.* July 21, 1954.
"Slayer of Girl Confesses." *The Indianapolis Star.* July 24, 1954.
"Police Hold Lively's Boss for Questioning in Murder." *The Indianapolis Star.* July 26, 1954.
"Dresser Drawer Killer Is Charged with First Degree Murder Today." *The Daily Clintonian.* August 12, 1954.
"Lively Attorney Plans 'Hushing' of Confessions." *The Indianapolis Star.* August 20, 1954.
"Lively Plea Hearing Set." *The Terre Haute Tribune.* August 26, 1954.
"'Ruth' Sought Anew in Hotel Slaying–Called Key Witness in Lively Case." *The Indianapolis Star.* August 30, 1954.
"Lively Murder Trial Set to Start Oct. 11." *The Terre Haute Tribune.* September 3, 1954.
"Lively Trial Is Postponed." *The Indianapolis News.* October 6, 1954.
"Lively Jury Panel Called for Monday." *The Indianapolis News.* November 13, 1954.
"The Trial Finally Starts." *The Indianapolis Star.* November 16, 1954.
"Maid Tells of Finding Girl's Body in Drawer." *The Indianapolis News.* November 22, 1954.
"Expert Gives Story of Dorothy's Death–Pathologist Says Victim Suffocated." *The Indianapolis Star.* November 23, 1954.
"Lively Jury Hears 'Sex Slaying' Story." *The Indianapolis Star.* November 27, 1954.

"'We Made Love and I Blacked Out'–Lively Said." *The Indianapolis News*. November 30, 1954.

"State Rips Holes into Lively Story of 'Gin Stupor' While Dorothy Died." *The Indianapolis Star*. December 1, 1954.

"Murder Trial of Victor Lively Ends Today, State Rests Its Case." *The Commercial-Mail* (Columbia City). December 1, 1954.

"Jury out More Than Nine Hours." *The Indianapolis Star*. December 2, 1954.

"Life Term Brings Smile to Lively." *The Indianapolis News*. December 2, 1954.

"Lively Taken to Prison at Michigan City." *The Indianapolis News*. December 3, 1954.

"Dresser Drawer Slayer Seeking to Gain Release." *The Indianapolis Star*. April 23, 1977.

Periodical

Eddie Krell. "I Know I'll Burn." *Front Page Detective*. November 1954, 23.

Chapter 2—The Case of the 'Flaming Youth' Murder

"Youth to Be Charged with Murder of Girl, 20, Near Camp, Prosecutor Asserts." *The Evansville Journal*. October 16, 1933.

"Youth Is Accused in Fatal Shooting of Girl After Dance." *The Evansville Press*. October 15, 1933.

"Staab Charged with Murder as New Shooting Facts Are Found." *The Evansville Press*. October 17, 1933.

"Funeral Is Held for Mary Elizabeth Robb." *The Evansville Press*. October 17, 1933.

"Seek Clues to Motive in Girl's Death." *The Evansville Press*. October 18, 1933.

"Indicted in Death at Tourist Camp." *The Indianapolis News*. November 2, 1933.

"Jury Started in Staab Trial." *The Evansville Press*. January 3, 1934.

"Whoopie Party Details Told by Beulah Bender." *The Evansville Journal*. January 5, 1934.

"Story of Fatal Party Is Told to Staab Trial Jury." *The Evansville Press*. January 5, 1934.

"State Seeks to Show Staab Had Used Gun Against Another Girl." *The Evansville Press*. January 6, 1934.

"Judge Balks Attempt of Defense to Attack Miss Robb's Character." *The Evansville Journal*. January 8, 1934.

"Defense Tries to Show That Miss Robb Fired Fatal Shot." *The Evansville Press*. January 9, 1934.

"Staab 'Fiend' or 'Scared Child.'" *The Evansville Journal*. January 10, 1934.

"Staab Case Goes to Jury." *The Evansville Journal EXTRA*. January 10, 1934.

"Staab Is Found Guilty in Death." *The Indianapolis Star*. January 11, 1934.

"Staab, Facing Life Term, Will Ask for New Trial." *The Evansville Journal*. January 11, 1934.

"Staab Unmoved as Life Sentence Is Read to Him." *The Evansville Courier*. January 12, 1934.

"Life Term Prisoner Release on Parole." *The Evansville Courier*. January 24, 1945.

Chapter 3—The Bloomfield Slasher

"Tragedy at Bloomfield: Dr. Ed Gray Stabs His Paramour to Death at Noon To-day." *The Daily Mail* (Bedford). December 29, 1898.

"A Bad Knife at Hands of a Vicious, Jealous Surgeon Takes a Girl's Life." *The Bloomfield News*. December 30, 1898.

"Indiana Mob Foiled–Dr. Gray Secretly Taken From Bloomfield to the State Reformatory." *The Fort Wayne News*. December 31, 1898.
"To Plead Insanity: Murderer Gray Preparing for His Defense at the Trial, Which Begins in February." *The Daily Mail*. January 2, 1899.
"Bold Crime Was the Wilful, Premeditated Murder of Melissa Skinner." *The Bloomfield News*. January 6, 1899.
"Will He Hang? Further Particulars of the Murder of Melissa Skinner by Dr. E.E. Gray." *The Bedford Weekly Mail*. January 13, 1899.
"Insanity Plea: Line of Defense in Behalf of a Murderer–Defendant Will Be Arraigned for Trial on Monday in the Green Circuit Court." *Logansport Daily Journal*. May 4, 1899.
"Dr. E.E. Gray, Murderer, Trial to Begin Monday." *The Indianapolis Journal*. May 6, 1899.
"Dr. E.E. Gray on Trial." *Muncie Daily Herald*. May 8, 1899.
"Evidence Against Dr. Gray: The Bloomfield Murder Case Is Now Fairly Started." *The Indianapolis Journal*. May 11, 1899.
"Gray Trial." *The Bloomfield News*. May 12, 1899.
"Dr. Gray's Defense." *The Argos Reflector*. May 18, 1899.
"Gray Trial." *The Bloomfield News*. May 19, 1899.
"Trial of Dr. Gray for Murder of Malissa Skinner Goes to Bloomfield Jury To-Day." *The Indianapolis Journal*. May 20, 1899.
"Gets Life Sentence" Jury Finds Dr. Gray Guilty of Murdering Mrs. Skinner at Bloomfield." *The Seymour Daily Republican*. May 22, 1899.
"Five Murderers Paroled by Gov. Marshall Monday on Recommendation of Board of Pardons." *The Bedford Daily Mail*. July 13, 1909.
"Slayer of Paramour Is Freed by Ralston: Bloomfield Physician Paroled, but His Petition to Go West Is Denied." *The Indianapolis Star*. July 19, 1913.

Chapter 4—Murder at the Lafayette Street Rooming House

"Winchester Girl Is Thought Slain." *Muncie Evening Press*. October 13, 1938.
"Suspect Held in Girl's Death." *The Muncie Morning Star*. October 14, 1938.
"Confesses to Slaying Girl in Ft. Wayne." *The Vidette-Messenger* (Porter County). October 14, 1938.
"Pleas of Insanity Prepared for Slayer of Indiana Girl." *The South Bend Tribune*. October 16, 1938.
"Miller Plans Insanity Plea, Hoping to Escape Death." *The Muncie Sunday Star*. October 16, 1938.
"Man Indicted in Girl's Death." *The Muncie Morning Star*. November 11, 1938.
"State to Ask for Death Chair for Miller." *The Times-Gazette* (Union City). May 3, 1939.
"Trial Opened in Girton Case." *The Muncie Morning Star*. May 2, 1939.
"Girton Case May Go to Jury by Noon." *The Times-Gazette* (Union City). May 6, 1939.
"Sex Murderer Is Sentenced to Die in Electric Chair on August 16." *The Times-Gazette*. May 8, 1939.
"Miller Pays for Murder of Alice Girton with Life." *The Times-Gazette*. August 16, 1939.

Chapter 5—Bushwhacked on Bittersweet Road

"Girl, 16, Slain in Mystery." *The South Bend Tribune*. October 13, 1937.
"Slain Girl's Fiancé Freed–Sheriff Says Stopper Has Told Truth." *The South Bend Tribune*. October 14, 1937.

"Hundreds Go to Rites for Melba Moore." *The South Bend Tribune*. October 15, 1937.
"Moore Death Probe Turns to Elkhart." *The South Bend Tribune*. October 16, 1937.
"Wife Slayer Held in Melba Moore Murder." *The South Bend Tribune*. October 19, 1937.
"Sheriff Releases Dr. Owen." *The South Bend Tribune*. October 21, 1937.
"Murder Probe Begins Anew." *The South Bend Tribune*. October 22, 1937.
"Moore Slaying Probe Is Again Near Dead End." *The South Bend Tribune*. October 24, 1937.
"Moore Verdict Stays Unsolved." *The South Bend Tribune*. November 16, 1937.
"Murder Will Out 41 Times out of 47, City Finds in Gory 10-Year Period Tragic Anniversary." *The South Bend Tribune*. October 12, 1947.

Chapter 6—A Bullet for Tacie Mang

"Grant County Youth Slays His Sweetheart." *The Indianapolis Journal*. September 25, 1897.
"Indicted for Murder." *The Logansport Journal*. September 28, 1897.
"Was Ready for the Mob." *The Indianapolis Journal*. September 28, 1897.
"Johnson Will Plead Insanity." *The Indianapolis Journal*. September 29, 1897.
"Shot His Sweetheart." *The Fairmount News*. October 1, 1897.
"Attorney Amsden Wants a Venire of 200 Men Summoned." *The Fairmount News*. December 31, 1897.
"For Killing a Woman." *The Indianapolis News*. January 3, 1898.
"Murderer Johnson: His Trial for the Killing of Miss Mang Begun." *The Logansport Journal*. January 7, 1898.
"Tacy's Bloody Clothing; The Gore-Stained Hat and Cape Wilted Young Johnson." *The Kokomo Daily Tribune*. January 14, 1898.
"Life Sentence Given Noah Johnson for Killing His Sweetheart." *The Logansport Journal*. January 21, 1898.
"Noah Johnson Dead in the Prison North." *The Muncie Morning Star*. January 31, 1903.

Chapter 7—The Deadly Affair of Nora Kifer

"Body of Young Woman with Stone About Neck Found in Creek." *The Evansville Courier*. May 24, 1900.
"Father Identifies Murdered Girl as Missing Nora Kifer." *The Evansville Courier*. May 25, 1900.
"Joseph Keith Arrested for Murder; His Young Son May Be Accomplice." *The Evansville Courier*. May 26, 1900.
"A Partial Confession." *The Indianapolis News*. May 28, 1900.
"J.D. Keith: Prisoner Charged with Murder of Miss Kifer." *Sunday Journal-News* (Evansville). June 3, 1900.
"Dead Girl's Hair & Slippers Found." *The Evansville Courier*. June 27, 1900.
"Hammer – The One Used to Kill Nora Is Found in Old Well." *The Evansville Journal*. June 29, 1900.
"Keith Taken to Warrick County." *The Evansville Courier*. July 7, 1900.
"Without Bond: Joseph Keith Is Held for Murder of Nora Kifer." *The Evansville Journal*. July 14, 1900.
"Keith Is Finally Indicted." *The Evansville Courier*. September 9, 1900.
"Keith Will Be Tried in Gibson County." *The Evansville Courier*. October 2, 1900.

"Keith Trial Is Under Way." *The Evansville Journal*. January 2, 1901.
"Will Keith's Wife Go on the Stand and Swear She Killed Nora Kifer?" *The Evansville Courier*. January 6, 1901.
"Joseph D. Keith Breaks the Long Silence; Declares He Is Not Guilty of Awful Charge." *The Evansville Courier*. January 9, 1901.
"Case Of Joseph Keith Will Go to Jury Late This Afternoon." *The Evansville Courier*. January 10, 1901.
"Joseph D. Keith Guilty of Murder; Penalty Is Fixed at Death." *The Evansville Journal*. January 12, 1901.
"Keith Is Condemned to Hang." *The Evansville Courier*. January 12, 1901.
"Keith Confesses Crime Before He Dies." *The Evansville Courier*. November 15, 1901.

Book
Garrison, C. Stanley. *The Keith Murder: The Horrible and Revolting Murder and Her Mysterious Disappearance*. Princeton Publishing Company. Princeton, Indiana. 1901.

Chapter 8—The Mysterious Murder of Madam X
"The Mutilated Body of a Woman Found in the Woods Near Terre Haute." *The Indianapolis Journal*. October 8, 1883.
"A Terrible Crime Unearthed in the River Bottoms–Remains of an Unknown Woman Found in a Lonely Ravine." *Terre Haute Weekly Gazette*. October 11, 1883.
"Mrs. Nelson's Mysterious Murder." *The Indianapolis Journal*. November 10, 1883.
"Susanna Nelson: A Woman Who Spent a Fortune in Debauchery after Fifty-eight Years of Age." *The Terre Haute Express*. November 11, 1883.
"The Nelson Murder: Jasper Nelson, Her Son, and Rev. Perry Manis Suspected." *The Indiana State Sentinel*. November 21, 1883.
"Reflections Caused by a Visit to the Spot Near St. Mary's." *Terre Haute Weekly Gazette*. November 29, 1883.
"Perry Manis Indicted." *The Indianapolis Journal*. December 14, 1883.
"The Murder Trial: The First Day's Proceedings in the Manis-Nelson Murder Case." *The Terre Haute Express*. January 25, 1884.
"Perry's Trouble: The Fourth Day of the Trial and the Prosecution Still Hammering Away." *The Terre Haute Express*. January 29, 1884.
"Convicted at Terre Haute." *The Evening Item* (Richmond). January 30, 1884.
"Perry Manis Agrees to Take a Life Sentence, and His Wishes Are Respected." *The Terre Haute Express*. January 30, 1884.
"Dead in Prison: Perry Manis, Who Murdered His Mistress in Cold Blood, Dies of Consumption." *The Indianapolis Journal*. May 15, 1887.

PART 2: VICTIMS / KIDS
Chapter 9—Little Girl Gone
"A Little Girl Is Missing." *The Fort Wayne Journal-Gazette*. July 3, 1901.
"Her Dead Body Found Floating in a Cistern." *The Fort Wayne Journal-Gazette*. July 8, 1901.
"Chas. Dunn Held For Murder." *The Fort Wayne Sentinel*. July 9, 1901.
"Charles Dunn Charged with Awful Crime." *Ft. Wayne Weekly Journal-Gazette*. July 11, 1901.

"Charles Dunn Held for Murder—Alice Cothrell Was Strangled." *The Fort Wayne Journal-Gazette*. July 14, 1901.

"Dunn Arraigned." *The Fort Wayne Sentinel*. September 25, 1901.

"Mother's Story: Mrs. Cothrell First Witness in Dunn Murder Trial." *The Indianapolis News*. October 24, 1901.

"State Plays Its Biggest Trump Against Charles Dunn." *The Fort Wayne Journal-Gazette*. October 30, 1901.

"State Rests." *The Fort Wayne News*. October 30, 1901.

"Denials Made by Dunn." *The Indianapolis News*. November 1, 1901.

"Sentenced for Life: Charles Dunn Found Guilty of Fiendish Child Murder." *The Fort Wayne News*. November 7, 1901.

"Dunn Is Taken Away." *The Fort Wayne News*. February 5, 1902.

"Dunn's Life Sentence Is Upheld on Appeal." *The Indianapolis News*. June 18, 1903.

"Dunn Verdict Is Again Reversed: Supreme Court for Second Time Sends Case Back for New Trial." *The Fort Wayne Sentinel*. June 8, 1906.

"Charles Dunn Is at Liberty." *The Fort Wayne News*. December 2, 1907.

"Dunn Murder Trial Monday." *The Fort Wayne Journal-Gazette*. December 6, 1908.

"Dunn Murder Case Ends, Prosecution Quits Fight." *The Muncie Morning Star*. December 17, 1909.

Chapter 10—The Private Hell of Harriet Dinkins

"Mother Kills 3 Children, Self." *Muncie Evening Press*. March 20, 1941.

"Four Die in Gas-Filled Room–Mother Finds Life Struggle Too Difficult." *The Muncie Morning Star*. March 21, 1941.

"Unable to Fight Life's Battles Any Longer, Mother Spares Her Children 'Hell on Earth.'" *The Kokomo Tribune*. March 21, 1941.

"To Bury Family from 'Friendly Little Church.'" *The Muncie Morning Star*. March 21, 1941.

"Pastor Speaks 'Kindly Words' at Rites for Dinkins Family." *The Muncie Sunday Star*. March 23, 1941.

"Burial to Mark Tragedy's Final Chapter Today." *The Muncie Morning Star*. March 24, 1941.

"Mother Rests in Final Peace; Estranged Father Attends Burial of Little Family." *The Muncie Morning Star*. March 25, 1941.

"Husband Tried to Aid Family, Story Reveals." *Muncie Evening Press*. March 25, 1941.

Chapter 11—Pandemonium at William Reed Elementary School

"Principal Slays 2 School Teachers." *The Indianapolis News*. February 2, 1960.

"Hartford City Classroom Slayer Ends Life with Murder Weapon." *The Muncie Star*. February 3, 1960.

"Gossip Blamed in Slaying, Suicide." *The Tipton Daily Tribune*. February 3, 1960.

"Classes Resume in Hartford City." *The Tipton Daily Tribune*. February 4, 1960.

"School Holds Nightmares for Hartford City Children." *The Evansville Press*. February 4, 1960.

"Hartford City Aftermath–Absence of Principal, Teachers to Be Treated as Normal Event." *The Alexandria Times-Tribune*. February 4, 1960.

"Horrified Pupils Get Comfort from Pastor–Children Return to Teacher Death Scene."

The Indianapolis News. February 4, 1960.
"What Led Up to Shooting of Hartford City Teachers?" *The Pharos Tribune and Logansport Press.* February 7, 1960.
"But Nobody Heard Him." *The Hammond Times.* February 9, 1960.
"Building Was Location of 1960 Double Slaying." *The Star Press.* February 6, 2015.

PART 3: KILLERS / KIDS
Chapter 12—When Murder Is Child's Play

"Boy, Age Nine, Is Held on Charge of Murder." *The Indianapolis News.* June 3, 1922.
"Boy Murdered by Companion." *The Muncie Morning Star.* June 3, 1922.
"Boy Slayer May Prove a Puzzle to Authorities." *The Muncie Evening Press.* June 3, 1922.
"Portland Boy Held on Murder Charge." *The Huntington Press.* June 4, 1922.
"Youth Gets Two to 21 Years for Killing Boy." *The Indianapolis Star.* June 4, 1922.
"Youthful Slayer to Be Taken to Boys' School." *The Indianapolis News.* June 5, 1922.
"Law Keeps Youthful Slayer from Prison, Though He Is Guilty." *Indiana Daily Times,* June 7, 1922.
"Silvers Boy Will Go to Plainfield." *The Indianapolis News.* June 10, 1922.
"Conduct of Silvers Boy Is Commended." *The Muncie Morning Star.* July 14, 1922.
"Lad, 9, Goes Free as Xmas Present." *The Indianapolis Times.* December 20, 1922.
"Prisoner, Age Nine, Is Ordered Sent Home by Governor McCray." *The Indianapolis News.* December 20, 1922.
"Boy Governor Released Writes of Appreciation." *The Indianapolis Star.* December 28, 1922.
"Charges Faced by Three Daytonians." *The Herald* (Dayton, Ohio). May 11, 1934.
"Police Quiz Man on Burglaries." *Journal Herald* (Dayton, Ohio). July 30, 1953.
"Arrests Here Lead to Breaking Up of Statewide Ring." *The Evening Journal-Tribune* (Marysville, Ohio). July 30, 1953.
"Dayton Man Convicted in 'Lootless Job.'" *Dayton* (Ohio) *Daily News.* November 20, 1953.
"Judge Orders Sentence Be Carried Out." *Dayton Daily News.* November 26, 1954.
"Robert F. Silvers." *Dayton Daily News.* March 12, 1984.

Chapter 13—The Mother Goose Murder Trial

"Child Accidentally Killed." *The Marion Chronicle.* December 2, 1920.
"Jurors Indict Child for Capital Offence." *The South Bend Tribune.* January 27, 1921.
"Boy of 11 Is Facing Gallows; Can He Have a Fair Trial?" *The Richmond Item.* February 12, 1921.
"Boy's Fate Depends on Boys' Stories." *Twin Falls* (Idaho) *Daily Times.* March 3, 1921.
"State Demands Child Be Convicted of First Degree Murder." *The Richmond Item.* April 2, 1921.
"Boy May End His School Before He Faces Court on a Charge of Murder." *The Muncie Evening Press.* April 4, 1921.
"Mother Against Mother in Boy Murder Trial." *The Richmond Item.* April 26, 1921.
"11-Year-Old Boy Goes to Trial for Murder of Playmate." *The Indianapolis Times.* May 31, 1921.
"Says He Saw Burkett Shoot Playmate." *The Indianapolis News.* June 1, 1921.
"Cecil Burkett Sticks to His Story on Stand." *The Muncie Morning Star.* June 2, 1921.

"Jurymen Hold Fate of Young Cecil Burkett." *The South Bend Tribune*. June 2, 1921.
"Jury in Case of 11-Year-Old Cecil Burkett Fails to Reach a Verdict." *The Richmond Item*. June 3, 1921.
"Brother Sobs Boy Slaying Story." *Los Angeles* (California) *Evening Herald*. June 2, 1921.
"Tots Feature Murder Trial." *Seattle* (Washington) *Star*. June 2, 1921.
"State to Try Burkett Boy Second Time." *Lafayette Journal and Courier*. August 24, 1921.
"Judge Says Burkett Case Has Gone Far Enough." *The Indianapolis Times*. October 12, 1921.
"74-Year-Old Says He Never Thinks of 'Tragedy Time Forgot.' " *The Muncie Star*. October 9, 1984.
"Ora Man Says He Is Living Reason Not to Execute Youths." *The Indianapolis Star*. November 16, 1986.

Chapter 14—The Saga of Sororicide Charles Messel

"Kills Sister to Hide Terrible Crime He and His Father Committed." *Evansville Press*. February 3, 1911.
"Admits Killing Sister." *The Indianapolis Star*. February 4, 1911.
"Charles Messel Trial Will Begin on Friday." *Evansville Journal-News*. March 15, 1911.
"Shields Brother Up for Murder." *The Evansville Courier*. March 18, 1911.
"With Rifle Poised, Chas. Messel, in Witness Box, Shows the Jury How He Shot His Little Sister." *Evansville Journal-News*. March 18, 1911.
"Sealed Verdict to Be Read Monday Carries the Fate of Chas. Messel." *The Sunday Journal-News* (Evansville). March 18, 1911.
"Messel Guilty of Manslaughter; Attorney Appeals for a Parole." *Evansville Journal-News*. March 20, 1911.
"Will Take Boy into His Home." *The Evansville Courier*. March 21, 1911.
"Attorney Who Defended Boy Slayer to Be Father to Him." *Evansville Press*. March 21, 1911.
"Another Death Takes Place in Messel Family." *Evansville Press*. April 15, 1911.
"Young Slayer, Given Chance, Makes Good." *Evansville Press*. January 31, 1917.
"Governor Commutes Sentences for Five." *The Anderson Herald*. May 18, 1919.
"Local Deaths." *The Evansville Press*. December 30, 1970.

Chapter 15—Remembering Nellie Maynard, the Girl on Fire; and Rosie Perkins, the Girl Who Struck the Match

"Almost Incredible Story Comes From Alexandria." *The Elwood Call Leader*. December 7, 1904.
"Girl on Deathbed Explains Mystery." *The Muncie Morning Star*. December 7, 1904.
"Investigation Will Be Made Today." *Anderson Morning Herald*. December 8, 1904.
"Entire Family Is Now Under Arrest at Alexandria." *The Elwood Call Leader*. December 8, 1904.
"Coroner Trueblood Orders Fourteen-Year-Old Girl Held for Death of Nellie Maynard." *Anderson Morning Herald*. December 9, 1904.
"Girl Charged with Murder." *The Elwood Call Leader*. December 9, 1904.
"Perkins Girl Confessed." *The Elwood Call Leader*. December 10, 1904.
"Rosie Perkins Is Sentenced by Court." *Anderson Morning Herald*. December 14, 1904.

PART 4: KILLERS / WOMEN

Chapter 16—Rock-a-Bye-Bye, Baby: The Unspeakable Crime of Nora Mosher

"Infant's Death Caused by a Fracture of the Skull." *Evening Herald* (Huntington). May 2, 1907.
"Mother of Child to Be Held for Murder." *Daily News-Democrat* (Huntington). May 3, 1907.
"Mosher Placed in the County Jail." *Daily News-Democrat.* May 4, 1907.
"On a Murder Charge: Mrs. Nora Mosher Placed in County Jail." *Evening Herald.* May 18, 1907.
"Mosher Is on Trial for Murder of Babe." *Daily News-Democrat.* June 11, 1907.
"Divorced Husband on Witness Stand." *Daily News-Democrat.* June 12, 1907.
"Emery Mosher a Suicide." *Evening Herald.* June 13, 1907.
"Struck Her Own Baby." *Evening Herald.* June 13, 1907.
"The Evidence Ends in Mosher's Trial." *Daily News-Democrat.* June 14, 1907.
"Again in September: Mosher Gets New Trial Following Disagreement." *Evening Herald.* June 17, 1907.
"Mosher Is on Trial." *Evening Herald.* October 7, 1907.
"D.A. Mosher Jury Is Dismissed Sunday." *Daily News-Democrat.* October 14, 1907.
"Mosher Case Opens." *Evening Herald.* October 21, 1907.
"Third Day of Mosher Trial: Question of Insanity Before Jury in Case." *Daily News-Democrat.* October 23, 1907.
"Nora Mosher Guilty of Manslaughter." *Daily News-Democrat.* October 26, 1907.
"To Women's Prison." *Evening Herald.* November 9, 1907.
"Nora Mosher Goes to Women's Prison." *Daily News-Democrat.* November 13, 1907.
"D.A. Mosher's Third Trial." *Daily News-Democrat.* March 4, 1908.
"Mosher Is Freed by Jury Verdict." *Evening Herald.* March 28, 1908.
"Nora Mosher Is Now a Free Woman." *Evening Herald.* August 5, 1911.

Chapter 17—The Prosecution of Alice Lawson: 'The Human Icicle'

"Murder Motive Is Sought by Police." *Lafayette Daily Courier.* September 22, 1906.
"Woman Slayer Is Under Indictment." *Lafayette Daily Courier.* October 8, 1906.
"Trial of Mrs. Lawson." *Lafayette Daily Courier.* April 9, 1906.
"Alice C. Lawson's Trial Underway." *Lafayette Daily Courier.* April 15, 1907.
"Russell on Stand; Tells of Tragedy." *Lafayette Daily Courier.* April 19, 1907.
"Counsel Outlines Woman's Defense." *Lafayette Daily Courier.* April 24, 1907.
"Tells Life Story on Witness Stand." *Lafayette Daily Courier.* April 25, 1907.
"Woman Tells Why She Shot Husband." *Indianapolis Morning Star.* April 26, 1907.
"State Seeking to Trap Mrs. Lawson." *Lafayette Daily Courier.* April 26, 1907.
"Defense Rests in the Lawson Case." *Lafayette Daily Courier.* April 29, 1907.
"Defense Wants No Halfway Verdict." *Lafayette Daily Courier.* May 2, 1907.
"Mrs. Lawson to Go to Prison for Life." *Lafayette Daily Courier.* May 9, 1907.
"Mrs Lawson Freed by Board of Parole." *Lafayette Daily Courier.* October 8, 1910.
"Life Termer Who Killed Husband Is Given Pardon." *The Indianapolis Star.* December 12, 1914.

Chapter 18—The Glasgo Fiasco

"Ed Glasgo Is Shot Three Times on Left Side of Head." *Daily Times* (Brazil). September 5, 1907.
"Community Startled by a Terrible Tragedy." *Daily Times*. September 6, 1907.
"Woman Excites Pity." *The Indianapolis Star*. September 9, 1907.
"Mrs. Glasgo and Lawrence Smith Are Indicted." *The Indianapolis News*. October 19, 1907.
"Large Crowd Attends Opening Day of Rose Glasgo Trial." *Daily Times*. November 4, 1907.
"Court Room Packed to Hear Testimony." *Daily Times*. November 5, 1907.
"Mrs. Rose Glasgo Tells Own Story." *The Indianapolis News*. November 6, 1907.
"Is Acquitted: Mrs. Glasco Given Her Freedom in Short Order." *Daily Times*. November 7, 1907.
"Rose Glasgo a Nervous Wreck." *The Indianapolis News*. February 28, 1908.

Chapter 19—The Contemptible Crimes of Clara Carl: Indiana's Female Bluebeard

"R.M. Gibson Is Dead." *Greenfield Daily Reporter*. March 23, 1920.
"Death of Frank Carl." *Greenfield Daily Reporter*. August 8, 1921.
"Exhumation Is Asked." *The Hancock Democrat* (Greenfield). January 12, 1922.
"Frank Carl Had Case of Love at First Sight." *The Hiawatha* (Kansas) *Daily World*. January 12, 1922.
"Frank Carl Has $3,000 Woodman Insurance." *The Hiawatha Daily World*. January 13, 1922.
"Arrest Woman as Poisoner of Father-in-Law." *The Indianapolis Sunday Star*. January 29, 1922.
"Clara Gibson Carl Faces Second Charge." *The Muncie Morning Star*. January 31, 1922.
"Mrs. Clara Carl Arrested for Murder." *The Hancock Democrat*. February 2, 1922.
"Village Is Agitated by Murder Charge." *The Hancock Democrat*. February 9, 1922.
"Arsenic in Gibson's Stomach." *Greenfield Daily Reporter*. March 20, 1922.
"State Seeks to Prove Greenfield Woman Slayer of Three Unsuspecting Victims." *Indiana Daily Times* (Indianapolis). March 23, 1922.
"Sold Arsenic to Mrs. Carl." *Greenfield Daily Reporter*. May 23, 1922.
"Brother of Dead Man Takes Stand." *The Indianapolis News*. May 25, 1922.
"Defense Rests Its Case in Carl Trial." *The Indianapolis News*. June 1, 1922.
"Mrs. Carl Found Guilty of Murder." *Indiana Daily Times*. June 3, 1922.
"Shows No Emotion at Court's Ruling." *The Muncie Morning Star*. June 13, 1922.
"Attempt to Release Mrs. Carl Is Reported. *The Indianapolis News*. November 13, 1922.
"Murderess Breaks out of Prison." *The Indianapolis Times*. October 5, 1925.
"Clara Carl Captured, Report from Columbus, Ohio, Nabbed Waiting for a Traction Car." *The Indianapolis Sunday Star*. October 11, 1925.
"Clara Carl Is Given Parole." *The Greenfield Daily Reporter*. May 26, 1937.

Chapter 20—Cornbread to Deathbed: The Delicious Revenge of Nellie Collins

"Dies After a Few Hours Illness." *The Evening Journal* (Monticello). March 7, 1924.
"Mrs. Aaron Collins Confesses Having Poisoned Husband." *The Evening Journal*. March 10, 1924.

"Mrs. Nellie Collins Indicted Today on Murder Charge." *The Evening Journal.* March 14, 1924.
"Pleas Not Guilty and to Being of Unsound Mind." *The Evening Journal.* March 15, 1924.
"Jury Tentatively Accepted in Trial of Mrs. Collins." *The Evening Journal.* May 9, 1924.
"Introduction of Evidence Starts in Collins Case." *The Evening Journal.* May 12, 1924.
"Mrs. Collins Pleads Guilty." *The Evening Journal.* May 13, 1924.
"Mrs. Collins Leaves for Prison Wednesday." *The Evening Journal.* May 14, 1924.
"Mrs. Collins Gives Warning of Jail Break of Woman." *The Evening Journal.* October 6, 1925.
"Local Woman Gets Parole." *White County Democrat.* June 9, 1939.
"Nellie B. Collins, William Greer Wed on Saturday Evening." *Monticello Herald-Journal.* September 6, 1944.
"Nellie Greer Taken by Death." *Monticello Daily Herald Journal.* October 7, 1955.

AUTHOR

Photo by Christy Clark

JANIS THORNTON is the Indiana-based, award-winning author of two additional true crime books, *No Place Like Murder* and *Too Good a Girl*; the historical nonfiction, *The 1965 Palm Sunday Tornadoes in Indiana*; as well as pictorial-history books for the communities of Tipton County, Elwood, and Frankfort, all of Indiana. In addition, she has written two cozy mysteries in the "Elmwood Confidential" series, *Dust Bunnies & Dead Bodies* and *Dead Air & Double Dare;* and a stand-alone mystery, *Love, Lies and Azure Eyes*. She is a member of The Authors Guild, Indiana Writers Center, the Women Fiction Writers Association, the National Sisters in Crime mystery writers organization, as well as its Indianapolis-based chapter, Speed City Sisters in Crime. For more information, please visit *www.janis-thornton.com*.

www.ingramcontent.com/pod-product-compliance
Lightning Source LLC
Chambersburg PA
CBHW071001160426
43193CB00012B/1866